DRUG COURTS

SOCIAL PROBLEMS AND SOCIAL ISSUES

An Aldine de Gruyter Series of Texts and Monographs

SERIES EDITOR

Joel Best, *University of Delaware*

DRUG COURTS
IN THEORY
AND IN PRACTICE

James L. Nolan, Jr.
Editor

ALDINE DE GRUYTER
NEW YORK

ABOUT THE EDITOR

James L. Nolan, Jr. is Associate Professor of Sociology at Williams College.

ALDINE DE GRUYTER
A division of Walter de Gruyter, Inc.
200 Saw Mill River Road
Hawthorne, New York 10532

This publication is printed on acid free paper ∞

Library of Congress Cataloging-in-Publication Data

   Drug courts: in theory and in practice / James L. Nolan, Jr.
        p. cm — (Social problems and social issues)
Includes bibliographical references and index.
   ISBN 0-202-30712-3 (cloth : acid-free paper) — ISBN 0-202-30713-1 (paper : acid-free paper)
   1. Drug courts—United States.   I. Nolan, James L.   II. Series
     KF3890 .D777 2002
     345. 73'0277—dc21

                                                                        2001007581

Manufactured in the United States of America

10 9 8 7 6 5 4 3 2 1

Contents

Preface

The rapid expansion of the American drug court movement is now a rather well-documented story. Practitioners, politicians, and academics alike acknowledge the profound impact drug courts have had on the American criminal justice system. From a range of disciplinary perspectives, contributors to this volume seek to make sense of this important judicial innovation. What follows in this introduction is a brief review of the drug court phenomenon and a summary overview of the chapters included in the volume.

In response to several developments—not the least of which was the growing number of drug cases crowding American courts and prisons in the 1980s—the first drug court was initiated in Dade County, Florida, in 1989. Judge Stanley Goldstein was the first judge to preside over what would become the essential model for over seven hundred similar courts established throughout the United States since. While drug courts vary from location to location, they share the same basic defining features: Drug courts offer drug offenders, as an alternative to the normal adjudication process, an intensive court-based treatment program. Unlike previous diversion programs, such as Treatment Alternatives to Street Crime (TASC), the courtroom, rather than the clinic, is the focal point of treatment. That is, participants or clients (as they are typically called in drug courts) return regularly to the courtroom, where they engage directly and personally with the judge.

In addition to these regular encounters with the drug court judge, clients participate in individual and group counseling sessions, Alcoholics Anonymous (AA) and Narcotics Anonymous (NA) twelve-step groups, and acupuncture treatment. Progress in these various treatment modalities is monitored by the drug court judge who, during court sessions, offers praise and prizes for success and admonitions and sanctions for noncompliance. Sanctions can vary from increased participation in weekly NA meetings, to community service, to several days of incarceration. Clients agree to participate in drug courts with the promise that successful completion will result in dropped charges or an expunged record of arrest. It is a process advertised to take one year, but that often lasts much longer.

In many important respects, drug courts depart from the practices and procedures of typical criminal courts. Prosecutors and defense counsel, for example, play much reduced roles. Often lawyers are not even present during regular drug court sessions. Instead, the main courtroom drama is between the judge and client, both of whom speak openly and freely in the drug court setting. Often accompanying the client is a treatment provider, who advises the judge and reviews the client's progress in treatment. Court sessions are characterized by expressive and sometimes tearful testimonies about the recovery process, and are punctuated with applause from those in attendance. Once completing the program, clients participate in colorful graduation ceremonies, which involve emotional speeches from graduating clients, the issuing of graduation certificates, and sometimes visits from the media and local luminaries.

Media coverage of the drug courts has been almost universally positive. Moreover, the movement has been supported by politicians across the political spectrum. Federal support for drug courts has increased steadily over the past seven years. In 1995 the Drug Courts Program Office (established within the Department of Justice in the same year) issued $12 million in grants to drug courts. During the Clinton administration this increased to $15 million in 1996, to $30 million in 1997, and then to $40 million in 1999. In February 2001, President Bush designated $50 million in his proposed budget for drug courts, the highest level of federal support to date. So popular is this new form of criminal adjudication that new domestic violence courts, juvenile drug courts, family courts, reentry courts, and community courts have been initiated based on the drug court model. Drug courts have even spread internationally: England, Scotland, Ireland, Australia, and Canada have, within the last several years, established programs inspired by the U.S. model. Moreover, in 1999 the United Nations Drug Control Program convened a meeting with representatives from eleven different countries to discuss the international implementation of drug courts.

Movement activists, therefore, do not overstate matters when they speak of drug courts as a movement, even a revolution, in the criminal justice system. Just over a decade after the first drug court was established Jeffrey Tauber, former president of the National Association of Drug Court Professionals (NADCP), wrote in a November 2000 letter to NADCP members that the drug court movement had "come of age," and that a vision to "change the face of the criminal justice system" through the movement had been largely realized. As evidence he noted the joint resolution passed by the Conference of Chief Justices and the Conference of State Court Administrators in August 2000 endorsing drug courts and "problem solving courts" based on the drug court model.

The resolution acknowledges the "rapid proliferation of drug courts" and the strong "evidence of broad community and political support" for the movement. Moreover, it commits the chief justices and state court administrators to "take steps, nationally and locally, to expand and better integrate the principles and methods of well-functioning drug courts into ongoing court operations." It also encourages the "broad integration over the next decade of the principles and methods employed in problem-solving courts in the administration of justice." Less than a year later, the American Bar Association (ABA) followed suit, adopting a very similar resolution at its annual meetings. Here the ABA called for "the continued development of problem solving courts" and went so far as to encourage "law schools, state, local and territorial bar associations, and other organizations to engage in education and training about the principles and methods employed by problem solving courts."

The available evidence strongly suggests that the intentions of these resolutions have been and are being realized. For example, by the summer of 2001, more than 1,200 drug courts had been initiated or were in the planning and implementation stages throughout the United States, with drug courts operating in all fifty states, the District of Columbia, Guam, and Puerto Rico. It has been estimated that more than 225,000 clients have enrolled in a drug court program and that more than 1,500 judges have served as a drug court judge. Also, as noted above, the model has spread internationally and has inspired the development of a host of other problem-solving courts. A sociological analysis of the emergence and impact of the American drug court movement was the focus of my book, *Reinventing Justice: The American Drug Court Movement* (2001). It was in the context of finishing this project that the idea for this volume came to mind. *Reinventing Justice* offers an overview of the sociohistorical developments leading to the initiation and growth of drug courts, a detailed ethnographic account of twenty-one drug courts around the United States, and a consideration of the unintended consequences of the movement. While the book helps explain why drug courts were developed and what they look like in practice and in effect, the work invites further research in several respects.

For one, the national focus of the earlier project welcomes additional empirical examinations at both the local and international levels. Thus, intensive locally focused empirical assessments of individual drug court sites are important to confirm common features and / or to tease out differences peculiar to certain locations. Also, as mentioned above, the U.S.-led drug court movement has recently become an international phenomenon, the full significance of which would profit from comparative assessments of emerging courts in very different national contexts. Moreover, *Reinventing Justice* raises, but does not directly address, a number of other questions more political, philosophical, and jurisprudential than sociological in nature. A fuller comprehension of the movement's complexity and consequences would, therefore, benefit from a diversity of disciplinary perspectives.

By widening the scope of empirical analyses and the breadth of disciplinary foci, this edited volume promises to advance our understanding of drug courts in important ways. For example, it investigates such questions as: How do punitive practices in drug court correspond to or depart from classical views of punishment and justice? What civil rights are ignored or undermined by this unique form of adjudication? How does the therapeutic jurisprudence endemic to the drug court program compare / contrast to previous rehabilitative practices in Anglo-American law? How do certain historical and legal differences determine the style and shape of drug courts in distinct cultural contexts? How do competing institutional interests affect the processes of a local drug court program? By pulling together scholars and practitioners from a range of disciplinary perspectives this edited collection takes up the diverse scope of questions that the burgeoning drug court movement invites.

While addressing a range of questions, it also aims to achieve a careful balance between focused empirical studies and broader theoretical analyses of the same phenomenon. The variety of questions requires a diversity of disciplinary expertise. Assembled in the volume is the necessary range of scholars and practitioners prepared to address these questions. Contributors include five sociologists, a law professor, a judge, two lawyers, a political theorist, and a criminologist. As one would expect in a volume comprised of both legal practitioners and academics, the chapters vary in the degree to which they offer policy prescriptions and / or maintain a more dispassionate analytical orientation. Moreover, not all contributors to the volume (as the reader will readily detect) are in agreement with one another. Though wide ranging with respect to the diversity of disciplinary approaches represented here, the volume maintains an analytical concentration on drug courts and on the important practical, philosophical, and jurisprudential consequences of this unique form of therapeutic jurisprudence.

The volume is made up of eleven chapters in two parts. Part I, Empirical Explorations, is comprised of five theoretically informed empirical examinations of local drug court sites. Four chapters examine U.S. drug court sites in Baltimore, a northeastern city, a western city, and Denver, respectively. The fifth chapter compares emerging programs in the United Kingdom with the American model. Each chapter employs useful conceptual / theoretical frameworks to organize engaging and sometimes portentous data.

Part I begins with William McColl's overview of the Baltimore city drug court. Among other matters, McColl discusses how drug court officials in Baltimore have successfully sustained public support for the program by deemphasizing "rehabilitation" (a criminological concept that came under severe criticism in the early 1970s and beyond), and highlighting the more politically acceptable notions of community safety and program efficacy.

The Baltimore case, as presented by McColl, usefully demonstrates the limitations of conventional political categories for making sense of the drug court phenomenon.

Combining organization and social control theory, sociologist Elaine Wolf provides an extensively researched assessment of a drug court in the Northeast. Based on observations of 104 court hearings between January 1997 and April 1999, Wolf shows how competing disciplinary perspectives and limiting budgetary and other systemic constraints influence the nature and scope of the drug court program. Competing interests of various drug court actors and difficulties in adapting to the unique qualities of the drug court format result in sometimes mixed messages and conflicting requirements for program participants. Wolf draws upon statements from various courtroom actors to illustrate these points, and provides an engaging case study of one client's nearly two-year-long journey through the northeastern drug court.

In Chapter 3, Sara Steen uses organizational compliance theory to explain how clients in two "western state" drug courts become morally involved in the drug court program. According to Steen the use of "normative power" rather than "coercive" or "remunerative" power best characterizes social control in drug courts, particularly for clients in the later stages of the program. Though clients may initially experience alienation in relationship to the court and may only participate according to a calculative (cost/benefit analysis) strategy, they eventually become morally committed to the program wherein they "internalize the goals and values of the organization." Steen's findings are based on six months of ethnography conducted during 1998 at the two drug court sites, including thirty-three hours of observation of courtroom activities and open-ended interviews with the main actors in the courtroom drama.

Morris Hoffman provides, in Chapter 4, a unique insider's view into the initiation and growth of the Denver, Colorado drug court program. In 1994 he participated in the decision to start a drug court in Denver and witnessed its development and (many unanticipated) consequences in the years thereafter. In direct contrast to the public relations rhetoric of drug court advocates, Hoffman documents how in Denver the drug court has had enormous net-widening effects and has failed to reduce recidivism rates among participating clients. Linking these findings to similar developments in other drug courts, Hoffman considers the consequences of judicial activism, as such, on the constitutional roles of the legislative and executive branches of government.

The final chapter of the volume's first section is my comparative work between the American and British models. As noted above, the U.S. drug court model has been adopted in several countries, including England. A comparison between programs in the United States and the United Kingdom reveals the extent to which important historical, cultural, and legal differences determine the unique style, substance, and scope of the programs in both places. Though sharing a common law tradition and a common language, the unique accents of Anglo and American cultures and legal histories go far in explaining why this uncommon legal innovation takes on a very different form when transplanted from one location to another.

Part II, Theoretical Assessments, contains six analyses of the larger drug court movement. While thematically related to issues raised in Part I, this part is more exclusively theoretical in scope. Attention is given to therapeutic jurisprudence theory, a new and expanding school of legal scholarship to which the drug court movement has been closely linked. Indeed, drug courts are the most advanced practical archetype of this legal theory, and as such provide fertile investigative soil for assessing the content and consequences of therapeutic jurisprudence.

The section begins with Richard Boldt's comparison of drug courts to previous rehabilitative practices in American criminal law. Here, Boldt argues that drug courts, like previous rehabilitative practices, have important legal consequences. He reviews earlier critiques leveled against the rehabilitative ideal, and considers these in relationship to the drug court movement. Of particular concern to Boldt is the substantive altering of the attorney's role, caused by the drug court's departure from the traditional adversarial model.

In Chapter 7, John Rosenthal discusses therapeutic jurisprudence theory, as realized in the drug court movement, in comparison/contrast to classical theories of punishment. Rosenthal, along with Peggy Hora and William Schma (both of whom are practicing drug court judges) published an important article in the *Notre Dame Law Review* (1999) linking therapeutic jurisprudence theory to the drug court movement. This was the first and most extensive written articulation of the relationship between the two related phenomena to date. Rosenthal's contribution here gives more focused attention to theoretical matters. That is, he provides a full explication of therapeutic jurisprudence theory in relationship to drug courts, and considers the substance of this theory and practice in comparison to traditional conceptions of justice and punishment.

In Chapter 8, Susan Shell responds to Rosenthal's arguments from a more traditional philosophic perspective. Her chapter considers, among other things, the complex relationship between punishment and therapy in such classical thinkers as Aristotle, Plato, and Kant. She raises concerns about the extent to which drug court and its theoretical affinity to therapeutic jurisprudence departs from classical understandings of the purposes of punishment, and offers a reconceived justification for drug courts based on an Aristotelian perspective.

James Chriss employs a theoretical framework inspired by Alvin Gouldner to uncover the tacit assumptions underlying the drug court movement. Chriss considers, for example, the extent to which certain practitioners (in both the legal and treatment communities) benefit from the movement. He also raises questions regarding drug court claims of program efficacy and cost effectiveness, and identifies the "net-widening" tendencies and circumvention of due process rights that the drug court's unique combination of "coercion and compassion" effects. Moreover, he discusses the inherent conflict between utilitarian and justice values, as played out in the drug court movement, a tension that has been debated for years, but that finds unprecedented form in the drug court's prototypical embodiment of therapeutic jurisprudence theory.

In Chapter 10, Frank Furedi reflects on drug courts in relationship to other recent legal and cultural developments in the United Kingdom. Legal programs, like all government interventions, must find resonance with dominant cultural sensibilities for their legitimacy and social acceptance. Thus, it is critical to demonstrate cultural change that makes corresponding legal change plausible. In his lively analysis of contemporary British culture, Furedi makes just this connection.

Finally, in Chapter 11, the British criminologist Philip Bean, like Richard Boldt, compares drug courts to previous rehabilitative practices. Bean raises some concerns that drug courts may be reproducing some of the same practices of the previously discredited rehabilitative model. He discusses, for example, the nonadversarial nature of the "team-oriented" drug court model and considers the activist orientation of the drug court judge in contrast to the Aristotelian ideal of "passionless reason." Bean recommends more deliberate efforts to limit judicial powers fostered by the procedural informalities of drug court. While focusing on the United States, he makes useful comparisons to the British legal system to underscore the significance of particular American tendencies.

Taken together, the chapters provide a variety of perspectives on drug courts, and extend our knowledge of the movement in important respects. Work on the project was aided through the assistance of several resources. During the 1999/2000 academic year, I was located at Loughborough University in England on a Fulbright scholarship. The Fulbright award facilitated much of the ethnographic and historical research represented in Chapter 5. It also provided time to assemble and organize the volume's other chapters, and supported my visiting position at the Midlands Centre for Criminology and Criminal Justice in the Department of Social Sciences at Loughborough University. Philip Bean, the Director of the center, proved a generous host and an invaluable consultant throughout all stages of the project. Teresa Nimitz, among other faculty in the Social Sciences Department, also helped make the time at Loughborough a collegial and welcoming place to work.

Williams College deserves my gratitude in several respects. A Herbert H. Lehman fellowship at the Oakley Center for the Humanities and the Social Sciences during the fall of 2000 provided a conducive environment to continue writing and editing the work. While at the center I profited from the input of several Williams faculty and Oakley fellows, including Gary Jacobsohn and Steve Gerrard, who generously read and commented on my chapter in this collection. Thanks also go to Darci Phillips for her editorial assistance, and to Richard Koffler at Aldine de Gruyter, for his support of the work.

James L. Nolan, Jr.

Contributors

Philip Bean is Professor of Criminology and Director, Midlands Centre for Criminology and Criminal Justice, University of Loughborough. He is the author/editor of over twenty books, mainly in the fields of drugs and crime, and mental disorder and crime. He has been reporting on drug courts for a number of years. From 1996 to 1999 he was President of the British Society of Criminology.

Richard Boldt is Professor of Law at the University of Maryland School of Law, where he teaches courses in constitutional law, criminal law, criminal procedure, and torts. He is a frequent lecturer and has published numerous articles in leading law journals, including *Michigan Law Review, University of Pennsylvania Law Review, Hastings Law Journal, Journal of Criminal Law and Criminology, Washington University Law Quarterly, Criminal Law Forum,* and *Journal of Health Care Law & Policy.*

James J. Chriss is Assistant Professor of Sociology at Cleveland State University. His major areas of interest are sociological theory, law, mental illness, and juvenile delinquency. His latest books are *Alvin W. Gouldner: Sociologist and Outlaw Marxist* (Ashgate, 1999) and an edited volume, *Counseling and the Therapeutic State* (Aldine de Gruyter, 1999). His most recent articles are "Alvin W. Gouldner and Industrial Sociology at Columbia University" (*Journal of the History of the Behavioral Sciences* 37(3):241–59, 2001), and "Gouldner's Tragic Vision" (*Sociological Quarterly,* forthcoming).

Frank Furedi is Professor of Sociology at University of Kent in Canterbury. He is the author of a number of books, including most recently, *Paranoid Parenting* (Alan Lane, 2001) and *The Culture of Fear* (Cassell, 1997). He is currently working on two interrelated texts, *The State of Emotion* and *Litigation and the New Subject,* both of which investigate the interaction between risk consciousness, blaming, and the ambiguities of contemporary morality. Articles written by Furedi have appeared in a wide range newspapers and periodicals, including *Guardian, New Scientist, New Statesman, The Independent, Daily Mail, Wall Street Journal, Times Higher Education Supplement, The Times Literary Supplement,* and *Die Zeit.*

Morris B. Hoffman is a District Judge in the Second Judicial District, Denver, Colorado. He is currently assigned to a civil division, and also presides over the Denver Grand Jury. He has been an Adjunct Professor at the University of Denver College of Law (1997 and 2000), and is a member of the Supreme Court Criminal Rules Committee (1997–present), CBA Criminal Law Section Executive Council (1997–present), and National Judicial College's National Mass Tort Directory (1996–present). He is the author of numerous law review articles, including "The Drug Court Scandal" (*North Carolina Law Review* 78:1437, 2000).

William D. McColl is the Director of National Affairs for The Drug Policy Alliance, a membership organization devoted to promoting drug policy based on science, compassion, public health, and human rights. McColl's interest in drug courts began as a student at the University of Maryland School of Law, when he helped work on the creation of the Baltimore City Drug Treatment Court. He has additionally served as the Executive Director of the National Association for Alcoholism and Drug Abuse Counselors (NAADAC).

James L. Nolan, Jr., is Associate Professor of Sociology at Williams College. His most recent book is *Reinventing Justice: The American Drug Court Movement* (Princeton University Press, 2001). He is also the author of *The Therapeutic State: Justifying Government at Century's End* (New York University Press, 1998) and the editor of *The American Culture Wars: Current Contests and Future Prospects* (University Press of Virginia, 1996).

John Terrence A. Rosenthal is an associate at Sidley, Austin, Brown & Wood. He clerked for Chief Judge Robert H. Bell and Judge Richard A. Enslen, United States District Court, Western District of Michigan. He is the coauthor of "Therapeutic Jurisprudence and the Drug Treatment Court Movement: Revolutionizing the Criminal Justice System's Response to Drug Abuse and Crime in America" (*Notre Dame Law Review* 74:2, January 1999):439–538.

Susan Meld Shell is Professor of Political Philosophy at Boston College. She is the author of *The Rights of Reason: A Study of Kant's Philosophy and Politics* (University of Toronto Press, 1980) and *The Embodiment of Reason: Kant on Spirit, Generation and Community* (University of Chicago Press, 1996). She is currently working on a book on punishment.

Sara Steen is Assistant Professor of Sociology at the University of Colorado, Boulder. Her research interests include the medicalization of deviance, racial and ethnic disparities in juvenile and criminal justice proceedings, and the impact of sentencing reforms on prosecutorial behavior. She has recently coauthored papers on these topics that have appeared in *American Sociological Review* and *American Journal of Sociology*.

Elaine Wolf is a Senior Research Associate at the Center for Community Alternatives in Syracuse, New York. She also holds a research appointment in the Sociology Department in the Maxwell School of Citizenship and Public Affairs at Syracuse University. Her research focuses on program implementation, the criminal justice system, and social inequalities.

I

Empirical Explorations

1

Theory and Practice in the Baltimore City Drug Treatment Court

William D. McColl

We punish, but this is a way of saying that we wish to obtain a cure.
—Michel Foucault, *Discipline and Punish—The Birth of the Prison*

After more than ten years of continual growth, it is now possible to say that drug courts have become institutionalized in the United States. These courts are interesting, not only as a dramatic departure from the United State's common law tradition of adversarial justice, but also as a community response through the criminal justice system to the overwhelming problems of addiction. In 1994, Baltimore City, Maryland, faced with a fraying and broken-down justice system, adopted this new justice approach with enthusiasm. Its relatively well-documented history offers lessons in both how and why the drug court came into being. Consequently, it is a good case study in which to explore some of the philosophical issues raised by the creation of a drug court.

In particular it is worth examining whether drug courts fit into the tradition of the "rehabilitative ideal" (Allen 1981:1–2). Critiqued heavily on both the right and left, the ideology of rehabilitation has been in decline for more than twenty years. This chapter argues that the history of the formation of the Baltimore court shows that drug courts do not fit neatly within the constraints of the rehabilitative movement in American jurisprudence. In fact, the widespread acceptance of these courts by both the right and left is based less on appeals to rehabilitation than on the gains achieved by drug court through cost savings, program efficiency, and community safety. Advocates only make occasional nods to the rehabilitative benefits of drug courts. Because of the drug court's emphasis on community safety, screening out violent offenders, and properly controlling the drug court population, the critics on the right have largely been mollified. Though the powerful "liberal" critique of the rehabilitative ideal is also applicable to drug courts, this criticism has been blunted by the popularity of the community-centered nature of these courts.

Despite this popular appeal it is worth exploring the inherent tensions between the nonadversarial orientation of the courts and defining democratic principles. To do so, this chapter looks at the formation, history, and current operations of the Baltimore City Drug Treatment Court. The chapter then discusses the nature of drug courts, noting that the court fits closely with the idea of "social defense," a blend of rehabilitation and incapacitation theory, rather than the more mainstream evocations of the "rehabilitative ideal." Initially developed in the 1960s, social defense theory emphasizes the need to protect society over the needs of rehabilitation, but it also medicalizes criminal behavior, emphasizing the treatment and eventual return of offenders to society upon their cure (Wootton 1963:168–69). Drug treatment courts may be the fullest realization of social defense ideas to date. Finally the chapter explores the inherent tension created for defense lawyers in the nonadversarial role they play in the drug treatment court.

THE BALTIMORE CITY DRUG TREATMENT COURT

On March 23, 1995, after a little more than a year of operation, the Baltimore City Drug Treatment Court celebrated the graduation of the first seven defendants to complete treatment through the program. Now, after six years of operation in the Baltimore City District (misdemeanor) Court, the style, form, and procedures of drug court are familiar and routine to its lawyers, judges, court personnel, and even defendants. Buoyed by the success of the District Court, a drug treatment court for Baltimore City's Circuit (felony) Court system began in October, 1994, and became fully operational on March 6, 1995.[1]

The thirty-fifth such court in the nation, the Baltimore City Drug Treatment Court was part of the second wave of drug courts established in the United States. Thus, the Baltimore court had the advantage of designing a program with the lessons of the first wave of courts in mind. The result was an ambitious undertaking, dealing not only with practical issues of funding and securing treatment facilities for offenders, but with the philosophical changes necessary to create a new nonadversarial court.

The public success of drug treatment courts in Miami, Oakland, and elsewhere, along with increased federal appropriations for the creation of drug treatment courts, precipitated the formation of the Baltimore City Drug Treatment Court. However, the true genesis of the drug treatment court in Baltimore is a wide ranging report, *The Drug Crisis and Underfunding of the Justice System in Baltimore City*, prepared in December, 1990, by a Special Committee of the Bar Association of Baltimore City chaired by former judge George L. Russell, Jr. (Russell et al. 1990:29–30). The report of the Russell Committee provided a compelling description of a legal system under siege by growing numbers of drug-related cases. That Baltimore was able to take advantage of increased federal funding, as well as lobby for increased state funding, was largely a result of the alarm created among decision-makers by this report.[2]

The Russell Committee was charged with addressing "the problem of increasing drug litigation and the chronically underfunded justice system in Baltimore City" (ibid.:5). The committee's description of the increase in drug prosecutions was stunning. For example, 50 percent of felony prosecutions in Baltimore City were direct drug offenses, while 85–95 percent of all felony prosecutions were drug-driven offenses. Fully 55 percent of murders were drug related (ibid.:3). Even the casual observer could not fail to recognize that the system was becoming less and less capable of meeting its burden.

The committee's more compelling conclusions, at least in terms of the formation of the Baltimore City Drug Treatment Court, were based on other equally alarming facts: 80 percent of Maryland's prison population had a history of substance abuse; 71 percent of the population at the City Jail had been there before; 40 percent of Baltimore City probationers violated their probations within a year, primarily due to drug-related offenses; 80 percent of Juvenile Court cases were drug related (ibid.). The conclusion was inescapable:

> The appalling fact is that because the system fails through lack of resources or resolve to effectively *treat* the problem of drug abuse when the offender first encounters the system, *the same individuals return over and over again. To simply house these offenders at great expense, is a short sighted and ultimately a prohibitively expensive and self-defeating approach* to the problem. To perpetuate an underfunded, ineffective, hurried and, on occasion, unfair criminal justice system for which those subject to the system have no respect, is little better than having no system at all. (ibid.:6, emphasis added)

Thus against a backdrop of funding cuts and failure, the committee made numerous recommendations. The fifth general recommendation is particularly noteworthy: "Whether one employs a cost benefit analysis or just good sense, effective *drug abuse treatment is the only answer to reducing drug related criminal cases*" (ibid.:46, emphasis added). The committee specifically recommended the study and establishment of "special drug treatment courts," which would divert first-time offenders into treatment (ibid.:47).

The Russell Committee spawned unprecedented change in the Baltimore criminal justice system. The committee remained in session for an additional two years, writing a supplemental report in 1992, mostly focused on the juvenile system. In its third year, the committee began to concentrate on a treatment-based drug court:

> We just called a meeting and invited people to come talk about [forming a drug treatment court]. George Russell presided over a symposium in November, 1992, along with numerous judges and corrections officials. After that, we just kept calling meetings. It took about a year, until Sep. of '93, for the money pieces to be put in place at the state level.[3]

The recognition that every facet of the system was being affected by drug cases led to numerous changes, including the formation of three courts to expedite drug offenses (but not to divert individuals into treatment), approval by the legislature for a new central booking facility, as well as a state takeover of the city jail. At the same time, the Bar Association of Baltimore City helped to create a Drug Treatment Court Working Committee led by judges, state's attorneys, and public defenders, working closely with health and corrections personnel. "In this jurisdiction they didn't need any persuading that punishment was not going to solve the problem."[4]

INITIAL AND CONTINUING OPERATION

Phase 1 of the Baltimore City Drug Treatment Court began operations in the District Court on March 2, 1994 (Tauber 1994). This program is called STEP, an acronym for Substance Abuse Treatment and Education Program (Williams 1994). On October 19, 1995, Phase II operation of the drug treatment court began at the Circuit Court level. Phase III, a special program for probation violators, began on March 6, 1996, in the Circuit Court drug treatment court.[5] All three phases are designed to reach essentially the same population, nonviolent addicts involved in criminal activity. Defendants from each phase share the same treatment and supervision facilities (ibid.:8).

Upon entry into the criminal justice system, defendants who are in jail or who are being supervised by pretrial services are "screened" for eligibility for the program from a criminal justice standpoint (ibid.). Defendants' current cases, convictions, and past records are examined and potential participants are excluded if there are signs of violence (ibid.:Appendix C).[6] Additionally, defendants are screened for security (likelihood of fleeing jurisdiction) and willingness to participate. If the defendant is still eligible at this point, the public defender (P.D.) is notified and if the defendant is in jail will attempt to visit the defendant to explain the program. In actual practice, the P.D. may not be able to reach the defendant prior to trial for a variety of reasons, usually having to do with scheduling. However, the P.D. is the defendant's spokesperson vis-à-vis the criminal justice system, and is responsible for providing the defendant with his or her various options (ibid.:9).

The defendant is then "assessed" to determine medical eligibility for alcoholism and drug addiction treatment. The assessment for substance abuse is made using the Addiction Severity Index (ASI), which identifies severity of needs on a 0–9 scale. The ASI measures the following needs: medical, employment/support, drug, alcohol, legal, family/social, and psychiatric (ibid.:Appendix E). Additionally the defendant is assessed for amenability to treatment on the Psychopathy Checklist Revised (PCLR) (ibid.).[7] Following assessment, the assessor sends paperwork for eligible defendants to the public defender and the state's attorney's offices. They review the packages and agree to terms for the participation of the defendant. The public defender then must interview the defendant, explain the terms and conditions, and ensure that the defendant agrees to the procedure (ibid.:9).

The Baltimore City Drug Treatment Court originally planned to have two tracks for entry into the system, a "diversion" track and a "probation" track. In practice the diversion track was abandoned soon after the drug court opened. This initial diversion plan would have allowed defendants who had relatively clean records and who completed treatment through the program to be granted a "Stet" by the prosecutor. By placing a case on the Stet docket, the state declines to prosecute a case but retains the right to reopen the case for any reason for one year. The case may be opened between one and three years upon a showing of good cause. To be eligible for a Stet, the defendant must waive his or her right to a speedy trial (Maryland Annotated Code 1995:Rule 4-248). By using a Stet, the drug court ensured that defendants would not receive a conviction on their records. This practice was abandoned soon after the drug court opened because when defendants flunked out, witnesses and others were unavailable to return for a trial, forcing the state to abandon cases.[8]

Thus the second track, probation, is the only track that is currently in operation. Defendants must now stipulate to the facts of the case (that is, they must legally agree to the state's version of the case) and are generally offered a Probation Before Judgment (PBJ). A PBJ allows defendants to plead guilty, after which the court defers further proceedings, including sentencing. The court then places the individual on probation subject to the terms of the plea (in this case, completion of treatment to the satisfaction of the drug court). Upon satisfactory completion of probation the court will discharge the defendant from probation and dismiss the case without a finding of guilt (Maryland Annotated Code 1995:Article 41 Section 641). This system is advantageous to defendants because, assuming success-ful completion, their records will not reflect a conviction. Defendants are supervised by the Baltimore City Parole and Probation Unit (Williams 1994:18).

Before going to court, the public defender and the state's attorney agree on a plan for the defendant. They then agree on a contract to be presented to the defendant, which details the program, including possible sanctions for treatment failure. After signing the contract, the defendant is ready to go to court. In court, the judge again explains the program to the defen-dant and offers a final chance to back out. If the defendant accepts the pro-gram by signing the contract created by the state's attorney and public defender, treatment begins the next day. Additionally, the defendant will report back to the judge every other week until a sufficiently good record permits an extension in the time between his or her courtroom visits (ibid.).

Violations of the provisions of the drug treatment court contract result in the imposition of a system of graduated sanctions, such as increased uri-nalysis testing, or even "shock incarceration," which are written directly into the contract (ibid.:Appendix H). Shock incarceration is usually the last step in a series of graduated sanctions designed to force a defendant into compliance with the terms of his or her contract. Judge Jeffrey S. Tauber (1993) notes that shock incarceration is a brief period of incarceration de-signed to force a defendant to realize that his or her behavior is incompat-ible with treatment and moreover that failure in treatment could result in the imposition of a jail sentence. The incarceration thus "shocks" the defen-dant into compliance. In treatment terms, shock incarceration is intended to help a defendant overcome his or her "denial," which is a symptom of the disease of alcoholism.

The sanctions are designed to create immediate consequences for the de-fendant, compelling a return to treatment. Under a medical model of sub-stance abuse treatment, it is considered normal for substance abusers to relapse. Consequently, the sanctions are designed to show the defendant that relapse in the drug treatment court has immediate, sometimes severe consequences (ibid.:6). In contrast to typical probation, violation of the drug treatment court contract (for example missing a meeting with a su-pervisor) will not result in a charge of violation of probation.[9]

Treatment is currently provided to drug treatment court defendants by eight private treatment providers. The treatment providers include three intensive outpatient facilities, which provide one to three day sessions per week, at a minimum, for at least six months. These facilities provide NA and AA support groups, detoxification, acupuncture, GED training, and vocational training services. There is a residential facility option at each of the intensive outpatient providers (Gottfredson and Exum 2000:16).

Other treatment modalities include two methadone maintenance facilities, two inpatient facilities, and a transitional housing facility. Methadone maintenance facilities provide methadone treatment six to seven days per week and, additionally, detoxification and GED/vocational training services. The inpatient facilities provide treatment seven days per week for as long as six months, with a twenty-eight-day minimum. In addition they provide HIV education, social skills development, psychological evaluations, and referrals for psychological treatment. Finally, the transitional housing facility is available seven days per week for a minimum of six months and a maximum of one year. The inpatient facilities additionally provide basic vocational training and general education programs (ibid.).

Judge Jamey Weitzman, the long time administrative judge of the District Court, offers the following description of the drug court clientele:

> Over the years we have targeted very intense, high-level, individuals in terms of criminal history and chronic addiction. I estimate the average person has 10–30 years addiction. Anecdotally they tell me that they spend between $50 and $200 (per week) on drugs and all of them have criminal histories. We try to take people who would be going to jail if not for the drug court.[10]

Gottfredson and Exum studied 235 arrestees who were randomly assigned to receive drug treatment court services or treatment as usual in the criminal justice system. The study participants on average had twelve prior arrests and five prior convictions. Sixty-nine percent of the participants had severe drug problems, and 18 percent had severe alcohol problems. Only 23 percent were employed and only 16 percent were married. Eighty-seven percent named heroin as their primary or secondary drug of choice. Seventy-two percent reported daily use of crack. Fewer than one percent of study participants were arrested for a violent crime. From these data, Gottfredson and Exum conclude that the intended population (nonviolent, addicted adults) is being reached (2000:17).

DRUG COURTS AND THE REHABILITATIVE IDEAL

Americans have had a long and fretful history of use and abuse of drugs. As David Musto (1987) points out, drug use is not "un-American" as has been claimed, but rather peculiarly American. Musto shows that the

United States has historically moved through cyclical patterns of rising drug use, followed by public concern and enactment of prohibitionary legislation, which have been followed by periods of relative tolerance (ibid.:240–50). It surely is no accident that the drug court movement began in 1989 at the height of the most recent popular antidrug sentiment following the emergence of crack cocaine in 1986 (Belenko 1993:13–15). As shown by the Russell Report in Baltimore, there was a growing frustration with the criminal justice system's failing efforts to adequately deal with the growing number of addicted prisoners.

This cyclical movement of drug addicts between society and the criminal justice system has long been a source of frustration to the criminal justice system. A class of people, clearly identified, is known to commit an exceptional proportion of crimes. In fact, attempts have been made to simply outlaw addicts and addiction. However, in *Robinson v. California*, the Supreme Court held that one's status as an addict cannot, in itself, be a criminal offense. There must be some act or omission of will to subject individuals to criminal liability [*Robinson v. California*, 370 U.S. 660 666–667 (1962)].

The most widely held medical model of addiction, that addiction is a disease, highlights the problems facing criminal law. The medical theory derives originally from the study of alcoholism, but has now been applied to other forms of addiction, including narcotics addiction. Although there are varying definitions of the disease, the most basic proposition, and the proposition important to drug treatment courts, is that the defining symptom of the disease of addiction is behavior by an individual that shows a "loss of control" in the ability to avoid or regulate the use of narcotics (Nemerson, 1988:397–99).

A rudimentary sketch of four traditional penal theories—incapacitation, retribution, deterrence, and rehabilitation—will serve to illustrate the theoretical problems posed by the criminal justice system's acceptance of the disease model of compulsive behavior. Incapacitation justifies imposing punishment upon an individual on the grounds that society has the right to protect itself from the harm of the defendant's possible future criminal behavior. A criminal who is incapacitated (by imprisonment or execution) cannot commit future crimes (Lafave 2000:24).

Even assuming the truth of the disease theory, the incapacitation of addicts would still be a desirable outcome in order to prevent harm. However, implicit in the definition of incapacitation is that the defendant's behavior must be a crime, which typically requires intent. Under the disease theory, it could be argued that the addict did not commit a crime, either because the intent was lacking due to intoxication or because the drug use was an involuntary act. If either alternative is true, then the defendant did not commit a crime and should therefore not be incapacitated. Additionally, incapacitating a blameless individual will not stop that individual from behaving under the compulsion. After the period of incapacitation is over, the individual still has the compulsion and thus the problem is not truly solved (Nemerson 1988:440).

Likewise, approaches from a retributive standpoint emphasize the assigning of blame. Under this theory punishment is assigned because society deems it is just and deserved. The justification is that one who causes harm to others must receive commensurate punishment to restore the peace of mind of others or, alternatively, to ensure respect for the law and suppress acts of private vengeance. In a sense, the punishment then is society's vengeance upon a criminal. Indeed retribution has been compared to simple retaliation (Lafave 2000:26). However, in the eyes of most observers, retributive sentencing requires proportionality to culpability. Thus the disease theory of addiction presents a problem for retribution similar to the one it presents for incapacitation. An individual must be guilty of the crime to be punished. If the defendant is blameless (because of an involuntary disease), punishment is not justified (Allen 1981:66).

Deterrence theory has two parts. "Specific" deterrence provides that punishment is necessary to prevent the individual from committing future crimes. According to this theory, an individual who has been punished and is now released, will remember the punishment and either will refrain from or reduce the commission of future crime. "General" deterrence provides that punishment will prevent others from committing crime because, having observed the punishment, they will seek to avoid a similar fate (Lafave 2000:23–25). Again, both parts of this theory founder with application of the disease theory. If an addict has a disease (a "loss of control"), the compulsive behavior is undeterrable. Thus, punishing an addict will not serve to deter that addict or other addicts from committing crimes. Some will argue that deterrence of compulsive behavior is not necessarily an either/or proposition. Perhaps an addict's behavior is moderately deterrable. This is clearly a possibility. However the argument illustrates a relatively narrow point, that the tenability of deterrence is undermined when employing a strict definition of addiction as a disease (Nemerson 1988:434).

Rehabilitation may be described as an effort to change the behavior (along with character and attitude) of offenders through the penal system. Classical rehabilitation theory founders simply because it has been recognized that mere imprisonment or mere punishment does not in itself constitute adequate treatment. Modified or mixed versions of rehabilitation generally emphasize some degree of criminal behavior and intent, but as shown for incapacitation, this conceptualization in made problematic when employing the disease model of addiction. If a person is not at fault, then reform is not necessary.[11]

If addicts are indeed under a compulsion to take narcotics, then they are blameless for the crimes that they commit. Yet the criminal justice system has repeatedly shied away from following this reasoning to its logical end, namely, an understanding of the behavior with no assigning of guilt. Perhaps this was most starkly shown in *U.S. v. Moore* (486 F.2d 1139, 1155: 1973). The court explicitly stated that Congress could punish addicts for the crime of possession of narcotics, even if addicts were in fact suffering from a disease. This tension has been inadequately resolved, and indeed Richard Boldt suggests that the question is unresolvable. He states that the criminal law, which is oriented toward assignment of responsibility and blame, ordinarily requires punishment of some sort. In contrast, the medical model of treatment avoids assigning blame and concentrates on relieving symptoms (Boldt 1992:2305).

Rehabilitation theory has most fully provided a framework for a frontal approach to addiction. The "rehabilitative ideal" has been defined broadly as "the notion that a primary purpose of penal treatment is to effect changes in the characters, attitudes, and behavior of convicted offenders, so as to strengthen the social defense against unwanted behavior, but also to contribute to the welfare and satisfaction of offenders" (Allen 1981:2). Implicit in this definition is the idea that the behavior (or character) of convicted offenders has some malleability and can be reshaped. More importantly, the use of the state's ultimately coercive powers to effect this change is also necessary.

Francis Allen notes that this formulation of the rehabilitative definition leaves questions of causation untouched (ibid.:3). In fact, persons who have argued that crime is a chosen expression of free will and those who argue that crime is determined either biologically or socially, or both, have argued in favor of some aspects of rehabilitation. The lack of emphasis on causation is particularly important to this discussion since, unlike other penal theories, the necessity of blame is also diminished. Thus a rehabilitative focus concentrates less on whether or not an individual had the free will to commit a crime or even whether the crime was particularly egregious, but rather on whether or not the individual is susceptible to reform and how to bring about a positive change.

Thus rehabilitative practitioners have felt free to use or discard the concept of blame as they deem necessary, sometimes doing a bit of both within the same program. For example, in drug court, offender addicts are considered to have committed their crimes, at least in part, due to the disease of addiction and thus are not "blamed" for their disease. Yet they are also required to admit that they have a problem. In treatment terms, they overcome denial of the problem. This can mean making up for past wrongs, including admitting to guilt (or fault) for those wrongs, which may involve court-ordered restitution to victims (which of course looks very much like punishment).[12]

Additionally, the drug treatment court seeks to hold offenders responsible for their current and future actions, reintroducing the concept of blame through the use of graduated sanctions. Having shown the connection between the crime and the disease, the drug treatment court then seeks to "reshape" the offender's lifestyle from addiction and irresponsibility to nonuse and accountability. Offenders are required to take charge of their lives by confronting addiction. However, despite an occasional look back to the behavior that required the defendant to enter the drug treatment court in the first place, the drug treatment court treatment process essentially focuses on the present and future behavior patterns of offenders.

Ultimately, the process becomes one of accountability as opposed to blame in the traditional retributive sense. In the retributive sense, blame is a means of determining the amount of punishment an offender receives. Blame in the drug treatment court sense is a tool to change the behavior of an offender. As such, as an offender becomes more self-motivated, the system may choose to refocus away from, or even discard, constant reminders of blame.

The treatment of crime as a disease is not particularly new to rehabilitation theory. Aristotle spoke of punishment as "a kind of cure," while nineteenth-century American writings often referred to prisons as "moral hospitals" (Allen 1981:4). The appeal of this type of theory is obvious in comparison to other formulations of penal theory. Instead of mere concern with the behavior of convicted offenders behind the walls of prison, rehabilitative theory addresses the relationship of offenders to society at large and details ways of reintegrating offenders into society. Thus the modern dominance of the rehabilitative ideal is associated with a number of innovations in legal and court systems such as juvenile courts, indeterminate sentencing, systems of parole and probation, youth authorities, therapeutic programs in prison, juvenile institutions, and mental hospitals (ibid.:6).

Rehabilitation theory places great faith in the malleability of human nature. It holds that when presented with the proper opportunity and source of individual's motivation can change. Thus, in a "pure" version of rehabilitation, the focus of the criminal justice system is on the prisoner and on returning him or her to society. Indeed, the institutions mentioned above were originally designed for the benefit of the offender, subsequent criticisms notwithstanding. The juvenile courts, for example, were intended to shield youthful offenders from the harshness of the criminal law (*In Re* Gault, 387 U.S. 1, 1966). Indeterminate sentencing was designed with the idea that offenders were to be treated as individuals and that shorter sentences were appropriate for those who could be shown to be reformed.

Such rehabilitative regimes have been heavily criticized as being ineffective. There has been serious debate about whether corrections officials or mental health professionals are actually capable of affecting the behavior of offenders. An extension of this criticism is that rehabilitation is too centered on the offender and not concerned enough about the community (Allen 1981:28–29).

Concern about the performance of the criminal justice system in an era of rising crime rates brought tremendous scrutiny upon the reigning model of rehabilitation. Conservative critiques are marked by the belief either that the nature of human beings is immutable and thus not capable of being rehabilitated, or that the expense of rehabilitation is too high for society. Retribution with an emphasis on punishment allows conservative theorists to express a moral code (ibid.:67). At the most extreme end of the conservative spectrum are those who propound a "war" theory, which is characterized by repressive penalties and frequently by philosophies that encourage a view of criminals as apart from the society. This "us against them" system is apt to regard rehabilitative regimes as weak (ibid.:62).

Finally, the granting of wide sentencing discretion to judges, to parole boards, and certainly to treatment personnel came to be regarded as subject to abuse. This "liberal" critique is grounded in the belief that the power of the state must be checked. Containment of state power extends to the courts and to the discretion of the judiciary (ibid.:67). Thus, critics directly took on the symbol of rehabilitationism, the indeterminate sentence. Flexibility in sentencing is a key factor in allowing drug courts to control defendants and to fashion individualized treatment plans. As a result, the indeterminate sentence is a prominent feature of the drug court.

The need to ensure control of the offenders became a point of contention during the formation of the Baltimore City Drug Treatment Court. The drug court initially planned to offer offenders in the "diversion" track the promise of a Stet (an indefinite postponement of prosecution) upon completion of treatment. As noted above, concerns were raised that this was not enough of an incentive to keep offenders in the program. If defendants are simply placed on the Stet docket, frequently the cases become difficult to prosecute as witnesses move, become uncooperative, or simply begin to forget the details of the case. Recognizing difficulties with diversion, as such, the court eventually abandoned the Stet track.

In contrast, defendants on the probation track have a guilty judgment against them. If they do not complete the program, their probation may be violated and they may face jail time. According to Alan Woods,

> the probation track defendants are noticeably more cooperative than diversion track defendants. They have the sword of Damocles hanging over their heads. In contrast, we're saying to the diversion track defendants, "if you mess up we'll hang the sword of Damocles over your head in the future." Except that if we need to hang the sword, frequently we can't find either the sword or the thread.[13]

To solve the problem, the drug treatment court decided to require all offenders to admit to guilt as a requirement for entry into the drug treatment court.

These defendants in particular would be at risk of receiving more time in jail through the drug treatment court process than they would normally face. This possibility of unrestrained arbitrary or discriminatory abuse of discretion by the court is the precise concern of the liberal critic (American Friends Service Committee 1971:27). Although treatment is acknowledged as the goal, since discretion actually resides in the hands of the judicial system, which is charged with the safety of society, punishment is the result even if it is called treatment. In fact the indefiniteness itself is a component of additional punishment, resulting in dehumanization and depersonalization of the defendant. Additionally, the expansion of discretion is problematic to the liberal critics concerned about the containment of state power (ibid.:46).

The potential for abuse is shown quite clearly in the Gottfredson and Exum study. Offenders who were randomly assigned to the drug court track received sentences that were in excess of control subjects. For example, drug court offenders who were judged guilty in the Circuit Court received an average sentence of 2,641 days. In contrast, control group members who were judged guilty received a sentence of 2,312 days. Thus, the drug treatment court defendants received an average sentence that was 329 days longer than the control group defendants. District Court had the same dynamic, with drug court offenders receiving 499 assigned days compared to 306 days for control group members. In both drug courts, these sentences were then suspended to allow treatment to take place. However, failure to complete treatment could result in the imposition of the full sentence. In addition, assigned days of probation were longer for drug court defendants as well. It is clear that drug court defendants are at risk of serving longer sentences (Gottfredson and Exum 2000:Table 5).

To be fair, despite the potential for serving more days, Gottfredson indicates that on average, drug treatment court defendants spend fewer days in jail than the control group. In the Circuit Court drug defendants actually serve a total of 137 days as opposed to 415 days for the control group. This is nearly eight months less than the control group. The difference is slighter for District Court defendants. Those assigned to the District Drug Court serve approximately fifty-nine days compared to eighty-five days for non–drug court offenders. In both the Circuit Court and the District Court, the vast majority of days served by drug court defendants are served awaiting entry into the drug court. In contrast, many more defendants in the control group received sentences that added additional jail time at the time of trial.

Thus the drug treatment court response to this critique is simply that the defendant is engaged in treatment, and a night in jail may, in the long term, be the key to the defendant's recovery. Particularly in relationship to the disease theory of addiction, it is understood that such measures are necessary to break through the mechanism of denial and to institute a feeling of responsibility in otherwise unresponsive defendants. Drug court advocates argue that although discretion is expanded slightly it cuts both ways and that defendants may actually end up with a better deal.[14] Such advocates point out that drug court offenders on average spend less actual time in incarceration, even if they spend more time on probation. The longer probation period is justified on the grounds that it helps defendants to maintain their recovery.

Advocates of drug courts might also note that the Baltimore City Drug Treatment Court has actually limited judicial discretion in some notable ways. In particular, defendants are screened by the Addiction Severity Index (ASI) to determine whether or not an individual is an addict. The ASI measures seven potential problem areas in substance-abusing patients: medical status, employment and support, drug use, alcohol use, legal status, family/social status, and psychiatric status (Williams 1994:Appendix E). If properly applied, only addicted candidates are brought before the judge. Thus, though the judge is not blindly required to follow treatment recommendations, the practical effect of the expertise of treatment personnel in the field is that the judge almost always follows the recommendations of treatment providers.[15]

The liberal skeptics, however, would be concerned about the discretion given to these providers and about the expansion of treatment programs. To a certain extent, they are concerned that therapy is in itself punishment (American Friends Service Committee 1971:97). Certainly, past prison-based rehabilitative programs have been shown to be highly punitive (Allen 1981:46).

The pressure on American courts in recent years to do more for the community with fewer resources has led to a number of developments. Out of a desire to change a particular aspect of their job, respond to community concerns, or help the defendants who come before them, judges have instituted innovative approaches to criminal justice in individual courtrooms. For example, frustration with the mass production of cases was one factor leading to the rise of drug treatment courts. Currently, in the political world, and even in the theoretical world, retributionist theory seems to have gained the upper hand. But in the trenches, driven by the crushing drug caseload, numerous jurisdictions have turned to drug treatment courts in an attempt to stem recidivism and to slowly reduce the overwhelming number of addicted defendants.

Because they are essentially a practical response to the overwhelming caseloads and the cycle of recidivism, such as that detailed by the Russell Committee in Baltimore, drug treatment court reform efforts are not guided by theory. Practitioners in the drug treatment courts are guided by what they perceive to be working; they discard what does not work. Thus as detailed earlier, when it became apparent to the Baltimore drug court that it could not maintain enough control over drug offenders through the Stet process, the court simply eliminated the Stet track, turning to the use of probation and probation before judgment instead.

Boldt has noted that the particularly powerful critique of the rehabilitative ideal is given force by a focus on individual liberty interests. In his conception, liberals place individual freedom as the highest core value, with individual rights of autonomy, privacy, and choice protected by rights against the state (Boldt 1998:1238). In contrast, the goals for a drug treatment court may be extremely utilitarian. In Baltimore, for example, the goals of the court are:

> (1) To reduce reliance on incarceration as a criminal justice response to the management of criminal defendants who present low risk to public safety;
> (2) To provide an alternative to incarceration for criminal defendants whose crimes are drug involved which in turn provides the judiciary with a cost-effective sentencing option, frees valuable incarceration resources for violent offenders, and reduces the average length of pre-trial jail time;
> (3) To provide the criminal justice system with a fully integrated and comprehensive treatment program;
> (4) To provide graduated levels of sanctions for defendants;
> (5) To reduce criminal justice costs, over the long run, by reducing addiction and street crime;
> (6) To facilitate where appropriate, the acquisition or enhancement of academic, vocational and pre-social skill development of criminal defendants; and
> (7) To divert pre-trial detainees who have been assessed as drug-dependent and who present low risk to public safety into treatment systems with close criminal justice supervision and judicial monitoring (Williams 1994:18).

In fact, it is relatively clear from these priorities that the drug court is responsive to priorities beyond an exclusive interest in protecting individual liberties. Safety of the community is perhaps the dominant concern as is clear by the focus on "low-risk" and "nonviolent" defendants and the emphasis on "close criminal justice supervision and judicial monitoring."

Interestingly, these goals are reminiscent of "social defense" theory, a blending of incapacitation and rehabilitation, which stresses the protection of society from criminal behavior (Wootton 1972; Ancel 1972:132). Social defense theorists criticize rehabilitative theory for its central focus on the criminal offender. Nevertheless, they emphasize rehabilitation and dismiss retribution as the proper goal for all criminals. Instead, they emphasize the treatment and eventual return of offenders to society upon their cure and after they no longer represent a danger to society. Essentially, upon conviction, social defense theorists "medicalize" the criminal justice system response to an offender. Under this system, offenders are essentially treated as sick members of the community, largely abandoning punishment as a goal of the penal system.

Drug treatment courts, which "sentence" offenders to substance abuse treatment, may be the fullest practical application of the social defense model. Social defense theorists, have themselves criticized the criminal offender–centeredness of rehabilitative theory (Ancel 1972:138). In their view, reform-minded experimentation emphasized an offender's interest in rehabilitation over society's interest in safety, resulting in greater risk to society than necessary or advisable. Consequently, in contrast to rehabilitation proponents, social defense theorists chose to frame the question as a community rather than an individual. Thus social defense theorists proposed that, as offenders reenter the community, the community must first be protected. Offenders therefore must be "neutralized," preferably through a treatment program, but also through incapacitation (if necessary to make possible further treatment) (ibid.).

This reorientation of viewpoints produced a startling shift in results. Instead of worrying about the welfare of the criminal, social defense theorists worried about the danger of the criminal to society. They argued that the "dangerousness" of the criminal offender must somehow be measured, and subject to this measurement, the criminal offender must be controlled through state intervention (ibid.). Only after the determination of the need for intervention did social defense theorists begin to consider the rehabilitation of the offender. Clearly the drug courts share these goals.

That social defense theory has not become more broadly accepted is at least partly a result of its reliance on therapeutic or medical intervention (ibid.:5). Thus in some measure, the serious debate, which continues today, about whether corrections officials or mental health professionals can actually change someone's behavior mitigated the influence of the social defense theorists. Today however, drug treatment courts appear to be challenging this skepticism.

Finally, the success of drug treatment courts seems to be rooted in the courts' successful adaptation of their operations to the needs of the community. Judges in treatment courts have not been reluctant to get other community members involved. Judge Jamey Weitzman notes that the Baltimore Drug Treatment Court actively seeks to work with community members. For example, the drug court started weekly Narcotics Anonymous (NA) meetings, which are held in a church. The drug court is now working with the church community to "adopt" drug court addicts. The idea is to "embrace them into a church community, help them with social issues and to build bridges between drug court and the community."[16]

The primary goal particularly from the criminal justice system's standpoint is the ultimate reduction of crime toward the community. Hidden in the subtext of forcing defendants to undergo treatment is a high element of community supervision, particularly by the treatment agencies. In fact, even before defendants are allowed into the drug treatment court, potentially violent offenders are screened out (Williams 1994:7). It is thus clear that in the trade-off between community safety and the needs of defendants, it is the community that has first priority. This emphasis on community is essentially the practical application of a social defense.

This community cooperation is even more evident when one considers the level of integration of the legal, correctional, and medical systems involved in the drug treatment court process. While the court retains ultimate decision-making power, the "sentence" is in all cases some form of treatment. The judge relies entirely on the advice of treatment personnel to decide what type of and how much treatment is appropriate and even where treatment will be performed. Corrections officials ensure that treatment is carried out. This integration of three formerly diverse fields has been referred to as a "systems approach." Although technical boundaries remain, the integration of medical, correctional, and legal systems is far-reaching enough to conclude that a "withering away" of conventionally distinct institutional spheres has taken place in the Baltimore City Drug Treatment Court.

The institution of graduated sanctions for offenders who are not making satisfactory progress also advances a change in the court's role. Thus, within the drug treatment court, "sanctions" are not punishment. They are simply "adjustments," a device by which the court teaches addicts responsibility for their actions (ibid.:Appendix H). Judge Jamey Weitzman highlights this tendency:

> The defendants are in drug treatment court because they are addicted to substances. Therefore, dirty urines are not unusual. The court is concerned that these defendants continue to follow program regulations and rules and attempt to strenuously address their addiction. If they continue positively, the court will work with them. However when they fail to comply with program requirements, such as missing treatment sessions, then the court will show them that there are consequences to their behavior and impose some form of increased supervision.[17]

The result is a type of separation of drug use from criminality that is highly clinical in outlook. In a strict legal sense, failure of a urinalysis test could result in a violation of probation and punishment (Maryland Anno-tated Code 1957:Article 27 §641).

As shown above, in some cases drug treatment court offenders experi-ence greater criminal justice system involvement than the ordinary nonvi-olent offender in a like position. As in other indeterminate sentencing situations, in drug court defendants can spend more time in treatment than they would have spent in jail, had they gone through the traditional crim-inal justice process. The probability of receiving jail time and years of court enforced treatment may mollify persons who favor punishment over other competing goals.

Although the "systems approach" used by the drug treatment court model in conjunction with the medical concept of the disease of addiction seems particularly apt for drug and alcohol addicts, the model clearly has implications beyond the drug treatment court structure. In fact, Washte-naw County, Michigan, uses the "systems approach" to coordinate courts with law enforcement in the area of domestic violence (Pope 1994:946). However, one does not see a movement toward specialized courts for other types of crimes such as "environmental" or "white-collar crimes" courts. Thus far, court officials have only attempted the "systems approach" where there seems to be some form of medical pathology such as addic-tion or battered spouse syndrome. Given the critique of indeterminate sen-tencing and officials' justifiable concerns about releasing dangerous offenders, the medical condition and partnership with treatment authori-ties may provide cover for the difficult decisions officials are called upon to make.

THE ROLE OF THE DEFENSE LAWYER IN THE DRUG COURT

Although the concept of guilt has not vanished, the drug treatment courts sidestep the problem of determining blame or fault by requiring an ad-mission of guilt to enter the program. The question then is no longer whether the crime happened, but rather, what is compelling the crime and how can it be stopped?

The defense lawyer's role in drug courts is often passive, a passivity that conceals a difficult burden. How may a defender combine his or her status as a full working member of an integrated treatment team, while remain-ing an effective lawyer for the defendant? There does not seem to be a per-fect answer to this question and it may be that there is an unbridgeable tension between the role of zealous advocate for a client and member of a treatment team.

This dual role places a tremendous burden on defense lawyers. First the defense lawyer must act to help the defendant gain entry into the drug treatment court during the admission process. During this stage the defense lawyer must help the client weigh the value of a relatively short jail term against the possibility of long-term (one year at least) involvement with the drug court. The client must understand that involvement with the drug court might include loss of liberty through shock incarceration and, in the case of complete failure, potential imposition of a sentence (Williams 1994:Appendices G and H). The defense lawyer must simultaneously cooperate with the state's attorney to help the defendant gain entry.

The second stage is in some ways even more difficult. Having gained "informed consent" during the first stage, the defender also is reduced to passivity in most situations. Typically the judge bypasses both lawyers and talks directly to the client. This can lead to complications, particularly as clients become emotional when talking about certain aspects of their lives. Generally the defense lawyer remains silent. If a client is in violation of a contract, there is a slight reversion to the adversary system and the defender—similar to the prosecutor—will typically seek to clarify the status of the client.[18]

Generally the defense lawyer will argue for leniency if a client is going into shock incarceration. By definition however, the defense lawyer is part of the "systems approach" team and is thus also responsible for treating the client. Therefore, since shock incarceration is defined as treatment (a device to teach the defendant that there are consequences to irresponsible behavior), the defender will frequently mute his or her dissent. Often the defense lawyer is reduced to making arguments destined to be disregarded, and therefore has no incentive to oppose the course of the proceedings. Consequently the defender has moved from partisan zeal to cooperation.

Judge Weitzman states that it is extremely important for the defense to assess the situation up front. Once the defendant moves into treatment, the defense lawyer becomes a part of the team, diminishing the vigor with which the defense lawyer might act if he or she were in an adversarial court. Still, Judge Weitzman maintains that the defense plays an important role in setting policy. As an example, she states that the public defender's office talked her into using the more lenient PBJ plea, as discussed earlier, rather than simple probation as an incentive for defendants. In addition, the public defenders also asked her to reconsider allowing defendants to be credited with time served when violations occur, thus reducing potential punishment for the defendants.[19]

Boldt notes that this places an extraordinary burden on the defense lawyer and suggests that it may be impossible to reconcile this conflicting role with duty to client (Boldt 1998:1286–1300). The importance of the role of the defense counselor is precisely that the defense counselor is the only actor in the system empowered to speak on behalf of the client. When the defense lawyer becomes a member of the treatment team, the process of treatment can too easily be debased into punishment. Indeed we have already seen through the Russell Report and in the goals of the Baltimore City Drug Treatment Court, that the creation of drug treatment courts have less to do with the offender than with the protection of the community and with creating an outlet for drug cases in order to lessen the burden on the criminal justice system.

Boldt states that this is precisely the point. Ironically, the individual focus on addiction by the drug courts merely obscures a policy choice to treat addiction through the criminal justice system rather than to put resources into the arguably more appropriate public health and medical systems (Boldt 1998:1304).

CONCLUSION

Now, more than twelve years after their original debut, there is no longer a question as to whether or not drug courts will survive. Rather, the question has become whether drug courts are making a justifiable trade-off between the liberty interests of defendants and the safety of the community. Drug court advocates strive to make the case that the potential loss of liberty interests is either not occurring or is worth the outcome of the process. In Baltimore there is some evidence of success on utilitarian grounds. According to Gottfredson and Exum, the Baltimore court has succeeded in "targeting high-rate, drug involved offenders who if left untreated on the streets have a high likelihood of reoffending" (2000:22–23). In addition they show that the mean nonsuspended incarceration sentence for drug court offenders is 163 days less than the control group. Thus the system reduces costs. Finally the system "improves offender behavior." Offenders assigned to drug court were rearrested at a rate of 44 vs. 56 percent among the control group. This difference is conservative since drug court offenders were more often out on the street and consequently had greater opportunity to reoffend.

For the public this may be enough. Drug treatment courts have been at pains to keep public relations positive and to maintain community involvement. Thus in Baltimore, politicians and the media were invited to the first graduation of drug treatment court offenders. A steady stream of studies has been released by the drug treatment court movement to show that the drug treatment courts are working. The message remains simple. Almost every advocate of drug treatment courts has a remarkably similar approach to the subject: "The old system of dealing with addicted offenders does not work [is in crisis], prevention and treatment are the only alternatives" (Goldkamp 1994:4). By worrying about community safety first, the drug treatment court movement seeks to align itself with the community. As a result, despite the high level of public hostility toward rehabilitative or social defense goals, the ability of the courts to point to reductions in case loads and to the successful recovery from addiction of participants has earned continuing funding and approval.

The political question for drug treatment courts no longer appears to be whether the experiment will survive, but rather whether it can be expanded to play a larger role in the criminal justice system. In January 2000, the Baltimore City Drug Treatment Court became the center of a political crisis in the Maryland legislature. Court officials were forced to stop taking new offenders after they had accepted more than one hundred offenders beyond their funding level (Francke and Dresser 2000). The court reopened in August 2000. As a result of the funding crisis, new state funds were found and the Circuit Court now plans to handle three hundred additional offenders (Francke 2000). Despite the closure and subsequent controversy, whether the drug court would survive was never in doubt. It is clear that there is political will to keep expanding the treatment availability through the drug court program in Maryland.

The political climate in Maryland has been relatively supportive of drug treatment courts in the past, due in large measure to the court's success in conveying the message of program efficiency. The current governor of the state is a supporter of the drug treatment court concept. Moreover, drug treatment court committee-members anticipate strong bipartisan legislative support for the program, given broad criminal justice and community-based support for drug courts. The issue of alcohol and drug treatment has been seen as important enough to merit the creation of a drug treatment task force under the direction of the lieutenant governor, Kathleen Kennedy Townsend.

Finally, although admissions to the program started out slowly, the program currently has developed enough momentum to completely fill nine hundred treatment beds. The budget fight and, more importantly, the continuing graduation of classes of defendants have given the drug treatment court a relatively high profile in the Baltimore City criminal justice system. The practical problems of court administration, that continue to drive the drug treatment court movement, remain and may actually be intensified as drug cases continue to flood the system. Punitive sentencing and law enforcement practices aimed at the casual or addicted drug user increase defendant populations beyond capacity of the criminal justice system's and jail programs' capabilities. The drug treatment court in this context is, at the least, a good supervisory program for this population.

In Baltimore, the focus of the drug treatment court on the community continues to align community interests with rehabilitative and social defense goals. As long as this alignment is maintained, the community is likely to continue to support the drug treatment court into its seventh year and beyond.

NOTES

1. Interview with Alan C. Woods, III, chief of the Research and Development Division, State's Attorney's Office for Baltimore City, in Baltimore, April 19, 1995.
2. Interview with David W. Skeen, past president of the Bar Association of Baltimore City, member of the Russell Committee and Drug Treatment Court Committee, in Baltimore, March 6, 1995.
3. See note 2.
4. See note 2.
5. Interview with Alan C. Woods, III, see note 1.
6. Disqualifying criteria include convictions for violent crimes defined in the Maryland Annotated Code for which mandatory sentences are required. These include violent felony convictions, domestic violence, assault and/or battery, possession with intent to distribute, and certain other serious drug charges, all within the last five years. Other criteria include use of a firearm in the present offense or convictions that involved the use of firearms in the last five years, and any convictions of sex offense or rape charges (Md Code Ann. Art. 27 § 643B, 1957).
7. Note that "assessment" of medical eligibility (e.g., a determination that a defendant is an addict—it does not make medical sense to treat people who are not addicted) is different from "screening," which determines legal eligibility (e.g., a determination that the person is nonviolent through review of criminal justice system records) for the program (interview with Robb McFaul, Assistant Program Director for Correctional Options, STEP, in Baltimore, March 8, 1995).
8. Interview with Judge Jamey Weitzman, Baltimore City District Court Judge for the State of Maryland, Baltimore City Drug Treatment Court, in Baltimore, July 10, 2000.
9. See note 1.
10. See note 8.
11. It should be noted that each theory has to some extent developed utilitarian components that help the theory to overcome the concerns raised above. Utilitarianism, very generally, states that punishment may be imposed where the benefits resulting from the punishment, whether incapacitative, retributive, deterrent, or rehabilitative, outweigh the evil effects of the punishment on the individual. Accepting the disease theory, this logic essentially creates strict liability for addicts who are incapable of avoiding these crimes. That is, we punish because the good of punishment outweighs the evil we do to the addict (see generally Nemerson 1988:434).
12. Telephone interview with Deborah Marcus, Assistant State's Attorney for

Baltimore City, Baltimore City Drug Treatment Court, in Baltimore, July 12, 1995. Interestingly, in the court system, the process of accountability, e.g., admitting guilt or making restitution, is the first step into the drug treatment court. Thus the admissions become a tool to get defendants to acknowledge their addiction.

13. See note 1.
14. See note 1.
15. See note 1.
16. See note 8.
17. Interview with Judge Jamey Weitzman, District Court Judge for the State of Maryland, Baltimore City Drug Treatment Court, in Baltimore, March 7, 1995.
18. Author's observation of Baltimore City Drug Treatment Court, Judge Jamey Weitzman presiding, Baltimore, March 7, 1995.
19. See note 8.

REFERENCES

Allen, Francis A. 1981. *The Decline of the Rehabilitative Ideal.* New Haven, CT: Yale University Press.

American Friends Service Committee. 1971. *Struggle For Justice, A Report on Crime and Punishment in America.* New York: Hill and Wang.

Ancel, Marc. 1972. "New Social Defense." *Contemporary Punishment: Views Explanations and Justifications,* edited by Rudolph J. Gerber and Patrick D. McAnany. Notre Dame, IN: University of Notre Dame Press.

Belenko, Steven R. 1993. *Crack and the Evolution of Anti-Drug Policy.* Westport, CT: Greenwood.

Boldt, Richard C. 1992. "The Construction of Responsibility in the Criminal Law." *University of Pennsylvania Law Review* 140:2245–2332.

Boldt, Richard C. 1998. "Rehabilitative Punishment and the Drug Treatment Court Movement." *Washington University Law Quarterly* 76(4):1205–1306.

Foucault, Michel. 1979. *Discipline and Punish—The Birth of the Prison,* translated by Alan Sheridan. New York: Vintage.

Francke, Caitlin. 2000. "Drug Court Will Reopen Next Month in Baltimore," *Baltimore Sun,* July 26.

Francke, Caitlin and Michael Dresser. 2000. "Drug Court Turns Away Admissions." *Baltimore Sun,* January 20.

Goldkamp, John S. 1994. Justice and Treatment Innovation: The Drug Court Movement—A Working Paper of the First National Drug Court Conference. Washington, DC: National Institute of Justice.

Gottfredson, Denise C. and M. Lyn Exum. 2000. *The Baltimore City Drug Treatment Court: First Evaluation Report.* College Park, MD: Department of Criminology and Criminal Justice, University of Maryland.

Lafave, Wayne R. 2000. *Criminal Law,* 3rd ed. St. Paul, MN: West Group.

Musto, David F. 1987. *The American Disease: Origins of Narcotic Control.* 3rd ed. New York: Oxford University Press.

Nemerson, Steven S. 1988. "Alcoholism, Intoxication, and the Criminal Law." *Cardozo Law Review* 10:393–473.

Pope, Charles J. 1994. "Domestic Violence and the Courts: The Systems Approach." *Michigan Bar Journal* 73:946.

Russell, George L., et al. 1990. *The Drug Crisis and Underfunding of the Justice System in Baltimore City*. Baltimore, MD: Bar Association of Baltimore City.

Tauber, Jeffrey S. 1993. *A Judicial Primer on Unified Drug Courts and Court Ordered Drug Rehabilitation Programs*. Address at the California Continuing Judicial Studies Program, transcript available through the Bureau of Justice Statistics.

Tauber, Jeffrey S. 1994. "Drug Courts: Treating Drug-using Offenders Through Sanctions, Incentives." *Corrections Today* 56(1):28.

Williams, Thomas H. 1994. *S.T.E.P. Up and Out* (Baltimore City Drug Treatment Program Manual). Baltimore, MD: Baltimore City Drug Treatment Program.

Wootton, Barbara. 1972. "Crime Responsibility and Prevention." *Contemporary Punishment: Views Explanations and Justifications,* edited by Rudolph J. Gerber and Patrick D. McAnany. Notre Dame, IN: University of Notre Dame Press.

2

Systemic Constraints on the Implementation of a Northeastern Drug Court

Elaine M. Wolf

The Northeastern Drug Court (NDC), like all drug courts funded by the Drug Courts Program Office (U.S. Department of Justice), provides chemical dependency services for defendants who have been charged with a nonviolent offense and either dismisses or reduces those charges in exchange for clients' compliance with court requirements. The main conceptual and operational difference between programs that conform to the drug court model and traditional probation or other forms of community supervision is that drug courts require the active involvement of a judge. The assumptions underlying a national policy of implementing such courts are that they intervene in individuals' lives for their own and society's good; that "buying into" recovery is preferable to just "doing what I have to do"; and that social control achieved through voluntary, cooperative means is more effective than control achieved through the use of coercion and adversarialness.

The drug court judge embodies the combination of criminal justice and public health concerns represented in the concept of therapeutic jurisprudence that provides the rationale for these courts.[1] The different goals of these two concerns present challenges to the court's implementation and ultimately play themselves out in the ways that individual clients experience their participation in the court, make decisions about their compliance with court requirements, and demonstrate behavior that is consistent with the court's view of recovery.

The NDC's goals are for its clients to gain control over their addiction, to remain free of involvement in the criminal justice system, and to achieve and maintain productive lives. In order for clients to achieve those goals, the court has been required to provide a variety of services in response to needs that are ancillary to clients' addictions. Its case managers have also been required to coordinate clients' navigation of the social service system (primarily public assistance, Medicaid, and welfare-to-work programs), which holds clients accountable at the same time that they are accountable to the court.

This chapter addresses the ways in which the organization of treatment, social service, and criminal justice systems presents systemic contradictions that impose constraints upon the court's ability to function in a way that is consistent with its design and its purpose. Differences among these systems and their subsystems exist not only in the ways that they define their goals (e.g., public safety in the case of the prosecution, protection of individual clients' rights in the case of the defense, effecting recovery in the case of chemical dependency treatment, and reducing clients' dependence upon public assistance in the case of welfare-to-work requirements), but also in their ideologies (e.g., whether drug abuse is a public health or a moral issue) and in the ways that they acquire and sustain financial support for their work. These fundamental differences affect the ways in which staff go about their work, defend their turf, assess the behavior of the court's clients, and view the purposes and responsibilities of the court.

The chapter begins with a presentation of a theoretical framework, a brief description of the court, and an overview of data collection and analysis. It next addresses the ways in which several key systems under the NDC's "umbrella" function and operate as entities unto themselves as well as in relation to each other. Then it presents a view of system functioning and effects from the perspective of one drug court participant, illustrating how contradictions can affect program participants and have unintended consequences with respect to the court's ability to achieve its multiple goals. It concludes with a discussion of the meaning of these findings for our understanding of drug courts and the contexts in which they operate and with some suggestions for further research to enhance those understandings.

THEORETICAL FRAMEWORK

The theoretical framework for this analysis is informed by scholarly work that is concerned with organizational behavior, particularly the ways in which organizational roles and behavior affect the implementation of social policy. Drug courts represent new ways of organizing existing systems and new definitions of the relationships among long-standing institutional stakeholders. Drug courts introduce new institutions and individual personnel into the stakeholder mix (such as treatment providers[2] and a drug court coordinator). As with the implementation of any innovative program, the implementation of drug courts is fraught with difficulties based on the introduction of new personnel to an existing system (Hage 1980). Such programs typically require behavioral adaptations by existing providers and administrators of services. These adaptations often lead to role, status, and power conflicts and resistance (ranging from passive noncooperation to active opposition) within the new organization. Conflicts are based upon the introduction of new values, new jargon, and new ways of thinking that present communication blocks and barriers to cooperation (ibid.:221). In the world of a drug court, these conflicts are reflected by values and perspectives that acknowledge relapse as inherent in the recovery process instead of as a predictor of recidivism (and therefore punishable, as in traditional probation models of community corrections); that view participants as individuals with needs and as potentially productive members of society rather than cases to be processed expeditiously; and that depend upon graduated sanctions and incentives in contrast to traditional practices that depend upon incarceration to motivate offenders' behavior. Consensus is achieved only upon intraorganizational agreement regarding the extent or depth of the crisis facing the organization. Hage notes that compared to status and power conflicts, role conflicts are less dramatic but more enduring and ultimately more threatening to effective implementation.

Musheno, Palumbo, Maynard-Moody, and Levine (1989) argue that those who implement alternative-to-incarceration programs typically encounter resistance from established governmental agencies. The extent to which policies can be successfully implemented depends upon the organizational conditions of a given setting. Musheno et al. identify four distinct organizational conditions that exist as ideal types only rarely in the real world:

- prospective rationality, in which the people at the top control people at the bottom of the organizational structure;
- inductive rationality, in which the day-to-day deliverers of services control the implementation of the intervention;
- political rationality, where power flows in both directions through the process of bargaining that takes place between the people at the top and the people at the bottom, resulting in benefits and costs to both sides; and
- transformative rationality, where the organization is comprised of a diffuse network of change agents committed to the policy's fundamental principles and who share decision-making.

While it might be possible to identify ways in which the NDC conforms to each of these ideal types, a modified form of the political rationality model is most applicable to this program. Although the criminal court component of the intervention has the legal authority to control the processing and outcome of drug court cases, in practice the judge often defers to treatment considerations in situations in which he or she has some decision-making discretion.

Sutton (1994:243–45) argues that in "decentralized and weakly bureaucratized polities" such as the United States, the boundaries of public agencies are "fuzzy" due to their overlapping interests and their indefinite authority to provide services for clients' ancillary needs. Because the delivery of services is "determined by informal rules, often in defiance of formal agency prescriptions," we have been unable to "rationalize and tame" social problems. Sutton's arguments are pertinent insofar as drug courts rely on disjointed state systems to promote a range of socially acceptable behaviors among a marginal group. The "fuzzily bounded" systems that are expected to work together in drug courts include the criminal justice system with its own disjointed subsystems; behavioral and mental health systems; welfare; and vocational and educational services. The behaviors that are the focus of drug court programs include criminality, drug dependence, unstable living situations, and unemployment, all of which demand a range of social and legal services that have not been designed to operate in concert.

Finally, Polsky (1991:5), arguing from a social control perspective, asserts that the delivery of social services is carried out by individual agencies that are disjointed and poorly coordinated, lacking a shared identity, a sense of mission (even though they are connected by an intricate web of working relationships), adequate funding, or a common dialogue. This fragmentation affects the implementation of drug courts with respect to their ability to provide coordinated services and ultimately their ability to retain participants.

These considerations of policy implementation form the groundwork for the empirical analysis that follows. This chapter addresses such basic sociological issues as the roles of bureaucratic competition, cultural values, and authority in the implementation of a drug court. While the NDC has justifiably been labeled a success in many respects by its major stakeholders, they are united in their concerns regarding the difficulties inherent in carrying out the court's day-to-day operational tasks, especially its inability to attract its targeted number of participants (two hundred per year). The particular barriers that the court has encountered may be unique to the local context in which it operates, but they are symptomatic of fundamental tensions that exist in the wider context of programmatic interventions that challenge the maintenance of traditional arenas of turf and performance of duties.

A DESCRIPTION OF THE COURT

The NDC, as of July 31, 2000, consisted of eighty-nine active clients.[3] A single judge has presided over it since its inception in January 1997, and since then 292 defendants have signed contracts with the court. Seventy-eight have graduated. The NDC is housed in the local court of limited jurisdiction and is administered by a coordinated effort of the court's administrative office and a private not-for-profit agency that also provides case management services to the court. Four substance abuse treatment agencies have established formal linkages with the court and serve most of the court's clientele, except those who need long-term residential care or otherwise have needs that cannot be met by one of the four core providers (e.g., services for participants with co-occurring disorders, services for participants without an alcohol diagnosis,[4] or women-only services). These four providers are required to attend court each week to report and make recommendations to the judge. The court has also established a connection with the local school district for General Equivalency Diploma (GED) and vocational services.

The city in which the court is located does not have a public defender office. However, indigent criminal defense services are provided by an Assigned Counsel Program (ACP). This agency contracts with a legal aid society, which provides legal services to defendants charged with misdemeanors and contracts with individual attorneys to provide services to defendants charged with felonies, to misdemeanor defendants who are involved in cases involving codefendants, or to misdemeanor defendants who already have an ACP attorney representing them on another pending charge. A single legal aid attorney is assigned to the courtroom for the NDC's weekly hearings to represent its clients. The court requests that individual attorneys representing nonlegal aid clients appear in court for all of their clients' appearances prior to their contract-signing, at graduation, and whenever the client's legal status is in question (e.g., when the judge is deliberating over whether to terminate him or her prematurely from the program). Otherwise, the director of ACP is present in court each week to provide "caretaker" representation for participants appearing routinely before the judge.

Except for a brief period during the court's earliest stage of operations a single senior assistant district attorney has represented the district attorney's office during the court's Wednesday afternoon hearings.

The court is administered by a program coordinator and her assistant. A Program Management Committee consisting of representatives of the court itself (the judge and coordinator), defense services (legal aid and ACP), the district attorney's office, treatment (the agency providing case management services), the probation office, the county's Department of

Mental Health, the Police Department, and City Court (the court clerk) functions as an advisory committee. This group assembles at least once a month to be informed about, and to make decisions regarding, the program's implementation and to provide long-range guidance.

Sixty-nine percent of the court's participants are charged with misdemeanors. Most misdemeanor defendants are referred to the NDC by their attorneys or arraigning judges, while felony defendants may be referred by their attorneys or through a daily screening process conducted by the program coordinator. The district attorney's office must approve all referrals before defendants are allowed to sign a contract with the court. At a defendant's first appearance before the NDC judge, she or he is instructed to be evaluated for substance abuse. Upon a case manager's determination of a need for treatment the defendant signs a contract with the court. This rather cumbersome process results in many opportunities for defendants to be lost to the court once they are determined to be eligible for enrollment. Recent data (February through June 2000) indicate that only 9 percent of defendants determined to be eligible for participation (on the basis of limited information that is accessible to drug court staff at the time of their screening)[5] were calendared for a NDC hearing (24/278). The reason for noncalendaring within two weeks of arraignment is mainly the nonresponsiveness of defense attorneys, the district attorney's office, and/or City Court judges to the court's requests for consideration of a defendant for enrollment. Some reasons for nonresponsiveness may be legitimate (e.g., the client's denial of a drug problem, a defendant's having been convicted in the past of a violent crime, inability of the defense attorney to determine the prosecution's intentions with the case, or the client's refusal to participate despite admitting an addiction) while others reflect a system that is apparently not yet prepared for changing its ways of doing business (e.g., defense attorneys' disinterest, unwillingness to be tied up with a case for an extended length of time without being paid, or expectation of "beating the case" on a technicality or achieving a nonincarcerative or short jail sentence; prosecutors' eagerness to pursue eligible cases even if they show little promise of conviction; and judges' desire to retain cases in which they have a personal interest or not to share authority with a "competitor" court).

METHODS

The data used in this analysis were collected as part of an evaluation of the court's implementation and a study designed to reveal situational determinants of recovery. These data came from three sources: observations of NDC sessions, interviews with NDC professionals, and observations of meetings among the members of the program management team and among treatment providers.

Either my graduate assistant or I observed 104 NDC hearings between January 1997 and April 1999 and wrote fieldnotes that focused on the interactions between individual clients and the NDC judge.[6] Each of these interactions lasted anywhere from less than a minute to twenty minutes or more, depending upon the number of problems the client presented to the court and the extent to which they demanded the court's attention. Altogether we compiled notes reflecting 2,523 scheduled appearances during this period.

We conducted seven interviews with members of the NDC program team representing the perspectives of defense, prosecution, treatment, and administration. These in-depth interviews consisted of open-ended questions related to the functioning of the court and were designed to elicit responses that would reveal facilitators of, and impediments to, its implementation.

Finally, we observed meetings and recorded the content of conversations relating to the operations of the program from December 1995 through June 1999. Having served as the program's coordinator during its planning phase, I was ideally situated to collect information on the court's initial development and to become a trusted partner in the program's implementation.

We electronically transcribed the notes from interviews and field observation and imported them into QSR NUD*IST (Qualitative Solutions and Research, Non-numerical Unstructured Data Indexing Searching and Theory-building), a software package for qualitative data analysis, which facilitated our coding of the data with respect to what they revealed about structural barriers to the court's implementation.

KEY SYSTEMS COMPRISING THE COURT

Certain categories of differences among the organizations that constitute the NDC emerged as predominant in my review of narrative data from interviews with professional stakeholders and observations of management meetings. These organizations differ not only with respect to the functions they serve but in the ways that they are funded (private vs. public), their goals (e.g., public safety vs. attending to the legal rights of the defendant), the incentives that they view as meaningful (e.g., personal earnings vs. political future), their cultures (e.g., one of adversarialness vs. one of wanting to create alliances), and their ideologies (e.g., viewing addiction as moral failure vs. viewing it as a medical problem). These differences form the basis of this portion of the analysis.

CRIMINAL JUSTICE SYSTEM

Not only are the criminal justice and treatment communities at odds in their views and practices, but the criminal justice system is itself by design a "contradictory institution." Prosecutors and defense attorneys are trained to distrust one another. Any program that offers an alternative approach can expect to confront challenges to its implementation, and overcoming these barriers is difficult in the absence of strong incentives or leadership.

Defense

Ever since the court's first planning discussions in 1995, the defense function has been perceived as a problem for the NDC in terms of its ability to attract participants and efficiently process those who *are* interested and eligible for it. This stems to some extent from the organization of defense services. As Hage (1980) notes, program innovation requires learning new values, roles, and even terminology. The wide variety of attorneys results in an uneven level of knowledge and commitment among the members of the defense bar. The likelihood of eligible defendants' enrolling in the NDC depends upon their attorneys' knowledge of the court, their interest in the court, their familiarity with issues of addiction, and their willingness to try a new approach.

Many attorneys are reported to dislike the idea of being a "caretaker" attorney in court for nonlegal aid clients after enrollment. Considerations of professional integrity and attentiveness to the interests of clients are powerful motivating forces for attorneys' decision-making behavior. The requirement of entrusting a client's interests to a "caretaker" attorney during the client's participation period (except in instances of serious noncompliance and the threat of a severe sanction) motivates many attorneys to advise their clients not to enroll.

A second possible reason for attorneys' reluctance to advise clients to enroll in the program relates to financial disincentives. Assigned attorneys are paid only after the disposition of a case, which for NDC clients averages about ten months (nine months for premature terminators and fourteen months for graduates). In contrast, non-NDC misdemeanor and felony cases are typically disposed within six weeks and five months, respectively, after arraignment and require the attorney to appear in court and work in other ways on clients' behalf during the period of adjudication. NDC participants' typical lack of a need for an attorney during their participation period creates a situation that is doubly unattractive to attorneys who may expect to retain NDC clients "on the books" for many months with no apparent activity. Despite their continued assignment to the case, such inactivity precludes opportunities to bill the ACP for services. Frustrations can also occur for an attorney when he or she is called in only to "clean up a mess" after months of losing touch with the case. Other more mundane procedural and organizational factors related to the defense function that have emerged as problematic for the court are (1) attorneys' dislike of the judge's procedure of not necessarily calling cases in the order of attorneys' arrivals, creating what attorneys perceive to be wasted time (one informant[7] described it as "a real turn-off"); (2) many attorneys' having small, even home-based, offices that lack even a fax machine to receive court documents such as contracts; and (3) the failure of most attorneys representing felony defendants to acquaint themselves with the case until the case is scheduled to go before a County Court judge three days after arraignment.

Attorneys' goals for representing their clients and the culture of "lawyering" have also interfered with the court's implementation, especially its ability to attract participants. One of the most significant of these barriers is attorneys' inability to "have the flexibility to alter their relationship with their clients," in the words of one member of the management team. Their training to protect the rights of their clients diminishes their interest in buying into the drug court model with its emphasis on the treatment of a disease that may have implications for their clients' legal status. Defense attorneys fear that allowing a client charged with a drug offense to admit to having a substance abuse problem too soon in the legal process may diminish the likelihood of the client's taking advantage of other dispositional opportunities that may be more attractive than spending a year in drug court. This dual focus of the court and its implications for the defense function has led one informant to note that the defense bar is "conflicted between the roles of counselor and counselor-at-law. They're faced with life issues and legal issues, and they're often in conflict." Another said that "attorneys think it's not practicing law, but I see it as a way out of the hellhole of substance abuse. You don't need to be quoting statutes all the time to be doing law."

Attorneys' commitment to their client's legal rights has also made it difficult for them to embrace the nonadversarial model of courtroom procedure that is central to drug courts. This adversarial orientation carries over even into their views regarding training formats and preferring not to have a prosecutor in the room who might inhibit the voicing of concerns. This unfamiliar format and attorneys' having to forfeit their assumptions regarding "business as usual" have had an unsettling effect on the local defense bar. They no longer know the rules and are confused as to who is in charge.

Prosecution

Several factors associated with the local prosecutor's office have affected the court's implementation. Since the early 1990s the district attorney has independently funded its own diversion program, which overlaps with the NDC for recruiting defendants. Although it was designed to be a program to divert "seasoned" defendants who would otherwise expect to serve substantial prison terms under state law, it has accepted some defendants charged with a felony for the first time and in some ways duplicates the work of the NDC in purpose if not in mode of operations (i.e., supervision by a prosecutor instead of the court). This diversion program, however, is a very small program, with only about fifteen active participants at any given time. Nevertheless, a spirit of turf competition that existed during the NDC's planning and early implementation periods remains. (One informant, in response to a question regarding whether the prosecution was accepting any defendants for diversion to whom they had denied enrollment in drug court, answered in the affirmative and added that "they swiped one just last week.")

Although a senior member of the district attorney's office has faithfully attended NDC management meetings since its inception and is present in court each week, he is not the person who "controls the folders" (i.e., makes decisions regarding pursuing the prosecution of cases) associated with felony cases.[8] His fellow assistant DAs who do have authority over these cases are thought by the management team to subvert the court's operations by both failing to respond to defense attorneys' requests for information regarding their intentions in certain cases as well as failing to approve the participation of eligible defendants who are either "good" (winnable) cases by the prosecution's standards or constitute a link to a larger investigation. This failure of the wider organization to play by the "team's" rules, as they have been defined by the court's planning and management committees, has frustrated the court and its efforts to recruit participants.

The district attorney himself has never been a visible presence in the court's implementation. As in the case with issues associated with the defense function, the theme of money is woven throughout the data that relate to the prosecution. These data indicate that some members of the management committee believe that the district attorney's office would have been more motivated to support the idea and operations of the court had the court included money for it in the grants that the court submitted to the Drug Courts Program Office. Such funding would have allowed the district attorney to hire an attorney to be assigned to the NDC, thereby allowing the court to be perceived as just another aspect of the work of the district attorney's office rather than an additional burden for an already overworked staff member. Others have noted the politics of his having sponsored a competing program, "interoffice dynamics" (a vaguely worded reason given by one informant, which I interpret to mean that the speaker viewed politics and rivalries as significant determinants of decision-making behavior within the office), failure of the court to provide adequate incentives [e.g., the court's failure to (1) find a way for the key players in the district attorney's office to obtain more visible credit for the court's successes, (2) specify in the program design that the prosecution "has first choice" in cases, (3) pursue assertively opportunities to nurture collegiality, or (4) persuade the prosecution of the importance of developing a reputation as an active, "team" player in this federally funded program], and the inherent difficulties associated with implementing a policy that requires the dedication of elected officials affiliated with different parties, as is the case with the NDC.[9] A comparison of the implementation of this court with others, like the Kansas City court, whose primary impetus came from the district attorney's office, suggests that more visible support from this stakeholder component would have strengthened the NDC's ability to attract participants.

Because of its goal to protect the safety of the public and a professional culture of focusing on the victim and the legal merits of each case, the prosecution is not inclined to be sympathetic to ideas related to treating offenders' addictions. Several informants identified the importance of this factor in creating barriers to the court's implementation. One asserted that the prosecution "confuses rehabilitation with punishment. From their perspective, the worse the crime, the longer they should spend in treatment. A client's disability is confused with his or her behavior in the community." Another said that "some essential elements of drug court that make it different aren't recognized by the prosecutor's office as being important—like immediacy of treatment," and another noted the resistance of prosecutors to the "rhetoric" of drug court.

Traditionally, public perceptions of prosecutorial success have been based largely on its conviction rates and its advocacy of tough sentences. Several informants noted that as an institution, the district attorney's office is unlikely to subordinate its own goals to those of the NDC. One asserted that the prosecution is compelled to prosecute good cases even though it apparently perceives itself as on board with the drug court. Any change in this orientation, one informant argued, is likely to come only from a directive from within, and no amount of outside technical assistance to educate the line staff about the benefits of the drug court concept will make a difference.

DEFENSE AND PROSECUTION INTERACTION IN THE CONTEXT OF LOCAL CRIMINAL JUSTICE PRACTICE

One practice, considered unique to this jurisdiction, has contributed significantly to the court's inability to attract eligible participants. The practice of the district attorney's office is not to pursue actively many cases involving felony-level offenses. Rather, it holds these cases in a state of "limbo," waiting for further evidence before sending them to the grand jury. As a result, local defense attorneys passively wait to see if the prosecution will act on a felony case, hoping that the prosecution will "forget" about it and that the case will "die on the vine" before the prosecution is able to strengthen its case sufficiently to obtain an attractive plea or a conviction. The local defense bar views this practice as a great advantage for its clients because it enables the defendant to be released from jail and increases the likelihood of the eventual dismissal of the charge. For the defense to approach the prosecution regarding enrollment in the NDC in such a case is seen not to be in the client's best interests. From the attorney's perspective, to spend a year in the NDC would be a more punitive outcome than would occur otherwise.

CHEMICAL DEPENDENCY TREATMENT

Chemical dependency treatment agencies are licensed by the state. Their operations are also governed by Medicaid regulations that are established by the federal government and the state Department of Health and interpreted and managed locally by the Department of Mental Health. As the state and locality have moved to Medicaid Managed Care, private agencies providing primary care services play a gatekeeper role in determining the services that are appropriate for a given client. Gatekeeper decisions may conflict with the preferences not only of the treatment provider but with the court as well. One treatment professional said that under Medicaid Managed Care a person could be denied inpatient services because she or he "hadn't had a drink for two days."[10] While all but a handful of drug court clients rely on Medicaid to cover the costs of treatment, providers and the court also must be prepared to comply with private health insurance providers' requirements.

The state licensing agency requires its providers, including those serving drug court participants, to adhere to an abstinence-based model of recovery and currently has separate licensing requirements for providers that treat persons with an "alcohol and other drug" diagnosis and those that treat persons who only abuse illegal drugs.[11] As the court's affiliated providers of inpatient services are licensed to serve people with a diagnosis of alcohol (or alcohol and other drugs) dependency, the court has been challenged by difficulties in referring those participants who are not abusers of alcohol. The solution has been to send them to out-of-town providers, thus subverting the court's efforts to provide community-based services.

Mental health conditions have emerged as a major implementation problem for the court. Case managers report that only 20 percent of participants at intake report a need for mental health services but that nearly all manifest a need for those services during the course of their treatment for chemical dependency. Several informants have recommended the administration of a thorough mental health evaluation at intake and for integrated services for those participants who need them. Unfortunately the bifurcation of mental health and chemical dependency treatment authority at the state level (where mental health services are regulated by the state's Department of Mental Health) means segregation of services at the community level. Only two local providers offer both services (albeit in a way that is not totally integrated), and neither is formally affiliated with the court and thus do not report directly to the judge in court each week. One informant has said that "when we began, we thought the problem was drugs. We can deal with some participants who are marginally crazy. The problem is with people who have more severe issues. We've had to tell some people, 'We can't help you.' It's kind of sad because everyone is there voluntarily and expecting help from us. When we say we can't help, that's sad."

However, even the court's ability to deal with those "marginally crazy" participants is not certain. A representative of one local provider of mental health services has eagerly approached the court about becoming affiliated with it and indicated that this provider was prepared to offer chemical dependency treatment for clients the court would refer to it but is limited in its ability to serve the court's Medicaid clients (nearly all NDC clients depend upon Medicaid) by virtue of Medicaid regulations that exclude the provision of inpatient behavioral health services to people aged twenty-one to sixty-four unless they are disabled. The court was hopeful that a change to (what it perceived to be) a more flexible system of Medicaid Managed Care in November 1998 would solve some of these problems, but securing the systematic provision of mental health services under Medicaid Managed Care (where the locus for decision-making has shifted to primary care providers) for the court's participants remains a problem.

While the court is very proud of its accomplishment of creating a network of providers who meet with the NDC coordinator monthly to discuss the court's implementation, share ideas about innovative procedures ("consciousness raising," according to one informant), "pool their talents and resources," and refer participants to one another when they perceive that a participant could be better served by another provider, the provision of treatment services remains within a competitive, market economy. The costs of attending court each week and participating in monthly meetings are hard to justify without a sufficient number of participants to make it financially worthwhile for these agencies. One for-profit agency was unable to sustain a commitment due to the lower-than-expected numbers of people who enrolled in the court during its first few months. Another has struggled to remain affiliated with the court and has made it clear that it will not be able to do so without an increased caseload. Treatment providers' concerns for reimbursement and related financial considerations have caused one informant to speculate that providers may retain participants in treatment longer than necessary in order to increase their income:

> We need clarity about what participants need to achieve. I don't know if the treatment providers like attorneys in there too much because they argue against their position. Participants need an attorney's voice to represent their interests. Everyone wants them to stay sober, but attorneys need to speak up if the participant doesn't want to follow a treatment provider's recommendation, like going inpatient. An attorney needs to ask "why?" Why do people need to do these recommendations? We represent the clients' voices in these decisions.

Providers affiliated with drug court also face financial difficulties as it concerns their dependence upon Medicaid reimbursement. Many clients have been cut off from Medicaid benefits as a result of their involvement in the criminal justice system or their failure to apply for benefits, especially in the case of the court's youngest participants. While committed to providing services for the court and to being flexible in their policy regarding payment for those services, systemic and individual barriers (e.g., participants' resistance to applying for benefits or for reinstatement of benefits) that limit access to Medicaid have frustrated providers in some cases and remains a barrier to smooth implementation.

The court's problems with the issue of Medicaid reimbursement are one consequence of the overall organization of health care delivery at the state level. While a few drug court programs have funding for chemical dependency treatment services, the NDC does not and depends upon Medicaid to reimburse its treatment providers for almost all of the participants it refers. Under Medicaid Managed Care, the county contracts with private providers for chemical dependency treatment services separately from other health care services. This bifurcation of services presents complications in service delivery for criminal justice system–involved clients who are more likely than the general population to have mental health and other physical health needs such as AIDS, HIV, TB, and Hepatitis C that may be associated with their chemical dependency.

A CASE STUDY

The case of "Jerry," a young man charged with a felony level drug offense, illustrates some ways in which system tensions and contradictions can shape a participant's experience of the court and attempts at recovery. The data discussed here come from observations in court and prehearing conferences. Jerry, like all participants, represents a case that overcame the prosecution's tendency to retention and the defense's tendency to be passive or resistant. The data collection was not designed to obtain information about people who would be excluded from the drug court program. This analysis, therefore, focuses on the experience of someone, once enrolled, who was affected by Medicaid regulations as well as the court's "multicultural" (conflicting) views of the role of abstinence and other forms of compliance in fulfillment of program requirements.[12]

Jerry's is actually a case that was enrolled in an exemplary way, at least with respect to achieving the court's goal of immediacy of treatment following arrest. He appeared in court eight days after his arrest and signed his contract with the court on the day of his first appearance. Upon signing his contract, the court referred him to the Alpha agency for drug treatment. His work schedule limited his treatment options, and this agency had the most flexible hours of the four outpatient treatment providers affiliated with the court at that time. Because his job failed to offer health insurance and because he earned too much to qualify for Medicaid, his case manager made plans to enroll him under his mother's health insurance policy.

During his first four months of participation, Jerry was generally compliant with the expectations set by the court and his treatment provider. He was abstinent, employed, and appeared to be uninvolved in criminal activity (as indicated by his failure to be arrested during this period). However, in the fourth month his work hours increased, and he had less time for twelve-step (Alcoholics Anonymous) meetings and therapy. He remained uninsured but was making an attempt to secure Medicaid. Alpha arranged a sliding payment scale due to his uninsured status. But with only a minimum-wage job he was still unable to pay his bills for treatment. As his debt to Alpha increased, it became an issue for the court as well as Jerry, and the judge confronted him about his payment record:

> Judge: What's going on? I'm not satisfied with your progress, and I'm getting reports that your attendance [at treatment] is slipping.
>
> Jerry: I can't get Medicaid while I live with my folks because my income and my pop's income together is too high. Now I got a bill from Alpha for something like $2,000. And my attendance hasn't fallen off. It's just that they won't even see me now because I owe them this money.

At his court appearance the following week, Jerry said that he was thinking of moving out of his parent's house in order to qualify for Medicaid. He added that Alpha had threatened to expel him but allowed him to continue on the condition that he pay at least a portion of his bill each month.

In the eighth month, Jerry did move out of his parents' house. A county agency that assists people who are denied Medicaid and have work but no insurance helped him in reapplying for Medicaid. He was transferred to another treatment provider (the Omega agency) because Alpha had grown increasingly impatient with him over his owing them several months of payments. He complained that treatment was interfering with his work and school schedules (he was working on a GED). He acquired and lost a number of jobs during this time.

In the tenth month the representative from Alpha told the court's treatment team that Jerry still had not made payments on his debt and that they were prepared to turn the case over to a collections agency. Another member of the team noted that although Jerry was still clean, he owned a car and appeared to have some money in the bank. "His behavior doesn't reflect his rising to accept responsibility for recovery." At the hearing, the judge instructed Jerry to stop at Alpha on his next payday and demonstrate a good-faith effort to pay his debt to them.

By the time he had been in the program a year, Jerry was making regular payments to Alpha but concurrently was falling behind in his payments to Omega. Given his record of compliance and engagement in treatment, he would have been considered eligible for graduation had this debt not been an issue. His treatment provider reported in chambers that although Jerry had been "doing good work he gets angry in group over his debt to Alpha." At this point Jerry's compliance generally began to regress. He even stopped working. In the fourteenth month his case manager reported that he was ready to complete treatment (one of the requirements for graduation) and that he was angry that he had not been scheduled to graduate yet. He confronted the judge on this issue in court:

Jerry: "Smith," [the judge's last name] how come I'm not scheduled to graduate?

Judge: You're almost done. It's where you are, not the amount of time.[13] What about a job? You need to be squared away financially.

Jerry: I'm working on that with my case manager, and I'm working on my GED but missed last month's test.

Prior to this exchange, in chambers, the treatment team agreed that Jerry should graduate soon (within the next three months). He needed only to secure stable employment and pay his debts. The judge remarked that once treatment was complete, "he'd be on the downhill track."

However, three months later Jerry was still in the program and lacked a steady job. Then he tested positive for marijuana, though he insisted that it was a false positive. Several members of the treatment team were concerned that he was spending too much time with the wrong "people, places, and things" (in twelve-step parlance). The judge asked Jerry to explain why his urine test was positive:

> Jerry: I took a trip and everyone in the car was smoking hydro [marijuana]. I just broke up with my girlfriend . . . all my friends smoked weed. I fell asleep in the car, and my friends started smoking. I'm not going to stop hanging with friends who smoke.
>
> Treatment Provider: Jerry tested positive three times and registered high levels of THC. He shouldn't register like that just from being in a car with a bunch of people who were smoking.
>
> Jerry: I'm not going to hang myself like that!
>
> Judge: You can't graduate from drug court right now! You need twelve clean urines. That's the number required for graduation.

The team decided to review the case, to put Jerry on a relapse prevention program, and to conduct more frequent random screens. However, his compliance did not improve. He began missing treatment appointments and court hearings, requiring the judge to sign a bench warrant for his arrest. When he finally did come to court, he exclaimed to the judge that he was sick of treatment, drug court, twelve-step meetings, and just wanted to do his time.

In the nineteenth month, his treatment provider reported that Jerry admitted smoking weed every day. She recommended that he be placed in an inpatient treatment program and then in a halfway house somewhere outside the city. The general consensus among the members of the treatment team was that Jerry had given up because he could not see an end to this process. The judge discussed this issue with him at his next scheduled court hearing.

> Judge: The deal is that you might have to go inpatient. You're not working, and you've caught dirty urines. We can't figure out what's going on in your head, Jerry. We're not concerned with treatment. It's what happens after [you leave treatment].
>
> Jerry: I might want to take my charges again. I've been here so long that I don't even know most of these people [he gestured to those sitting in the gallery]. I've been here too long and I'm getting tired of this. It ain't fun no more! I've done everything that I've been asked to. The only reason that I'm here right now is because of the money that I owe Alpha. I never even knew I owed money to Alpha until after I'd been there for a while and built up debt.
>
> Judge: Squaring your responsibility for debts and obligations to treatment are a sign of a recovery lifestyle. The persons, places, and things issue is also a problem for your recovery.

Jerry: [voice getting louder, almost shouting] My people have no bearing on all this. How do you know who I'm hanging with? Do you have me on tape? I'm living my life! Y'all are more concerned about my gold and car than you are about me.

Judge: These are issues from the past that you haven't touched yet. I've never held a gun to your head. I've always let you take the lead. We don't want to lose you! We understand that you are getting frustrated and have been here a long time. We are willing to do anything to help you end this thing right now and walk out the front door.

Jerry consented to trying inpatient treatment one more time. However, he left the facility after just one day because he felt the staff treated him unfairly. At his next hearing he explained his absconding from treatment to the judge:

Jerry: They treated me like a street thug. I've taken a long path through this program. I think what I need now is outpatient treatment, not inpatient. I've got some job interviews lined up, but I have big financial problems. I'm stressed out that my creditors might take me to court.

Judge: Jerry, what do you really want? Where do you stand?

Jerry: My mind is on the right track now. I want to get out there and prove that I can do it.

Judge: I'm willing to give you that chance, but I got to tell you something, Man you push people against the wall! How you present yourself to people is how they understand you at first. If you dress and talk like a street thug, they're going to think that you are one. This might not be fair, but it's reality. Fight your battles on the straight and narrow, and treat others with respect, and it will all follow.

The following week, Jerry's graduation status was still unresolved. The treatment team spent several minutes discussing his case in the pre-hearing meeting. One member of the team said that she felt that "we are beating this young man down and pushing him back into the streets." Another agreed, suggesting that "the court should take some responsibility for withholding graduation due to his long-standing bill to Alpha." She added, "This was a problem that was not emphasized to him while he was running up the debt." The judge said that they would reinforce the steps Jerry needed to take to complete the program and "force him out the front door."

In Jerry's remaining three months of participation his compliance did not markedly improve. However, he did complete the steps prescribed by the court and was permitted to graduate nearly two years after he signed his contract.

DISCUSSION/CONCLUSIONS

Although the different organizational missions, institutional responsibilities, and cultures represented within the court challenged its ability to achieve its self-defined goals and objectives (especially the number of referrals it was able to attract), it was nonetheless able to reconfigure criminal justice and treatment resources in a way that allowed the introduction of an innovative program in keeping with the key elements prescribed by the Drug Courts Program Office (National Association of Drug Court Professionals, Drug Court Standards Committee 1997). As indicated by its retention rate; responses to relapse; fostering a spirit of collegiality and cooperation among its affiliated treatment providers in a marketplace environment; dedicated adherence to an accountability-based model of implementation that consists of extensive qualitative and quantitative data collection; intensive case management; provision of pretreatment counseling; giving acupuncture a solid boost in the community; judge's attention to the individual participant and his or her recovery; meaningful graduation ceremonies; and institution of an alumni group it has attended to its responsibilities and demonstrated creative ways in which to manage problems that have arisen during the initial years of its operations.

The data used in this presentation, however, reveal that some thorny, even threatening issues have interfered with the court's functioning. In particular, its failure to reach its targeted number of eligible defendants has at times threatened its survival. Issues of turf, of expertise, of financial incentives, of ideology, of culture, of purpose, and of bureaucratic inertia all present disincentives to overcoming the segmentation that threatens the effective operations of the court and its ability to help its clients. The data presented support many of the theoretical assumptions identified earlier in the chapter as critical to an understanding of the process of policy implementation.

This court conforms to Polsky's (1991:6 note 5) description of the social service "apparatus." The agencies comprising this " nonsystem" maintain separate connections to different branches of government and have different purposes, but nevertheless depend in certain ways upon one another. Because the individual systems of the NDC exist under different organizational conditions, the NDC as a whole is organizationally diffuse (Musheno et al. 1989). Its operations have depended heavily upon bargaining between actors representing criminal justice and treatment interests. For example, the judge has surrendered some discretion to satisfy the interests of case managers and treatment providers but has gained the ability to participate in a national movement that is consistent with his ideas of social justice, and treatment providers have relinquished the authority to discharge clients prematurely from treatment but have gained the ability to retain a reliable caseload.

The organizational-level data also support the assertions of Sutton (1994) regarding the fuzzy boundaries that separate service delivery agencies and impede their ability to identify clear lines of authority in cases that present multiple and overlapping needs for services. Likewise, these data provide evidence of the enduring nature and problematic consequences of role conflicts, which Hage (1980) argues is inherent in the formation of organizations that require the coordination of new personnel.

The organizational and philosophic tensions that are exemplified in Jerry's story include those surrounding the financing of provider services, decision-making regarding participants' compliance with program requirements, and the extent to which the court's ability to fulfill its intended purpose is better achieved through supporting or requiring accountability of its participants. While treatment-related concerns are not traditionally within the purview of the criminal justice system, an innovative program like this drug court finds itself immersed in them. The judge encounters a wide variety of problems regarding participants' experiences in treatment and recovery that challenge his ability simultaneously to meet the program's criminal justice and public health goals (e.g., Jerry's involvement with people, places, and things that his treatment provider interpreted as incipient noncompliance but that are of no immediate criminal justice consequence).

The consequences to the NDC of the organizational barriers to full commitment on the part of the defense and prosecution are also illustrated in the case of Jerry. Although the court is designed to be cooperative and non-adversarial, the absence of input on the part of the prosecutor and defense counsel regarding Jerry's obligations and the extent to which he complied with essential NDC requirements left the judge alone to determine the extent to which his nonpayment of debt was a reflection of his success in the drug court program.

Jerry's case also illustrates some ways in which organizational inconsistencies can undermine the court's ability to achieve its goals of retaining participants and promoting recovery. His situation demonstrates the ways in which organizational-level conflicts play themselves out in the lives of program participants and threaten the likelihood both of successful recoveries and of remaining free from future involvement in the criminal justice system. His early achievements in complying with court mandates—attendance at treatment, abstinence, and a lack of criminality—soon were eclipsed in the minds of his treatment providers and the judge by the financial needs of his treatment provider. The contradictions among the various systems including private sector employment, Medicaid rules, and the treatment provider's treatment recommendations hampered the court's ability to achieve its own goals. Jerry's work schedule at first made it necessary for him to attend treatment at Alpha (which could best accommodate his schedule), but Alpha's sliding scale was not as forgiving as some of the other affiliated treatment providers. Since his jobs did not provide medical benefits and his parents' benefits would not cover him, he was left in a tenuous position. He was confronted with several possible choices: to quit working and move out of his family's home in order to achieve eligibility for public assistance, to work out the treatment payments on his own, or to terminate his participation in the program and risk a substantial prison sentence.

This chapter has focused on the implementation of a policy designed to respond to drug abuse and criminal involvement from a local organizational perspective. This response is driven by overloaded court systems willing to acknowledge the necessity for a fresh approach to the problems that judges see every day. It has required a substantial investment in resources and community-level adjustments that are as yet of uncertain consequence. Some possible long-term consequences of the drug court movement will be a "marriage" between criminal justice and public health functions that will serve to decriminalize and destigmatize its participants as well as those who are at risk of criminal justice involvement; a shift of resources from correctional to public health agencies; or (at worst) an increase in frustration for drug court constituent agencies as they attempt to carry out traditional modes of operations and achieve traditional goals.

Although some aspects of the structure and purpose of drug courts are consistent with total institutions (Goffman 1961) (i.e., they attempt to care for and limit the activities of their participants), they do not constitute a single bureaucracy. Based upon the evidence of the NDC, we might identify it as a "partial institution." It is constrained in its ability to achieve its goals and objectives because its constituent elements have difficulties communicating, cooperating, and understanding one another. The court as an institution acknowledges the necessity for compromise (one informant in a management committee meeting said, "We've all got to give a few things up"), but its constituent members have nevertheless found it difficult to shed their traditional roles and to adapt their requirements in ways that facilitate the court's operations.

The issues identified in this chapter suggest a need for better analytic models of service organization. This would help us understand the ways in which people respond to the provision of various kinds of services and the factors that influence the effectiveness of delivery systems. Network analysis can reveal the ways in which agencies relate to each other and how those relationships are mediated by the relationships that those agencies have with other related agencies. The identification of these patterns could provide answers to some of the problems that beset this court. For example, modeling the ways in which the provision of Medicaid benefits relates to the court, the ways in which the court relates to the provision of mental health services, and the ways in which the provision of Medicaid benefits relates to the provision of mental health services through a common set of variables, could indicate some ways in which these systems could be integrated and centralized in ways that are consistent with all of their goals.

The foregoing analysis suggests a number of questions related to the implementation of innovative programs. Addressing and finding answers to these possibly overlapping questions would enhance our understanding of the mechanisms that govern the implementation of drug courts in particular. These findings lead to fundamental questions about issues of bureaucratic competition and about who stands to gain from the retention (or even the creation) of obstacles to organizational innovation; the role of money with respect to the decision-making practices of the constituent agencies; the operation of incentives and disincentives to effective implementation; the ways in which authority structures are built and maintained; the ways in which drug courts negotiate their roles as promoters of public health interests and as protectors of public safety; and the consequences of the exercise of social control that is inherent in the drug court movement (Nolan 1998).

ACKNOWLEDGMENTS

I am very grateful to Corey Colyer for contributing substantially to the analysis and interpretation of "Jerry's" data; James Nolan, Kathryn Sowards, and Marsha Weissman, who read a draft of the manuscript for this chapter and provided many helpful comments; and The Drug Courts Program Office (grant number 97-DC-VX-0115), the National Institute of Justice (grant number 98-IJ-CX-0041), and the Unified Court System of the State of New York for supporting the research that led to this product. I assume full responsibility for the analysis of the data and the conclusions contained in this chapter.

NOTES

1. This connection was first articulated by Hora, Schma, and Rosenthal (1999). It is noteworthy, however, that the Department of Justice sponsored the drug court initiative with no involvement of any division of the Department of Health and Human Services.
2. Throughout this chapter I have used the term "treatment providers" to rep-

resent public and private agencies that provide treatment for chemical dependency as well as the personnel (management and staff) employed by those agencies.

3. A more typical population for the court at any given time during the past few years has been 100 to 110. It was somewhat lower at the time this chapter was written because of a recent graduation ceremony.

4. The state's Office of Alcohol and Substance Abuse Services requires its residential treatment licensees to limit its clientele to those who use alcohol in combination with other drugs.

5. Information as to a defendant's drug abuse history is not available to the court at the time of arraignment. While a defendant may have indicated that he or she uses drugs to a Pretrial Services staff member in the morning prior to being arraigned, this information is neither mentioned in court nor contained in any paperwork that drug court staff receive that would allow them to screen defendants on this basis.

6. We also recorded interactions between the judge and treatment providers and case managers when they took place in the courtroom as well as those that took place in the judge's chambers prior to each hearing.

7. Because the number of informants is spread thinly across functional roles, I have been forced in many instances to attribute a quotation or idea to an "informant" rather than a representative of a particular agency in order to protect an individual's anonymity. I have attributed the speaker's functional role whenever possible, however, in order to provide the reader with a context for the idea.

8. The NDC targets defendants charged with felonies because diverting people from prison will have the highest impact on costs to the criminal justice system.

9. The NDC judge and the Supervising Judge are Democrats whereas the district attorney is a Republican.

10. The court, however, has the authority to "trump" a decision by a managed care provider and mandate care of a type that its case managers recommend. (It also has the authority to activate Medicaid Managed Care in cases when it has been denied to a participant.) The program coordinator reports that the judge issues such mandates on average about once a week when in any typical week an average of about eight participants initiate treatment, either because they have recently enrolled in the court or because they are transferring from one treatment provider to another.

11. The licensing agency's regulations are currently being revised to eliminate this distinction.

12. Codes identifying problems either that participants mentioned in court, or that were mentioned in chambers by the treatment team, revealed three general types of problems encountered by participants: those associated with the individual (e.g., physical or behavioral problems); those associated with the participant's immediate social surroundings (e.g., people, places, and things); and those associated with the larger social structure in which the participant navigates his or her everyday life (e.g., public assistance, treatment, and the NDC). I selected Jerry as the case study for this

argument because the record indicated that he far surpassed any other program graduate with respect to his chronically mentioning having to deal with structural problems during the course of his participation period.

13. The NDC *Participants' Handbook* specifies that "the program length is determined by individual progress but will be no less than 12 months." This is reinforced to prospective participants at their orientation where they are told to expect to spend at least a year in the program. Even though the judge repeatedly tells participants that drug court is "not time driven, it's progress driven," most participants anticipate the twelfth month with the expectation of graduation without regard to their program status.

REFERENCES

Goffman, Erving. 1961. Asylums: Essays on the Social Situation of Mental Patients and Other Inmates. Chicago: Aldine.

Hage, Jerald. 1980. Theories of Organizations: Form, Process, and Transformation. New York: John Wiley and Sons.

Hora, Peggy Fulton, William G. Schma, and John T. A. Rosenthal. 1999. "Therapeutic Jurisprudence and the Drug Treatment Court Movement: Revolutionizing the Criminal Justice System's Response to Drug Abuse and Crime in America." *Notre Dame Law Review* 74:439–537.

Musheno, Michael C., Dennis J. Palumbo, Steven Maynard-Moody, and James P. Levine. 1989. "Community Corrections as an Organizational Innovation: What Works and Why." *Journal of Research in Crime and Delinquency* 26:136–67.

National Association of Drug Court Professionals, Drug Court Standards Committee. 1997. *Defining Drug Courts: The Key Components*. Washington DC: Drug Courts Program Office, Office of Justice Programs, U.S. Department of Justice.

Nolan, James L. 1998. The Therapeutic State: Justifying Government at Century's End. New York: New York University Press.

Polsky, Andrew J. 1991. *The Rise of the Therapeutic State*. Princeton, NJ: Princeton University Press.

Sutton, John H. 1994. "Children in the Therapeutic State: Lessons for the Sociology of Deviance and Social Control." Pp. 227–48 in *Inequality, Crime, and Social Control*, edited by G. S. Bridges and M. A. Myers. San Francisco: Westview.

3

West Coast Drug Courts: Getting Offenders Morally Involved in the Criminal Justice Process

Sara Steen

Drug courts in many ways represent a qualitatively new phenomenon in the area of criminal justice. While the criminal justice system in the United States has historically been based on an adversarial model, drug courts rely on courtroom players acting out a script that is nonadversarial in nature (Hora, Schma, and Rosenthal 1999). Not only do the traditional players (the judge, defense attorney, and prosecutor) adopt new roles in a drug court, but the defendant him- or herself also plays an active role in decision-making (Satel 1998). This research looks at the nature of courtroom behavior in this new environment, focusing on the question of whether alternative models of courtroom behavior can affect the investment of the defendant in the criminal justice process.

To be successful, agencies of social control must induce some form of compliance from the subjects of control. Often, compliance is forced, as when subjects of control are incarcerated: such individuals have no choice but to comply. In general, criminal justice systems induce compliance forcibly, but this need not be the case. Drug courts represent a new way of doing justice, in part because they require defendants to "opt into" the program. Drug court participants are given a *choice* as to how to comply with the dictates of criminal justice. In most drug courts, defendants choose between a traditional sentence based on some combination of jail time, community service, and community supervision, and participation in the drug court program. The choice, of course, is minimal, since they must do one or the other, but it is nonetheless a defendant's choice, something that is rarely seen in the administration of criminal justice.

Defendants participate not only in the decision about whether or not to enroll in drug court, but also in treatment decisions once they have opted into the drug court program. The participation of defendants in criminal justice decision-making is highly unusual, and suggests that this is a qualitatively different kind of justice. Organizational theories of compliance suggest that, by adopting different strategies of compliance, organizations can influence the investment of the lower participants in the organization (Etzioni 1961). If drug courts represent an avenue to get participants more deeply invested in criminal justice operations, they could serve not only to help people with their drug addictions, but also to break through some of the alienation that frequently exists between criminal offenders and criminal courts.

In this chapter, I draw on organizational theories of compliance relations and courtroom workgroups to explore the ways in which drug courts involve offenders in the justice process. Using observational and interview data from two West Coast drug courts, I describe organizational strategies for involving participants and the nature of the resultant involvement of offenders in the drug court program. I conclude that, by relying on less coercive methods of getting offenders committed to the goals of the organization (in this case, treatment of the offender's drug addiction), drug courts are able to induce a higher level of involvement by offenders than are traditional criminal courts.

THEORETICAL AND HISTORICAL BACKGROUND

Compliance Relations

Amitai Etzioni theorizes organizational compliance relations as consisting of two parts: the *type of power* adopted by the organization to induce compliance, and the *"orientation* of the subordinated actor to the power applied" (1961:3, emphasis added). Etzioni lays out three distinct types of power used by organizations to induce compliance by lower participants in the organization: coercive, remunerative, and normative. Coercive power "rests on the application, or the threat of application, of physical sanctions such as the infliction of pain, or the deprivation of physical needs such as food, sex, comfort" (ibid.:5). Incarceration is a clear example of the use of coercive power. Remunerative power "is based on control over material resources and rewards through allocation of [for example] salaries and wages" (ibid.). Employers often adopt remunerative power strategies to induce compliance from their employees. Normative power "rests on the allocation of symbolic rewards, such as acceptance and positive response" (ibid.). Normative power is often used in organizations where participants have chosen to participate, such as volunteer or religious organizations; compliance depends on participants' internalization of the norms and goals of the organization.

The second element in the compliance relationship, the involvement of lower participants, will vary depending on the type of power used to induce compliance (Etzioni 1961). Coercive power most often generates an alienative involvement, wherein the participants have an intense negative orientation toward the organization and its goals. Calculative involvement results most often from the exercise of remunerative power. Here, the participant is involved, but in a very calculated way (e.g., "I will do this so that I receive the benefits from doing it"). Finally, moral involvement, wherein participants are strongly devoted to the organization and its goals, results from the successful application of normative power.

Etzioni argues that, although organizations may use more than one type of power to induce compliance, they "tend to emphasize one means of power. This is because when two kinds of power are emphasized at the same time, over the same subject group, they tend to neutralize each other" (ibid.:7). Coercive power, for example, would not be very effective in combination with normative power, as the use of force is likely to alienate participants from the organization, while the success of normative power depends on participants' commitment to the organization.

The Drug Court Movement and Normative Power

The type of power an organization adopts will depend on a variety of factors, including the goals of the organization, the characteristics of its lower participants, and the cultural and structural conditions within which it operates. To understand why drug courts have been able to rely on normative power strategies and to identify the content of the norms underlying such strategies requires a brief history of the drug court movement within the context of criminal justice in the United States.

Drug courts were first developed in the United States in response to the "War on Drugs" of the 1980s, which resulted in phenomenal increases in court cases involving drug offenders (Goldkamp 1994). Drug courts developed in part "out of a sense of frustration that law enforcement and imprisonment policies alone were not having the impact on drug supply or demand that the proponents of the 'War Against Drugs' of the 1980's had hoped for" (ibid.:i). Part of the challenge for court reformers, then, was to find a way to cope with resource issues. The development of drug courts was an attempt to confront this issue by providing drug offenders with supervised treatment programs in an attempt to reduce recidivism and thereby stem the flow of future drug cases.

While resource concerns may have provided the trigger for a change in the criminal justice response to drug offenders, the recognition that drug offenders are addicts and should be treated as such was also invoked to support a shift in policy. Hora et al. argue that the "traditional structure [of the adversarial system] conflicts with the therapeutic foundation of the drug treatment court, and . . . may actually reinforce or facilitate addictive behavior" (1999:472). A shift away from the use of purely coercive power is due in part to the recognition that drug offenders are addicted individuals and are therefore unlikely to respond well to coercive tactics. Rather, their addictions necessitate a system in which they are "forced to confront their denial of substance abuse, accept their addiction problem, and embrace the recovery process" (ibid.:472–73). Because of the alienative effects of coercive power, courts will have to rely on different tactics to encourage such behaviors.

One of the central elements distinguishing drug courts from other criminal courts is that offending behaviors are characterized not as moral transgressions, but rather as addictive behaviors that are largely out of the control of the offender. In the system of "guiltless justice" (Nolan 2001:140) that underlies drug courts, the emphasis shifts away from placing blame and administering appropriate punishment, toward identifying the underlying causes of the offending behavior, and working to address those causes through treatment. While drug courts are deliberately structured to deemphasize guilt (for example, one of the common benefits of successful completion of drug court treatment is having the offense removed from one's criminal record), responsibility remains a central element in the normative structure of the court. Offenders are viewed as responsible for, though not entirely in control of, their offending behavior. Rather than viewing offenders as passive victims of addiction, drug courts purposely frame offenders as active participants in both their offending behavior *and*, more importantly, in their recovery.

The drug court model has proven tremendously popular as (at last count) close to eight hundred new drug courts have become operational based on the pilot project originally created in Dade County, Florida (Drug Court Clearinghouse and Technical Assistance Project 1999; Nolan 2001). While part of the success of the movement is undoubtedly related to the kinds of issues raised above, it may be argued that the popularity of drug courts is also derived from the fact that the philosophies underlying the movement do not truly challenge the fundamental principles of the criminal justice system in the United States.

First, drug courts maintain a focus on individuals rather than institutions as the appropriate target for a social response to the drug problem. Boldt (1998) argues that, by developing treatment *within* the criminal justice system, the public discourse about addiction remains focused on individuals. "Social constructs regarding individual blame and responsibility," he argues, "make it extraordinarily difficult to generate a public discussion about addiction that does not also impose a vocabulary and a set of policy imperatives directed toward treating addicts as criminals" (ibid.:1304). A treatment program developed within and directed by the criminal justice system (with its focus on individual responsibility) will, he argues, be more acceptable to the American public than a public health program based on the premise that drug addictions have broad social causes.

Second, drug courts, while representing a move away from the coercive practices involved in punishment, do not completely renounce such practices. Indeed, one may argue that the "treatment" practices advocated by drug courts have effects that are fundamentally punitive in nature. At a general level, some social critics would argue that all rehabilitative programs endorsed by the state are designed to regulate and constrain individual behavior (Foucault 1979). More specifically, critics of drug courts have argued that the "treatment" provided by drug courts is likely to be more oppressive than a standard sentence involving short-term incarceration and probation (Boldt 1998). While drug courts may use different tactics to maintain offender compliance over time, virtually all rely on fundamentally coercive tactics such as incarceration as a threat for noncompliance with court orders.

Courtroom Workgroups

To apply Etzioni's theory of compliance relations to criminal justice, it is instructive to look at the literature on courtroom workgroups. Eisenstein and Jacob (1977) developed the idea of courtroom workgroups to talk about the important interactions that occur inside a courtroom among various "players," including the judge, the prosecutor, and the defense attorney. They define a courtroom workgroup as "a complex network of ongoing relationships that determines who in the courtroom does what, how, and to whom" (ibid.:21). In the context of this study, it is helpful to determine what kinds of characteristics of courtroom workgroups might affect the likelihood that a particular workgroup will be able to implement some form of compliance strategy other than a purely coercive one.

Eisenstein and Jacob suggest that the stability of a courtroom workgroup will be an important factor in determining how justice is done in a particular time and place. Specifically, they argue that "the more familiar courtroom members are with each other, the more likely it is that they will agree about courtroom values and goals and the less they will conflict with one another" (ibid.:35). This is a critical prediction for the present chapter because the exercise of normative power will quite clearly require a low level of conflict among courtroom workgroup members.

Etzioni's theory of compliance and Eisenstein and Jacob's discussion of courtroom workgroups form the basis for the present chapter. I argue that drug court participants typically begin with an alienative, or at best, calculative involvement in the criminal justice process (often based on their experience of its coercive power in the past). Drug court workers, however, in part due to the stability of the courtroom workgroup within a drug court, are able to rely heavily on normative power in the treatment of participants. Because of this, and because the individuals who opt into drug court are likely to be at least nominally committed to the organizational goals of treatment, I argue further that many leave drug court with a moral involvement in at least this aspect of the criminal justice system. Moral involvement, wherein participants internalize the goals and values of the organization, is clearly the goal of drug courts, and I argue that they are at least somewhat successful in achieving this goal.

DATA AND METHODS

The data sources for this study include courtroom observations and interviews with courtroom personnel. The research was conducted in the first six months of 1998 in two county drug courts in a western state. As my research involved spending a lot of time inside the courtrooms, I selected the two drug courts based on their proximity to me. While the bulk of my data come from the closer of the two courts (which I subsequently refer to as the "primary court"), I spent a significant amount of time in the secondary court to check my conclusions in another setting, and thereby increase the validity of my results. While the courts differ somewhat in their culture (one operated somewhat more cooperatively than the other), they both clearly emphasized the use of normative power in place of coercive power.

Because most of my data are based on observations, and because drug courts in the state studied are open to the public, I did not experience any difficulties gaining access to the research site. I did, however, introduce myself to the regular courtroom actors early on, and was given a spot in the front row (sometimes in the jury box, sometimes at the public defender's table) so that I could better hear the courtroom exchanges. By sitting at the front of the courtroom and talking to the courtroom actors during breaks, I became an ordinary (and, to some degree, trusted) part of the courtroom audience.

The five types of activities I observed in drug court include arraignment hearings, status hearings, review hearings, termination hearings, and graduation ceremonies. I observed a total of thirty-three hours of courtroom activities. Of this time, twenty-three hours were spent in the primary county, and ten hours were spent in the secondary county. Rather than tape-record the proceedings (about which several courtroom actors expressed concerns), I took detailed notes during my observations and transcribed them immediately following my time in the courtroom. None of the courtroom actors involved are ever referred to by their real names (where names were used, I substituted pseudonyms to protect research subjects).

Toward the end of my courtroom observations, I conducted interviews with the public defender, the prosecutor, and the drug treatment coordinator in the primary county. Because of the regular nature of the courtroom workgroup (during the six months I observed, the core actors remained the same), it was possible for me, through interviewing these central actors, to obtain a fairly complete picture of the workgroup (although I requested an interview with the judge, she was unable to work me into her schedule). The timing of these interviews worked to my advantage, as all three individuals were fairly familiar and comfortable with me, and I was familiar with the kinds of issues they face in the courtroom and could compose my questions accordingly. Each interview lasted approximately one hour.

To analyze the data, I used a computer program called Atlas-ti for use with qualitative data. The first stage in analysis involved reading through a sample of the fieldnotes and developing a coding scheme. The second stage involved coding the interviews. At this stage, I read through each interview, identifying places in the interviews where a particular theme or question was touched on, and marking those passages using the appropriate code. The results of this analysis were coded interviews, which I could then analyze in a broader sense using the entire set of fieldnotes.

COMPLIANCE RELATIONS IN DRUG COURT

Before exploring the type of compliance relations used by an organization, it is important to first establish what the goal of the organization is (that is, to what end the organization is trying to induce compliance). The goal of drug courts, not unlike other types of courts, is to prevent the individual from reoffending. Drug courts, however, were founded on the belief that the most effective way to reduce recidivism among drug offenders is to provide comprehensive treatment for drug addictions. Thus, rather than leaning on the deterrent potential of punishment (as do most traditional criminal courts), drug courts rely on treatment to reduce recidivism. The ultimate goal of drug court is to get the individual offender invested in treatment, so that he or she will be able to stay clean (and not reoffend) after his or her time in drug court has ended.

The question addressed in this section is *how* drug courts go about getting offenders invested in treatment. Etzioni predicts that the kind of moral involvement that would indicate a real investment in treatment would most likely result from the use of normative compliance strategies. In this section, I provide evidence that drug courts do rely on normative strategies to induce compliance, and demonstrate that these strategies are successful in inducing moral involvement from at least those offenders who are successful in the drug court program.

NORMATIVE APPROACH TO JUSTICE

Courtroom Setting

Given that the primary goal of drug courts is to get offenders invested in their own treatment, how do drug courts set about attaining this goal? One of the most basic things that courtroom actors can do is set up the courtroom itself in a way that downplays an adversarial approach to justice and encourages the defendant to feel that he or she is part of the decision-making team. In the primary court studied, the drug court judge positioned the various actors in her courtroom to make manifest the team approach to justice. Specifically, the prosecutor, defense attorney, and defendant all sit together at a long table in front of the bench (rather than sitting at separate tables). When the case is heard, all three players stand close together immediately in front of the judge. By standing close to the judge (maintaining, in essence, a perpetual state of approaching the bench), the judge is also brought into decisions as a member of the team. Furthermore, the defendant stands between the prosecutor and the defense attorney, physically breaking down the idea that the defense attorney is present to protect the defendant from the prosecution. This physical setting represents and encourages a team approach, with the defendant as a central part of the team (in a study of fifteen drug courts, Satel found that all paid careful attention to the physical setting as an important element in the "directing of courtroom theater" (1998:65).

Courtroom Workgroup

The workgroups in both drug courts discussed in this study were very stable. In both of the county courts, one judge was assigned to drug court duty, and that judge was expected to serve in drug court for at least a year. This is generally seen as a critical element in the success of drug courts, as defendants are interacting with the drug court judge over a relatively long period of time. By retaining the same judge in drug court over a period of at least a year, the defendants are working with the same judge through-out much of their treatment program. The prosecutor is also a regular fix-ture in drug court. In both of the drug courts I observed, the prosecutor had been in the drug court for at least six months. The office of the public defender has also established two regular positions for drug court, so that the same two individuals are in charge of all drug court cases. This kind of stability means that a small group of people are working together on a reg-ular basis (which is a common element of drug courts; see Hora et al. 1999).

Because the courtroom workgroups in drug courts are relatively stable, and because the primary goal of the drug court is treatment of an addic-tion, workgroup participants behave very differently than they do in most criminal courts. The stability of the workgroup allows for a low level of conflict among players. This nonadversarial atmosphere is an important part of what enables drug courts to do what they are designed to do: treat offenders. In a drug court, everyone in the workgroup is pulling for the same outcome: getting the defendant enrolled in drug court and having him or her successfully complete treatment. This is, of course, quite differ-ent from the situation in most criminal courts, in which each courtroom ac-tor has a different goal.

Members of the courtroom workgroup in drug court want to make clear that the way justice happens in their courtroom is very different from tra-ditional courtrooms. One way they do this is by making justice a coopera-tive effort (this is another hallmark of drug courts across the country; see Drug Courts Program Office 1997). This approach is very different from the more traditional, adversarial approach to justice. Decision-making in the courtrooms studied is seen as a team effort. For example, to avoid dis-agreements in the courtroom among the various actors, the courtroom workgroup engages in backstage decision-making in the judge's cham-bers. In an interview, the prosecutor said:

> Most of what we do, we figure out in the back room so that when we come out, we present a united front. We do that because of the nature of drug ad-diction. Drug addicts are used to manipulating things. They are surrounded in the courtroom by people who are all pushing them to treatment.

This backstage decision-making allows the courtroom workgroup to main-tain the non-adversarial, cooperative approach that is characteristic of a drug court.

The team approach used in drug courts leads to dramatic changes in the allocation of courtroom roles. Rather than playing the distant authority, the judge in the courtroom studied usually plays the role of a supportive and understanding parent (for a detailed description of changes in the judge's role in drug courts, see Satel 1998). In the following case, the defendant has failed many times to comply with treatment rules, and a new plan has been developed for him.

> Judge: So, things change from moment to moment. I guess we're on, what, plan C now? I've been told you're going to try outpatient treatment now.
>
> Defendant: That's my understanding.
>
> Judge: You think this will be enough for you. You don't think you need the inpatient right now?
>
> Defendant: I know what to do now.
>
> Judge: All right, good luck. If things aren't going well, come and let us know.

Here we see the judge not only exercising understanding, but also trying to incorporate the offender himself into decision-making. Rather than taking the position that she knows best, the judge solicits the opinion of the defendant, and defers to that opinion.

The prosecutor, rather than pushing for punishment, is also seen as a member of the team. In an interview, he responded to a question about the team approach:

> You must recognize that that is done with a purpose. They're not necessarily going to see me as an ally. If they see me as an enemy, they see the team as an enemy.

The actors in this courtroom make an active effort to change the traditional image of the prosecutor. For example, the prosecutor pays close attention to personal details about the defendants' lives—things like names of family members and what they do—and brings them up in the courtroom.

The public defender is also seen as a member of the team, rather than as an advocate for the client: "I don't defend, I collaborate. A defense attorney is usually a mouthpiece for the client, here I am more like a guardian ad litem."

A guardian ad litem is an individual designated by the court to look after the "best interests" of the client, which in many cases may not be in accordance with the client's wishes. This shift in the traditional role of the defense attorney has been the cause of some concern to legal scholars. Indeed, Boldt (1998:1257) argues that "the conflict between zealous advocacy and membership on the treatment team" leaves the drug offender, still technically a criminal defendant, without the necessary legal protection mandated under the law. Because the defense attorney is expected to have an allegiance with the drug court "team," his or her allegiance to the client is compromised.

Decision-Making

Opting into Drug Court.   One way to get individual participants involved in the organizational goals is to involve them in the decision-making process. The first hearing that occurs in the drug court is one in which the judge gives the defendants information about the drug court treatment program, and asks offenders if they might be interested in opting into the program. The typical exchange is as follows:

> Judge: Let me tell you what your options are. You can take your case to trial and make the state prove the charges. Or, you can plead to a reduced charge, which would be a misdemeanor instead of a felony, and you would have no more jail time. Or you can choose treatment. If you successfully complete a treatment plan, then the charges against you will likely be dropped. You don't have to make the decision today; you can check out the treatment, come back in two weeks and let me know.

If the offender expresses an interest in treatment, he or she has an initial meeting with the drug treatment coordinator, and is given a series of tasks to follow for two weeks (such as attending meetings of Narcotics Anonymous). After these two weeks, the offender comes back to drug court and either opts into the treatment program officially, or pleads guilty to the offense and is sentenced accordingly.

A defendant's decision to opt into drug court alters their status in the eyes of the court. When someone opts into the drug court program, court officials stop referring to the individual as an "offender," and change their language to "client" [this kind of linguistic exercise occurs in other drug courts as well, with offenders sometimes being referred to as "participants" (Satel 1998)]. This marks a turning point in the offender's involvement in the criminal justice organization. While "offender" implies someone outside the law—someone opposed to the laws that are the basis of criminal justice—"client" suggests an individual who is being served by the organization. The shift in language points to a more important shift, as the defendant becomes an important part of the drug court team.

Responding to Violation of Court Rules.   The court has a set of strategies at hand to encourage compliance with the treatment program. Rather than focusing on punishing clients who violate treatment rules, the court tries to focus on rewarding good performance and understanding lapses. Even in cases where a sanction is imposed, the judge often tries to shift attention away from the lapse and focus on the overall success of the client. In the following situation, a defendant has had a relapse, which showed up in a "dirty" (drug-tainted) urinalysis test:

Judge: I think the only alternative is to give you a day in jail. This is a pretty serious breach. This is a bump in the road, and we'll get past it. I'm not going to take you into custody today, you can choose the date in the next week or so, and report to us then. Don't be discouraged. You're doing well otherwise. The important thing is you're staying clean and sober.

The focus of this exchange is on the decision-making community (including the client) understanding the lapse, and praising the client for generally successful behavior in the program. Furthermore, to reduce the alienation the client may feel at receiving a punitive sanction, the judge gives the client a choice of when to serve the sanction, reminding her that she is part of the decision-making team.

The judge, however, is not always this understanding of violations of court rules. Particularly in the secondary court studied, the judge relied heavily on sanctions, such as jail time, and clearly felt the need to be stricter and less understanding of violations than the primary court judge. In the following case, the defendant had a drug relapse, a clear violation of drug court rules. In trying to explain the relapse, the defendant says:

Defendant: I just had a really awful three weeks. Dealing with my divorce, trying to take care of my kids, working lots of overtime. I made a bad choice.

Judge: That's a bumper sticker. I understand all that. I don't take excuses. If I did, I might as well take off my black robe. This is a good recommendation—one day in jail, one day community service. Don't do this to you or me ever again. I don't know what you're going to do about your kids or your job. You should have thought of that before. You hate me now, a year from now you're going to love me. Have a seat in the jury box.

Here the judge takes what one might call the tough love approach—focusing on the violation of rules, and remaining strict in the face of excuses. He justifies this, however, as a reasonable, almost parental, strategy that will eventually work in the client's favor.

Completion of Program Stages.   One of the characteristics of normative compliance strategies is the use of ritualistic symbols to emphasize success (Etzioni 1961). In drug court, the court presents clients with small tokens of accomplishment (such as coffee cups) as they move from one stage of treatment to the next. Because drug treatment is a lengthy process, courtroom actors want to make sure that clients recognize that small steps are critical in overall success. By emphasizing these steps, the drug court is clearly trying to sustain client involvement throughout the process.

Drug court actors also use the success of some clients to show other clients (or potential clients—people who have not yet opted into the program) how successful the program can be. One of the sanctions for violating program rules involves sitting in drug court for some period of time. The goal of this sanction is to show errant clients that there are many successes in drug court.

Finally, when a client completes his or her treatment program, there is an elaborate graduation ceremony. This kind of ceremony is held once every three months or so, and celebrates all those individuals who have successfully completed the drug treatment program during that period. The ceremony involves handing out certificates of completion, statements that the drug charges have been dismissed, and small prizes (e.g., t-shirts). In addition, at graduation, each of the central courtroom actors (judge, prosecutor, and defense attorney) gives a brief speech about the success of the group, and each of the graduating clients is given the opportunity to speak. This ceremony is largely symbolic, but is clearly important in reminding clients of their own personal investment in the program.

CLIENT INVOLVEMENT: FROM CALCULATIVE TO MORAL INVOLVEMENT

Early Stages: Calculative Involvement

Offenders often enter the drug court courtroom with little understanding of the drug court program. Upon learning that successful completion of treatment results in dismissal of the drug charges against them, many offenders who claim not to have a drug problem suddenly become interested in drug treatment. Those who express an interest in treatment (for whatever reason) are generally encouraged to consider drug court as an option. There are many reasons why an individual might be interested in drug court. While some offenders may be truly interested in receiving drug treatment, many have more calculated reasons for desiring the drug court option. Specifically, drug court allows defendants the opportunity to pay for their crime without having to be locked up (at least initially; drug court sanctions often include incarceration, but this element of drug court is rarely emphasized during the offender's decision about opting into the program). Participation in drug court also allows defendants the opportunity to have their offense dismissed from their criminal record through successful treatment [Satel (1998) also finds that defendants enter drug court based on such calculations].

This calculative involvement generally does not prohibit defendants from having the opportunity to try the drug court program. Even though the judge recognizes that many individuals are interested in drug court for reasons other than treatment, she generally allows people who express an interest in treatment (even though she realizes it may not be genuine, or the primary reason the individual is interested in drug court) to opt into the program. In a few cases, however, where it is clear that the defendant's *sole* interest in drug court is something other than treatment (such as in the following example), the judge may discourage the individual from opting into the program:

Judge: Mr. D., do you have a drug problem?

Defendant: No. But I don't want a felony on my record.

Judge: You might want to take your case mainstream if you want to challenge the case. If you don't have a drug problem, then treatment is going to be tough.

If the court senses that the defendant's interest is *purely* calculative, the individual may be discouraged from enrolling in drug court. Without at least an acknowledgment of a drug problem (genuine or not), as the judge states here, treatment will likely be unsuccessful.

Later Stages: Moral Involvement

For drug court to be successful in achieving its goal of treating drug-addicted offenders, the offenders themselves must get morally involved. Specifically, they must internalize the goals of the organization for treatment to be a lasting success. This poses a serious challenge to drug courts, as *many* defendants enter drug court for calculated reasons (rather than moral reasons).

The results of this study demonstrate that clients who are successful in their treatment programs *do* seem to become morally involved in drug court. Evidence of this involvement was clear at the graduation ceremony held for those individuals who successfully complete the treatment program in drug court. At the ceremony, the clients all have the opportunity to speak about their drug court experience. The following quotations show what some of them had to say:

John: This has been a great opportunity and a real privilege. I was very fortunate to be accepted into the drug court program. . . . Without my counselor Michael's direction, I don't know where I'd be now. It was pretty hard to fail when everyone was so damn nice. This whole program is just a wonderful, wonderful opportunity. With that, good luck to everyone else.

Xavier: I'd like to thank the system. It saved my life (crying). I'd like to thank Judge Martinez. When I came in, I couldn't stay awake. I kept passing out. I want to thank this court for getting me from one place to another.

Terese: When I got arrested, I thought it was the end of my life. In fact, it was the beginning of a new life for me. To be honest, I don't have much faith in the system, but we are proof that the system can work. I started looking forward to coming here; isn't that strange?

These testimonials suggest that drug court is successful in getting clients morally involved in the goals of the courtroom workgroup. It is a rather remarkable experience to sit in a courtroom and listen to offenders bestow praises on the court that has imposed so many rules on their lives over a period of at least a year. Satel also notes this kind of change in the drug court participants she studied: "While they are literally captive to the program, they acquire genuine, internal motivation" (1998:59). That the drug court is able to induce this kind of devotion from offenders suggests that the court is doing something quite effectively.

DISCUSSION

This study provides support for Etzioni's assertion that normative power can result in moral involvement. The results suggest that, by involving offenders in decision-making, and by treating them patiently instead of punitively, drug courts are able to do what criminal justice organizations are rarely able to do: get the offenders invested in the goals of the organization.

The results provided here demonstrate that, through a variety of techniques including manipulation of the courtroom setting, of courtroom roles, and of decision-making practices, drug courts are able to exercise strategies based primarily on normative power. This in itself is rather remarkable, given that criminal courts have traditionally relied on coercive power, which lies at the opposite end of the spectrum in Etzioni's classification scheme.

Further, the results show that, while most clients enter drug court with a calculative or even alienative involvement in the goals of the criminal justice system, those who make it through the treatment program successfully emerge morally invested in their own treatment. It must be noted that the testimonials demonstrating such moral involvement all come from individuals who have successfully completed the drug court program. It is perhaps this moral involvement that keeps clients in the drug court without having their cases moved into the mainstream. The hope is that, as these individuals move out of the organizational environment (that is, as they move back into their own lives without the supervision of the drug court), they will be able to sustain this investment in the organizational goals of treatment.

REFERENCES

Boldt, Richard. 1998. "Rehabilitative Punishment and the Drug Treatment Court Movement." *Washington University Law Quarterly* 76:1205–1306.

Drug Court Clearinghouse and Technical Assistance Project. 1999. "Looking at a Decade of Drug Courts." American University supported by Office of Justice Programs, U.S. Department of Justice. www.american.edu/justice

Drug Courts Program Office. 1997. *Defining Drug Courts: The Key Components.* Washington, DC: Office of Justice Programs, U.S. Department of Justice.

Eisenstein, James and Herbert Jacob. 1977. *Felony Justice: An Organizational Analysis of Criminal Courts.* Boston: Little, Brown.

Etzioni, Amitai. 1961. *A Comparative Analysis of Complex Organizations.* New York: Free Press of Glencoe.

Foucault, Michel. 1979. *Discipline and Punish.* New York: Vintage Books.

Goldkamp, John S. 1994. "Justice and Treatment Innovation: The Drug Court Movement. A Working Paper of the First National Drug Court Conference, December 1993." National Institute of Justice, Office of Justice Programs, U.S. Department of Justice, Washington, DC.

Hora, Peggy Fulton, William G. Schma, and John T. A. Rosenthal. 1999. "Therapeutic Jurisprudence and the Drug Treatment Court Movement: Revolutionizing the Criminal Justice System's Response to Drug Abuse and Crime in America." *Notre Dame Law Review* 74:439–537.

Nolan, James L., Jr. 2001. *Reinventing Justice: The American Drug Court Movement.* Princeton, NJ: Princeton University Press.

Satel, Sally. 1998. "Observational Study of Courtroom Dynamics in Selected Drug Courts." *National Drug Court Institute Review* 1:43–72.

4

The Denver Drug Court and Its
Unintended Consequences

Morris B. Hoffman

INTRODUCTION

As a Colorado state district judge since February 1991, I participated in the decision to begin the Denver Drug Court in 1994. Since its inception on July 1, 1994, I have also observed its operations and its impact on the rest of our bench. Like its popular predecessors, and now its popular offspring, the Denver Drug Court began on a note of optimism, sparked in our case by the deeply held convictions of a single judge and a handful of prosecutors, police officials, and probation officers. Like its predecessors and offspring, the Denver Drug Court was founded on the twin principles that drug defendants' high recidivism rates could be significantly reduced with treatment rather than imprisonment, and that the costs of the treatment could be more than offset by the savings in reduced prison populations (Murphy 1997).

Seven years later, the Denver experiment has gone terribly wrong. There has been no measurable reduction in recidivism, and massive net widening has had the effect of dramatically increasing, rather than decreasing, the number of drug defendants sent to prison. The caseload has mushroomed beyond all pretense of control. Less than three years after its inception, its jurisdiction had to be arbitrarily slashed by 25 percent. Despite these cutbacks, the docket has remained unmanageable, though the addition of magistrates and the delegation of many tasks to the magistrates have improved the situation.[1] Few judges volunteer to be assigned to the drug court, and it is a challenge for those who do volunteer for the job to serve out their one-year term. Our chief judge is coming close to running out of volunteers, and the program may soon be discontinued or shuttled off to the county court simply because no more district court judges may be willing to preside there. Effective May 1, 2000, our chief judge was forced to make yet another drastic change in the way our drug court works—transferring some pretrial functions to our county courts—in an attempt to make drug court palatable enough to attract some district judge volunteers, and to avoid its termination or wholesale transfer to county court.

Federal funds—so freely made available to us at the beginning of our drug court—are drying up as we move from pilot program to permanent drug court.[2] The combination of the increasing loss of federal funding and "the reluctance of judges to work [in drug] court" has prompted our probation department to suggest that remaining funds be directed away from drug court and toward a probation department's special drug program (Denver Adult Probation Department 2001). Under this proposal, drug defendants would be sentenced from *all* the criminal courts, not just from the drug court, and the probation department would take back much of the supervision function from drug court. We have appointed a committee of judges not only to study the probation department's proposal but also to consider the alternative of doing away with our drug court entirely. The experience of the Denver Drug Court provides us with important and sobering lessons about the drug court movement in general and about the way drug court theories are actually implemented.

THE FORMATION AND OPERATION OF THE DENVER DRUG COURT

The judges on our court approved the Denver Drug Court in early 1994, and it began operations on July 1, 1994. All felony drug cases filed in Denver with an arrest date after July 1, 1994, were assigned to the Denver Drug Court.[3] Consistent with the objective that drug court would be a self-contained institution designed to handle all felony drug cases (from cradle to grave), the drug court initially heard all second advisements,[4] bond returns, and preliminary hearings in all felony drug cases—proceedings that in Denver are otherwise routinely handled by our county courts rather than our district courts (Long 1996). This, anyway, was the practice until the changes implemented on May 1, 2000.

Unlike most drug courts, however, the Denver Drug Court was, as least in the beginning, a so-called all-comers drug court. There were no eligibility criteria (for example, a limitation on a defendant's number of prior felony convictions) to qualify for assignment to the drug court. Indeed, our drug court even captured cases in which a drug charge was just one of multiple charges against a defendant (ibid.).

Like most recent drug courts, the Denver Drug Court is both a differentiated case management (DCM) court (a court with an accelerated case processing structure) and a treatment court. All defendants arrested on a felony drug charge undergo a standardized drug and alcohol evaluation while in jail. The results of that standardized evaluation are then used by the drug court judge to set bond and to decide the appropriate treatment program for each defendant. Our treatment and reporting regimen is not unlike most DCM- and treatment-based drug courts.

Drug court defendants are typically released on bonds that contain as conditions the requirement that the defendants submit to, and pass, drug testing. Positive urinalyses or failures to report will result in revocation of the bond, imposition of a short (two- to five-day) jail sentence and then reinstatement of the bond. Defendants who agree to plead guilty are typically offered dispositions that involve either a deferred judgment or probation. In either event, their continued and successful participation in a designated treatment program is made a condition of the deferral or probation. The drug court judge has several alternative treatment programs to choose from, depending on the perceived nature of a defendant's drug problem and the prognosis for recovery.

The treatment program is coupled with an in-court monitoring program. At the court appearances, the drug court judge reviews the results of the drug tests and the defendant's general progress in treatment. The monitoring program proceeds in three phases. At least as originally designed, a defendant in Phase I must submit to drug tests twice every week and must appear in court once every other week. In Phase II, the drug tests are done once every week and the in-court appearances once every month. Phase III defendants are subjected to random drug tests and must report to court only on an as-ordered basis (Long 1996).

Missed drug tests, positive drug tests, or other failures of treatment are punished quickly—as at the preadjudication stage—with the imposition of short jail sentences as additional conditions of the deferral or probation. Repeated violations can also result in regression into a stricter monitoring phase or even relocation into a different treatment program. At some point, determined on a case-by-case basis by the drug court judge, the ultimate sanction for repeated treatment failures is revocation of the deferral, revocation of probation, then imprisonment.

Defendants who successfully complete their treatment program and proceed through all three monitoring phases are said to have "graduated." Although they may no longer be required to submit to regular drug testing or court appearances, the terms of their deferral or probation typically extend for several years, subjecting them to traditional revocation should they violate the conditions of their deferral or probation postgraduation.

THE FOUR GOALS

The Denver Drug Court was formed on the strength of four central goals articulated by its proponents: (1) it would not greatly widen the nets; (2) it would be self-contained, and would handle most of its own trials and motions hearings; (3) it would substantially reduce drug defendant recidivism; and (4) it would reduce the numbers of drug defendants being sentenced to prison. None of these four goals has been achieved.

The Denver Drug Court Would Not Greatly Widen the Nets

We underestimated the enthusiasm with which our police and prosecutors would embrace the idea of the drug court. We expected that the drug court would stimulate some modest increase in the number of drug filings, but instead of modest increases we got massive, unprecedented increases. Drug filings nearly tripled after the drug court's first full year of operation. There were 1,047 drug cases filed in the Denver District Court in 1993, the last full year before the drug court. In 1995, the first full year of drug court, that number jumped to 2,661. In 1996, drug filings increased still further, to 3,017 (Flesche 1999). Although there are no published data on recent filings, I understand that they have leveled off in the last few years near the 2,400/year range, still more than twice the pre–drug court level.

This increase in drug filings was not merely a reflection of the overall increase in criminal filings. On the contrary, from the moment our drug court was created the *percentage* of drug cases filed in our court has exploded. In 1993, the first full year before drug court, drug filings represented 27.8 percent of all criminal filings in the Denver District Court. In 1995, the first full year after drug court, that percentage skyrocketed to 51.6 percent, and has remained at that high level ever since. The complete figures for the eight years 1991 through 1998 are given in Table 1 (Flesche 1999).

It is clear that the very presence of drug court, with its significantly increased capacity to process cases, has caused police to make arrests in, and prosecutors to file, the kinds of ten- and twenty-dollar hand-to-hand drug cases that the system simply would not, and could not, have bothered with before. It is not just a matter of intensifying existing arrest and charging policies; since the adoption of drug court the Denver Police Department

Table 1.   Drug Filings in the Denver District Court, 1991–1998

Year	Criminal Cases	Drug Cases	Drug Cases (%)
1991	3,795	958	25.2
1992	3,790	1,014	26.7
1993	3,762	1,047	27.8
1994	3,907	1,260	32.2
1995	5,154	2,661	51.6
1996	5,814	3,017	51.9
1997	5,458	2,825	51.8
1998	5,089	2,585	50.8

has embarked on an extensive and unprecedented campaign of under-cover "buy-bust" operations (Ritter 1999).

Because the purpose of the drug court is to treat drug users, its presence has obligated police to concentrate their efforts on small-time users and dealers, and to deemphasize larger traffickers. The buy-bust operations put in place after drug court are designed not so much to reduce drug trafficking as to provide the drug court with a continuing supply of patients. Of the many drug court trials and motions I have heard as a transfer judge over the last seven years, only one involved trafficking in more than a fraction of an ounce.

The massive and underestimated net-widening triggered by the drug court has had immediate and drastic impacts on its operations. The un-controlled caseload has compromised the morale of the drug court judge and staff, forced a cookie-cutter approach to sentencing, and impacted the overall quality of drug court justice. The sheer number of defendants run through drug court every day is taking an enormous toll on the drug court judge, the drug court staff, sheriffs, prosecutors, and public defenders. In 1997 and 1998, an average of ninety-one defendants were on the drug court docket each day (*Denver Drug Court Statistics 1997 and 1998*). In 1999, that average climbed to ninety-five (Denver Drug Court 2000). By contrast, non–drug criminal district courts in Denver handle an average of eight to twelve nontrial matters every day, in addition to our regular trial dockets (Hoffman 2000). Even our county traffic courts do not see daily numbers approaching the numbers seen in drug court.

Except for its Herculean founder, no judge has been able to remain in the Denver Drug Court for more than one year, and even then it has been necessary for judges to take regular and substantial breaks. We have even discussed a formalized sabbatical program, where the drug court judge is relieved on a regular and frequent basis. Denver's experience with judge burnout in drug court is certainly consistent with what some prescient drug court proponents have predicted:

Incentives for judges to preside over the special drug court may need to be created by the judicial administrators if a highly skilled volunteer judge cannot be found. This assignment may be viewed as boring or repetitive, a certain route to frustration and burnout. (Belenko and Dumanovsky 1993:10)

Treating serious felonies like traffic tickets has also meant that the drug court judge has been forced to adopt cookie-cutter sentencing practices as a substitute for the kind of particularized sentence to which every criminal defendant, and especially every felony defendant, is entitled. The dispositional algorithm in the Denver Drug Court, at least for defendants charged with simple possession, is fairly rigid: (1) if you have no prior violent felonies and were arrested with a small so-called personal amount of drugs, you get a deferred judgment; (2) otherwise, you get probation (Long 1996). This isn't sentencing, it's triage. It is what we must all expect when the volume of cases allows the drug court judge to spend only a few minutes on each case.

Predictably, quality has also suffered. The drug court docket simply does not allow us the time to be the kind of deliberative and careful judicial officers—or prosecutors or defense lawyers—that all felony proceedings demand. Two examples will illustrate the point. When I was on the criminal bench in 1997, I agreed to take a transfer of a motions hearing from drug court. The public defender and the defendant appeared promptly after I agreed to take the transfer, but the district attorney (DA-1) never showed up. After some calling around, my staff determined that DA-1 thought DA-2 was handling the hearing, and vice versa. DA-2 finally showed up (an hour late), did the hearing, and requested at its conclusion that he be allowed to file posthearing briefs, a request I granted. I set a briefing schedule, which DA-2 then missed. When he finally filed his brief (one week late), he filed a draft, which had no caption, no case name, and no signature.

The second example is more troubling. In June 1997, a drug court defendant confessed his probation violation as part of an agreement in which he was to receive a four-year community corrections sentence instead of a prison sentence. But a clerical error in the minute order, repeated in the mittimus (the order directing the sheriffs to deliver custody of a prisoner to correctional facilities), resulted in the defendant being given a four-year *prison* sentence. A surprised defendant was transported to prison instead of to community corrections. He sent a letter to the drug court judge complaining about the mix-up. The overworked drug court judge misread the letter, treated it as some other kind of routine request, and issued a form order denying the request. It took an emergency appeal to get the matter straightened out. In the meantime, the defendant served more than eighteen months in prison when he should have been in community corrections.[5]

These examples are not the sort of isolated incidents that darken even the most diligent of busy urban courtrooms. They are what we can all expect from the volumes that are generated by treating serious felonies like traffic tickets. Even after sloughing off all its trials and most of its motions hearings, the Denver Drug Court could still not keep its head above the rising tide of filings. In 1997, the then presiding drug court judge decided that something drastic had to be done to cut the caseload by roughly 25 percent. Effective February 18, 1997, he excluded from drug court all cases in which the defendant was either a two-time felon or an illegal alien.

However, these cutbacks were made only at the drug court level—by district attorneys filing the excluded cases in the regular courtrooms rather than in drug court. No change was made at either the street level, in terms of who was getting arrested, or at the charging level, in terms of who was getting prosecuted. The nets stayed wide, and 25 percent of the catch was thrown over to the regular courts.

Trying to reach an arbitrary 25 percent reduction by slashing so broadly to exclude all two-time felons and illegal aliens fundamentally altered the original "all-comers" philosophy of the Denver Drug Court. Every two-time felon is not an unacceptable drug court risk. Before February 1997, the Denver Drug Court regularly gave dispositions to two-time felons if they were otherwise appropriate candidates for treatment. Indeed, drug court proponents have long argued that the hardcore addict—who more often than not has been through the revolving doors of prison on many other drug and drug-related convictions, and therefore is likely to have two or more prior felonies—is precisely the kind of person drug courts were intended to reach (Belenko 1998).

There is, by contrast, a sensible justification for excluding illegal aliens: defendants subject to INS custodial "holds" will be ineligible for outpatient treatment. But their ipso facto exclusion from drug court should make us all wonder about the fairness of a system that makes these kinds of arbitrary and suspicious distinctions simply because drug court proponents have bitten off more than they can chew.

Even the 25 percent reductions made in 1997 have not reduced the caseloads enough to change the fundamental "mill" nature of the drug court. We are fast running out of volunteer judges willing to spend even a one-year term in the drug court. The prospects have become so bleak that our new chief judge decided to make even more fundamental changes in the way the drug court operates. Effective May 1, 2000, all drug cases are now filed initially in county court, and county court handles the cases until either a disposition is reached and the case is then sent to the drug court, or, if no disposition is reached, probable cause is found and the case bound over to a regular district court for trial. The chief judge hopes that by separating, early on, the cases that will and will not go to trial, the drug court will be freed to concentrate on the treatment and reporting aspects of cases that do reach dispositions.

These changes are too new to evaluate, although the current drug court judge reports that they have made a dramatic difference and made his job considerably more tolerable. But the apparent savings in in-court time spent by the drug court judge probably comes at the cost of losing one of the key aspects of drug courts: early intervention. Now that the already overworked county courts must also do initial advisements in all drug cases, not only is the drug court judge not involved in any reviews while the case is pending in county court, but the time between arrest and preliminary hearing has increased from one or two weeks to three or four weeks. Thus, the "savings" in drug court time may simply be the result of an unstated abandonment of the fundamental therapeutic axiom of early and frequent intervention.

In any event, very little pretrial drug court time was spent on cases that eventually went to trial. After all, the most time-consuming pretrial event in any criminal case is the motions hearing, and most of those are already being done outside drug court, as discussed below. Moreover, many criminal cases do not reach a disposition until after the defendant loses his or her motion to suppress. This latest reform may thus merely be formalizing what is already happening in drug court: the motions hearings are being heard in other courtrooms, then the disposition and all other postdisposition monitoring happen in drug court.

The Denver Drug Court Would Be Self-Contained, and Would Handle Most of Its Own Trials and Motions

Part of the way the drug court idea was sold to our bench was the promise that it would relieve the other six criminal divisions of a significant and depressing portion of their caseload. The idea in the beginning was that drug court would be entirely self-contained, doing its own motions and trials, and seeking outside assistance only on the occasions when its docket required it. In a matter of weeks, however, it soon became clear that the massive net widening caused by the drug court was making it impossible for it to do *any* of its own trials. All drug court trials were transferred to the other courts, a practice that has persisted over the life of our drug court.

The explosion of drug filings caused a similar, though somewhat less dramatic, sloughing off of motions hearings. Our first drug court judge managed to do most of his own motions hearings, but that became impractical as the numbers of people in the reporting pipeline accumulated year after year. The drug court judges in years three and four were transferring virtually all of their motions hearings. The drug court judge in year five attempted to reacquire the motions, but his successor abandoned that approach. At this writing, the bulk of drug court motions are still handled outside the drug court. Indeed, two of our three domestic judges have agreed to a formal system of hearing drug court motions every Friday afternoon, their domestic dockets permitting.

Thus, the Denver Drug Court has increased, rather than decreased, the workloads of the other divisions, precisely by the amount of the new cases that are captured by the widened nets and that end up going to motions hearings or to trial, less any increased disposition rate enjoyed by drug court. But the disposition rate is already high in non–drug criminal cases, and there is no evidence that drug court cases reach plea bargains so much more often than regular criminal cases as to counteract the two- or three-fold increase in drug filings.

There has been a less direct, but no less troubling, impact on our bench from the drug court's inability to handle its own docket. We have a long tradition on our court of judges helping each other out when one of them has more than one trial or hearing set to begin on the same day. We have kept statistics on these transfers, and before the adoption of drug court the transfer rate—the rate at which litigants in need of another judge to hear their case were able to find such a judge—consistently hovered around 80 percent. Since the implementation of drug court, that number has plummeted to 50 percent (Hoffman 2000). As a result, both civil and criminal litigants in Denver are substantially more likely today than they were seven years ago (when the drug court began) to have their hearings and trials continued simply because the drug court cannot handle its own cases.

Our collective unwillingness to accept drug court transfers reached such heights that in mid-1999 we adopted a change in procedure in which drug cases are no longer set for trial until the deadline for disposition passes. They are then assigned for trial to one of the regular criminal courtrooms, on a rotating basis, without waiting for a volunteer transfer judge.

The Denver Drug Court Would Significantly Reduce Recidivism

One of the most important promises of all treatment-based drug courts is that they should interrupt the drug/crime cycle (Brown 1997). Most studies use arrest recidivism as the impact measure. They compare the percentage of drug court defendants who are rearrested in a given follow-up period with the percentage of non–drug court drug defendants rearrested in the same follow-up period (Belenko 1998).

The independent impact study done of the Denver Drug Court in 1997 showed a pre–drug court one-year recidivism rate of 58 percent, and a drug court one-year recidivism rate of 53 percent (Granfield and Eby 1997).

When the evaluators looked at the somewhat more sophisticated measure of average number of arrests in the follow-up period, the results were even less encouraging: drug defendants suffered an identical average of 0.8 arrests in the one-year follow-up period regardless of whether they came out of a regular court or out of the Denver Drug Court.

The Denver Drug Court Would Reduce the Number of Drug Defendants Being Sent to Prison

One of the most troubling aspects of the Denver Drug Court is that, despite the crucial reformist promise that drug courts will reduce prison populations (Granfield and Eby 1997), the Denver Drug Court is sentencing more drug defendants to prison than the traditional courts ever did, by a factor of more than two.

In 1993—the first full year before the Denver Drug Court—265 drug defendants were sentenced to prison out of the Denver District Court. In 1995—the first full year after drug court—434 defendants were sentenced to prison sentences out of the Denver Drug Court. In 1997, 625 drug court defendants received prison sentences in the Denver Drug Court (Office of Planning 1998). In other words, although the percentage of drug defendants receiving prison sentences has remained remarkably constant pre- and post–drug court, the raw number of drug defendants going to prison has more than doubled since the adoption of drug court.

The apparent paradox of more drug defendants going to prison out of a court designed specifically to send less drug defendants to prison is not surprising at all. It is a direct and entirely predictable consequence of high recidivism rates coupled with massive net widening.

WHAT DENVER'S EXPERIENCE SHOULD TEACH US ABOUT THE DRUG COURT MOVEMENT

When considering this question, we should remember Mark Twain's admonition: a cat who sits on a hot stove never sits on a hot stove again, but it also never sits on a cold one. There may be many unique things about the Denver experience that make it a dangerous base from which to generalize. For example, the original "all-comers" nature of our drug court no doubt contributed to its poor recidivism results.

But there is also no doubt that the Denver experience can teach us some valuable lessons about how drug courts really work when the rubber of the theoretical treatment model hits the road of the criminal justice system, and why drug courts continue to spread despite their lack of demonstrable effectiveness.

Recidivism

Although Denver's recidivism results were particularly unimpressive, what is most telling about them is that they are entirely consistent with the remarkably unimpressive results achieved by most formal impact studies. One of the first of those studies, of the seminal Dade County, Florida, Drug Court sponsored by the ABA in 1991, reached conclusions even less positive than Denver's: drug defendants convicted in Miami before the implementation of their drug court suffered a one-year recidivism rate of 33 percent; drug defendants convicted in the drug court suffered a one-year recidivism rate of 32 percent (Smith and American Bar Association 1991).

Many subsequent impact studies have had similarly sobering results, as the samples in Table 2 illustrate. It is true that a few impact studies have reported significant reductions in recidivism. Most of those, however, like most of the informal studies done by drug court personnel themselves, make an incorrect comparison between the control group of drug defendants before drug court and the target group of drug court *graduates,* a comparison most experts agree is flawed (Belenko and Dumanovsky 1993; Shaw and Robinson 1999). The handful of evaluations that do make the correct comparison suffer from a host of other methodological defects, including using unacceptably short follow-up periods, using different follow-up periods for the control group and the target group, and failing to randomize the control or target groups (Hoffman 2000).

On the whole, it is certainly fair to characterize the reliable formal impact studies as showing statistically insignificant reductions in recidivism (Nolan 1998, 2001). Indeed, most evaluators themselves characterize the state of the research in exactly this way. Two of the most comprehensive and important drug court metastudies, one done at Congress's request by the University of Maryland and one done by the General Accounting Office, reached identical conclusions about the data on drug court recidivism:

Table 2. Drug Court Impact Studies

	Recidivism (%)	
Drug Court	Pre–drug court	Drug court
Baltimore, MD		
district	27.1	22.6
county	30.4	26.5
Maricopa County, AZ	48.7	33.2
New York, NY	50.5	53.5
Travis County, TX	41.0	38.0
Wilmington, DE	51.1	33.3

Source: Belenko (1998), Belenko and Dumanovsky (1993).

despite the existence of literally hundreds of drug courts, only a handful of formal impact studies have been done that measure the correct target group of *all* drug court defendants rather than drug court *graduates*, and there is simply insufficient data to conclude that drug courts reduce recidivism (Sherman et al., 1997; GAO 1997).

Intrabranch Problems

As discussed in some of the sections above, the Denver Drug Court has put tremendous and unacceptable stresses on all our judges and court staff, and it is not just a matter of the uncontrollable caseload. Do we really want judges acting as glorified probation officers? And, to the extent they are more than just glorified probation officers, do we really want to institutionalize their individual sentencing philosophies?

Drug court judges spend most of their time doing things that could and should be done by probation officers. This criticism is not meant to denigrate the efforts of probation officers or to overvalue the efforts of judges. On the contrary, our roles have become muddled in drug court not because judges have stepped into a vacuum created by incompetent probation officers, but rather because the very purpose of drug court is to blur the adjudicative and probationary functions. It is a blurring that not only violates basic notions of adversariness, as discussed below, but that also makes no practical organizational sense. Drug courts have crowned the drug court judge as a kind of super probation officer, with direct probationary responsibility over thousands of defendants rather than with supervisory responsibility over a few dozen probation officers. This kind of probationary micromanagement is terribly inefficient, even ignoring the fact that the crowned super probation officer is by definition a rank amateur.

Even if there were an inherent value in a judge, rather than a probation officer, performing probation functions in drug court (and many drug court proponents claim that defendants pay more attention to judges than to probation officers) we must all recognize that we pay an institutional price for that supposed added value. Judges, trained in the nuances of procedure and evidence and supposedly appointed for their temperament and their ability to do justice, spend their days in drug courts looking at urine sample results and deciding how many days of jail time to impose on the reluctant patient. Is this really the kind of work the judicial branch wants its judges doing? Is this really the kind of work most judges want to be doing?

In addition to his or her role as a glorified probation officer, the drug court judge also imposes sentence. To the extent that this is an exercise of judicial discretion (and, as discussed above, in drug court the massive dockets have turned the sentencing process into much more of a mechanical, nondiscretionary process), do we really want the sentencing philosophies of a single judge institutionalized for an entire year?

The act of sentencing a defendant is intensely personal. One of the reasons most multi-judge criminal courts do not have specialized burglary courts or forgery courts or sexual assault courts is to avoid enshrining a single judge's sentencing philosophy. Of course, differences between judges necessarily result in inconsistent sentences. By continuing to vest in judges some meaningful sentencing discretion, most state legislatures are expressing the public policy that sentencing inconsistency is a price worth paying for a system that, at least in theory, has the capacity to make individual adjustments when necessary to achieve a just result. Within limits, one person's sentencing inconsistency is another person's justice.

An important check on the awesome sentencing responsibility with which judges are invested is to spread around the sentencing duties in multi-judge courts, either by insuring that all judges do all kinds of cases (the so-called integrated approach) or, in specialized courts, by insuring that judges regularly rotate from one specialty to another (the so-called nonintegrated approach). Otherwise, our gain in consistency is paid for with an unacceptable concentration of sentencing power in a single judge.

Drug courts are the worst of both of these worlds. They fix an individual judge's sentencing philosophies for a long period of time, and then the whole bureaucracy must adjust to a new sentencing philosophy when the drug court changes judges. It is true that traditional courts face this same challenge whenever there is a change of judge. However, the problem is substantially worse in drug courts, not only because the judges will tend to burn out more frequently but, more importantly, because drug courts, unlike other felony-level criminal courts, typically occupy an entire criminal field. For the whole period of time Judge Jones sits on the Metropolis Drug Court, every defendant charged with a felony drug crime in Metropolis must face Judge Jones and her particular sentencing philosophy. This is a dangerous concentration of judicial power, and one most multiple-judge courts are specifically designed to avoid.

Moreover, judicial power is more sharply exercised in drug courts than in traditional courts. The very purpose of drug courts is to coerce treatment, and the drug court judge is the chief coercer. His or her powers are not only grounded in the inherently intrusive act of forcing people to undergo quasi- and pseudomedical treatment, but those powers are brought to bear much more frequently than in traditional courts. Drug court judges are, and are meant to be, a regular and unpleasant force in the daily lives of drug court defendants. The particular sentencing predilections of any given judge are therefore much more likely to express themselves in drug court than in traditional court.

Nor are drug courts a sensible antidote to judicial frustration over mandatory minimum sentencing laws. No drug courts of which I am aware are the product of legislation.[6] That is, they do nothing to alter existing sentencing structures. Mandatory minimum sentences that are avoidable in drug courts through the imposition of deferred sentences or probation are likewise avoidable in traditional courts through those same alternatives.

Separation of Powers

The most profound defect in the drug court model is that it dissolves, and is expressly designed to dissolve, the boundaries between the three branches of government. It does this not only by forcing the three branches to act in dangerous concert, but also by forfeiting to the judicial branch legislative and executive powers it does not possess and should not exercise.

The Unholy Alliance.   Perhaps there is no better measure of the institutional impropriety of drug courts than their proponents' expressed ideas about their purpose. The chief deputy district attorney assigned to the Denver Drug Court put it as bluntly as anyone by explaining that the purpose of drug courts is "the cost-effective curtailment of drug abuse" (Long 1996:29). But of course no court's purpose should be to curtail any perceived social problem, no matter how lofty the curtailers' motives or how scurrilous the perceived problem. Our function is to insure that the rule of law is justly enforced. The job of curtailing a particular crime, or achieving any other particular social end, is a legislative and executive function, not a judicial one.

There is a palpable, day-to-day face to this unholy drug court alliance between the three branches. The entire drug court milieu is constructed as a single, unified institutional response to the scourge of drugs. Prosecutors, defense lawyers, and judges are meant to meld together into a kind of single public service institution designed to do what is best for the drug defendants, or "clients" as they are referred to in many drug courts. Indeed, it is *de rigeur* that drug courts cannot operate successfully without the cooperation of judges, prosecutors, police, sheriffs, and defense lawyers. The very instant this cooperation is achieved, the bedrock protections inherent in the adversary nature of our criminal justice system and the independence of the judiciary are put seriously at risk.

In the Denver District Court, this alliance between branches has evolved into a daily ritual, euphemistically called "staffing." These staffing sessions happen almost every morning before the drug court opens. They are attended by the drug court judge, the prosecutor, the public defender (but not private defense counsel), probation officers, and sometimes personnel from the drug court coordinator's office. Their purpose is to inform the judge of the issues in all dispositional, sentencing, and revocation matters for that day. The judge, after hearing from everyone, reaches a presumptive decision, and rarely changes that decision in open court. Defendants are not present and the staffing sessions are not on the record. Quite apart from the obvious constitutional concerns,[7] these staffing sessions symbolize what is wrong with the drug court institution: substantive decisions about a felony defendant are being made by some interbranch committee acting more like a support group than a court.

It is one thing for a defendant facing a few days or even a few months in county jail for drunk driving or misdemeanor domestic violence to be confronted by an alliance of prosecutors, defense lawyers, and judges unified in an effort to reeducate and treat him. But it is quite another thing when the defendant faces felony charges that could put him in prison for decades. We may be willing to sacrifice age-old traditions of adversariness and judicial independence for the former, but we should not be for the latter. If we are going to continue to treat some drug use as a felony, punishable by many years in prison, then we have an obligation to treat drug cases seriously—not like parking tickets in a mill in which the judge, prosecutor, and defense lawyer spend their days trying to push as many people through as possible.

Intrusions into the Legislative Function.   Drug courts are an attempt to answer one of the most beguiling public policy issues of our time, indeed of any time: at what point does the use of a particular drug break the social contract and become punishable by the criminal law, and even then, at what point is that particular drug use so involuntary as to become a medical issue rather than a legal one? The very existence of drug courts represents a policy determination that involuntary treatment efforts should be undertaken, at least for some defendants, before the full fury of the criminal law is unleashed. This may or may not be sound drug policy, but it is *policy,* and should come from elected lawmakers after an open and vigorous public debate, not from judges operating in the cloak of judicial pseudoscience.

Not only do drug courts represent a judicial intrusion into state legislative power, they also represent a federal legislative intrusion into state judicial power. As a condition of obtaining federal drug court funding, newly proposed drug courts must now meet a host of design and implementation criteria set by the Department of Justice in Washington (Drug Courts Program Office 1997). Drug courts—born in the laboratories of individual states and municipalities—have become increasingly federalized and homogenized. It is a dangerously short distance from the federal government telling us what the broad outlines of our drug courts should look like to telling us how they should be operated.

   Intrusions into the Executive Function.   Providing medical treatment
to people convicted of crimes, or even to people in custody awaiting trial,
is an executive function, not a judicial one. By mechanically imposing testing and treatment conditions on all criminal defendants before they have
even entered a plea, drug courts blur the fundamental distinction between
the accused and the convicted, and therefore between the judicial function
of determining guilt and imposing sentences and the executive function of
carrying out sentences and treating prisoners.

   This critique does not rest simply on the fact that judges are untrained
in these areas or that their judicial talents are being sadly wasted. It is a
more fundamental matter of defining the judicial function. The courts are
the third branch of government, given sobering powers designed to protect citizens not only from each other but also from the excesses of the other
two branches. We ought not become robed therapeutic administrators just
because some of us have convinced ourselves we are acting for the public
good.

   If we are truly serious about drug treatment, sufficient resources could
and should be directed to the executive branch's corrections facilities. If we
continue to believe that possession of some drugs is serious enough to warrant incarceration, then that incarceration should be imposed without further therapeutic hand-wringing, but it should be coupled with intense
in-custody treatment programs and draconian parole conditions. Parole eligibility, and the threat of parole revocation, can serve an important and
entirely appropriate coercive role in giving inmates and parolees incentives to take part in treatment programs, *after* they have been found by
judges to be deserving of some punishment.

The Political Appeal of Drug Courts

Drug courts are popular precisely because they are ambivalent about what
is fundamentally a legislative question: is drug use a disease or is it a
crime? Drug courts appeal to both ends of the political spectrum because
they are designed specifically to finesse this troubling question. Liberals
and the treatment community love drug courts because drug courts treat
drug users instead of punishing them (at least in the beginning). The treatment community is also making millions of dollars from drug courts. Con-
servatives and the law enforcement community love drug courts because
drug courts widen the nets, capture the drug users we used to pretend
were not there, and ultimately send many more of them to prison. The law
enforcement community is also flush with billions of federal and state dollars being thrown at the drug problem. Judges love drug courts because
they give us the illusion of treatment, then free our consciences to imprison
drug users when the treatment fails. Drug courts also benefit from millions

of federal dollars, at least in the beginning of the programs, and from inflated filing numbers used to allocate judicial resources between judicial districts within a state.

The attempt by drug courts to bridge this unbridgeable gap between crime and disease is having serious consequences, many of them unanticipated. In our paternalistic efforts to throw the criminal nets wider and wider in hopes of finding more treatable defendants, we have harvested a vast number of defendants we now deem untreatable. As discussed above, our nets in Denver are now so wide that there are more than double the number of untreatable defendants going to prison than there were in the old days, when we did not pretend to be able to distinguish the treatable from the untreatable.

It is not just a matter of the *number* of drug defendants going to prison. Drug courts have the paradoxical effect of sending the *wrong* people to prison. There is a powerful moral dimension to addiction: at what point, if any, does the desire to disengage from life's pain by taking drugs become an uncontrollable compulsion? Despite all of our modern bluster about the disease model of addiction and its alleged neurochemical bases (Levinthal 1988), the answer to this fundamental question is in large measure a moral one, implicating our common (or, in the case of drug policy, our rather balkanized) social views about free will and criminal responsibility. For all its weaknesses as the precursor to the disease model of addiction, at least the Alcoholics Anonymous model recognized this terribly central moral component to addiction (Seeberger 1993; May 1988).

Drug courts, whatever their benefits, do not perform this function of moral screening. On the contrary, their unstated central assumption is that modern treatment modalities are so effective that if a defendant fails treatment three or four times it must be the defendant's "fault," and he or she must be one of those "volunteer" addicts against whom the sword of the criminal law may morally swathe, and not a truly "diseased" addict. We judges can then sentence that defendant to prison, smug with the knowledge that our experts can separate the diseased from the criminal simply by offering treatment a certain arbitrary number of times.

Of course our treatment efforts are hardly so effective that a mere three or four failures indicate an intentional failing. This approach also grossly oversimplifies, and indeed largely eliminates, the distinction between compulsion and free will, and the reflection of that distinction in the fundamental *mens rea* requirement central to the definition of most crimes.

In any event, a case can be made that if addiction really is a disease, then the most diseased defendants are precisely the defendants most likely to fail many, and perhaps even all treatment attempts. Drug courts thus may be performing a kind of reverse moral screening. Those defendants who do not respond to treatment and therefore may be the most diseased go to prison. Those defendants who respond well to treatment and whose use of drugs may truly have been voluntary, escape prison.

This half-crime approach to drug control also has troubling implications at the crime end of the disease-crime axis. Once we have made the social decision that crack, for example, is such an addictive, dangerous drug that smoking it should be a felony, it makes little moral sense to excuse that crime for a certain number of times in order to try to treat it. We don't do that with shoplifting or with sexual assault on a child or with a host of other behaviors whose extremes we label as psychiatric diseases. Instead, we have made the clear social choice, without apology or guilt, that shoplifting and sexual assaults are crimes; that is, behaviors that we do not tolerate, regardless of their etiology. Issues related to kleptomaniacal or pedophilial compulsion are dealt with where they should be, at sentencing. These defendants are not given cookie-cutter deferrals or probation in the hopes of curing their "diseases." They are sentenced on a case-by-case basis. Some go to jail or prison, some do not; some are given probation with treatment components, some are not. We punish the criminal act and, if appropriate, consider issues about compulsion only at the sentencing phase and only after the primary consideration of punishment is vindicated. We should treat drug offenses no differently.

Instead, drug courts have, in effect, temporarily decriminalized drug offenses. In today's modern drug courts, it is no longer a punishable crime merely to *use* drugs. The punishable crime is to use them and then resist our mandatory treatment efforts.

Drug courts are perhaps the most visible real-world manifestation of the movement that calls itself "therapeutic jurisprudence" (Hora, Schma, and Rosenthal 1999; Wexler and Winick 1991). These ideas emanate from the proposition that the judiciary can be a powerful force for social change, not just in the traditional way of applying the law in individual cases or even by pushing the existing law to new enlightened boundaries, but rather by actively intervening in the day-to-day lives of litigants in an infinite variety of nontraditional ways that go well beyond what is necessary to decide the case at hand. A full discussion of these controversial notions is beyond the scope of this essay, but Boldt (1999) has suggested, at least in the context of drug court, that they are a repackaging of long-repudiated (Allen 1981) notions of rehabilitative criminology. Nolan (1998) has analyzed them as part of a broader sociological pattern he calls "the therapeutic culture." My problem with them is more institutional than criminological or cultural. If the idea of therapeutic jurisprudence is to free judges not only from the constraints of the separation of powers doctrine, but even from the limits of our own expertise, it is a dangerous idea indeed. I cannot imagine a more dangerous branch than an unrestrained judiciary full of amateur psychiatrists poised to do "good" rather than apply the law.

CONCLUSION

The Denver Drug Court has not worked. It has not reduced recidivism or incarceration. What it has done is triggered an unprecedented explosion in drug filings and prison sentences, fused the three branches of government into one giant case processing machine, made the drug court judge a small cog in that machine, usurped the legislative prerogative of deciding what is and is not a punishable crime, usurped the executive prerogative by focusing on treatment rather than guilt and punishment, become such an unpleasant place to preside that no one will volunteer to preside there, and taken on a self-sustaining bureaucratic life immune to the realities of its own ineffectiveness.

Its failures should teach all of us that there is a wide gap between the politically attractive promises of drug courts and their harsh reality, and that there are good reasons our founders were committed to the idea of an independent judicial branch populated with generalists of limited powers.

ACKNOWLEDGMENTS

The views expressed here are of course my own, and do not necessarily reflect the views of the District Court for the Second Judicial District or any of my colleagues on that Court. This essay is based on Judge Hoffman's article in the *North Carolina Law Review* entitled "The Drug Court Scandal," 78 N.C.L. Rev. 101 (2000), and is published with the permission of the Board of Editors of the *North Carolina Law Review*.

NOTES

1. The Denver Drug Court had no magistrates at its inception in 1994. It added one in 1997 and a second in 1999, but lost the second position in 2000 when some federal funding dried up. See note 3. We are currently funded for 1.5 magistrates, but the half-time position has remained unfilled so that the funds for that position could be used for other more pressing administrative expenses. The magistrate does a variety of things including advisements, bond settings, compliance reviews, revocation hearings on misdemeanors, and guilty pleas. The actual work he or she does has varied greatly according to the particular judge presiding in drug court.

2. In the early years we received a wide variety of federal funds, principally through the LEAA, to defray the considerable administrative costs of drug court. Although we still received federal funds in the form of a Local Law Enforcement Block Grant and a Byrne Grant as late as 2000, federal funds have been dwindling, and our state legislature has declined to make up the differ-

ence. As federal funds have dwindled, the bulk of the administrative costs have been shouldered by the City and County of Denver. The Byrne Grant expired September 30, 2001, and as of the date of this writing we are struggling with the problem of making up those lost funds from either the City and County of Denver or from our own judicial budget, or a combination.

3. Thus, the Denver Drug Court, like most drug courts, occupied the entire field of felony drug charges, at least before its jurisdiction began to be cut back in response to unexpectedly high volume.

4. Second advisements typically cover the appointment of the public defender's office for indigent defendants, bond reduction hearings, and the setting of a date for the preliminary hearing.

5. People v. Gendron, Case No. 98CA0789 (Colo. App. 1999). Unpublished. Copy on file in the offices of the *North Carolina Law Review.*

6. The only exception, and it is a big one, is California's Proposition 36. It became effective in July 2001, and requires that all defendants convicted of nonviolent possession offenses be given probation and treatment. It is too early to tell whether this will, in effect, turn all of California's superior courts into drug courts, or whether these drug defendants will get lost in an already overburdened probation system, as they typically do in traditional courts.

7. Criminal defendants have a right under the Sixth Amendment to have counsel present at all "critical stages" of a criminal prosecution [Powell v. Alabama, 287 U.S. 45, 68-71 (1932)].

REFERENCES

Allen, Francis A. 1981. *The Decline of the Rehabilitative Ideal.* New Haven, CT: Yale University Press.

Belenko, Steven. 1998. "Research on Drug Courts: A Critical Review." *First National Drug Court Institute Review* 1(1).

Belenko, Steven and Tamara Dumanovsky. 1993. *Program Brief: Special Drug Courts.* Unpublished. Copy on file in the offices of the *North Carolina Law Review.*

Boldt, Richard C. 1999. "Rehabilitative Punishment and the Drug Treatment Court Movement." *Washington University Law Quarterly* 76:1205.

Brown, James R. 1997. "Drug Diversion Courts: Are They Needed and Will They Succeed in Breaking the Cycle of Drug-Related Crime?" *New England Law on Criminal and Civil Confinement* 23:63.

Denver Adult Probation Department. 2001. "Proposal for an Enhanced Drug Treatment Program in Denver Adult Probation Department." Unpublished draft, June 10. Copy on file in the offices of the clerk of the District Court, Second Judicial District, State of Colorado.

Denver Drug Court. 2000. "1999 Year End Report." Unpublished. Copy on file in the offices of the clerk of the District Court, Second Judicial District.

Denver Drug Court Statistics 1997 and 1998. Unpublished. Copy on file in the offices of the *North Carolina Law Review.*

Drug Courts Program Office, U.S. Department of Justice. 1997. Defining Drug Courts: The Key Components. Washington, DC: U.S. Government Printing Office.

Flesche, Miles M. 1999. "Denver District Court Criminal Filings." Unpublished. Copy on file in the offices of the *North Carolina Law Review.*

General Accounting Office. 1997. Drug Courts: An Overview of Growth, Characteristics, and Results. Washington, DC: Office of Justice Programs, U.S. Department of Justice.

Granfield, Robert and Cindy Eby. 1997. "An Evaluation of the Denver Drug Court: The Impact of a Treatment-Oriented Drug Offender System." Unpublished. Copy on file in the offices of the *North Carolina Law Review.*

Hoffman, Morris B. 2000. "The Drug Court Scandal," *North Carolina Law Review* 78:1437–1534..

Hora, Peggy F., William G. Schma, and John T. A. Rosenthal. 1999. "Therapeutic Jurisprudence and the Drug Treatment Court Movement: Revolutionizing the Criminal Justice System's Response to Drug Abuse and Crime in America," *Notre Dame Law Review* 74:439.

Levinthal, Charles F. 1988. *Messengers of Paradise: Opiates and the Brain*. New York: Anchor.

Long, Gregory F. 1996. "Denver Drug Court: New Approach to Old Problems", *Colorado Lawyer* 25:29.

May, Gerald G. 1988. *Addiction And Grace*. San Francisco: Harper & Row.

Murphy, Sheila M. 1997. "Drug Courts: An Effective, Efficient Weapon in the War on Drugs." *Illinois Bar Journal* 85:474.

Nolan, James L., Jr. 1998. *The Therapeutic State: Justifying Government At Century's End*. New York: New York University Press.

Nolan, James L., Jr. 2001. *Reinventing Justice: The American Drug Court Movement.* Princeton, NJ: Princeton University Press.

Office of Planning and Analysis, Colorado Department of Corrections. 1998. "Denver Drug Court Convictions D.O.C. Sentenced Offenders Fiscal Years 1993 Through 1997." Unpublished. Copy on file in the offices of the *North Carolina Law Review.*

Ritter, A. William. 1999. "Denver Looks to Hire Drug Czar." *Denver Post* April 1, p. 38.

Seeberger, Francis F. 1993. *Addiction and Responsibility: An Inquiry into the Addictive Mind*. New York: Crossroad.

Shaw, Michelle and Kenneth Robinson. 1999. "Reports on Recent Drug Court Research." *National Drug Court Institute Review* 2:107.

Sherman, Lawrence W., Denise Gottfredson, Doris MacHenzie, John Eck, Peter Reuter, and Shawn Bushway. 1997. *A Report to Congress: Preventing Crime: What Works, What Doesn't, What's Promising*. Unpublished. Copy on file in the offices of the *North Carolina Law Review.*

Smith, Barbara E. and the American Bar Association. 1991. *Strategies for Courts to Cope with the Caseload Pressures of Drug Cases* 1991. Unpublished. Copy on file in the offices of the *North Carolina Law Review.*

Wexler, David and Bruce Winick. 1991. *Essays in Therapeutic Jurisprudence*. Durham, NC: Carolina Academic Press.

5

Separated by an Uncommon Law: Drug Courts in Great Britain and America

James L. Nolan, Jr.

As discussed in the introduction of this volume, the U.S.-led drug court movement has now become an international phenomenon. Drug courts, based on the U.S. model, have been initiated in Australia, Canada, England, Ireland, and Scotland. In December 1999 the United Nations convened a meeting in Vienna, Austria, with representatives from eleven countries to discuss the international implementation of drug courts. This chapter offers a comparison between the American and British versions of the movement, and considers the important historical, cultural, and legal factors that shape the distinct forms the programs assume in both places.

England is among the countries furthest along in implementing the U.S.-inspired judicial innovation. Through visits to England by American drug court judges and trips to the United States by British officials, the English took a keen interest in the movement and its potential applicability to the United Kingdom.[1] The introduction of drug courts and drug court–like programs have taken two forms in England. These related initiatives vary only in degree and are currently realizing a sort of conflation with the national rolling out of the New Labour government's Drug Treatment and Testing Order (DTTO)programs, a development I will discuss more fully below.

One transplantation of drug courts to the United Kingdom was initiated in Wakefield and Pontefract, two West Yorkshire cities, approximately two hundred miles north of London. The West Yorkshire drug courts—also referred to as STEP (Substance misuse Treatment and Enforcement Program)—came into being following a 1995 visit to the Miami drug court by Keith Hellawell, then chief constable of West Yorkshire Police (and currently the U.K. antidrugs coordinator or "drugs czar"). Hellawell was inspired by what he saw in the United States, and subsequently invited Miami drug court judge Stanley Goldstein to speak at a British police conference in the following year. Val Barker, the assistant director of public health of the Wakefield Health Authority, attended the conference. She describes what happened next:

> I first heard about drug courts when I went to an Association of Chief Police Officers conference in 1996, and I saw Judge Goldstein speak with such passion and emotion about how his drug court worked. And those people who know me, know that I am a very determined woman. And I was pretty determined to go see what happened in Dade County. So, in February of 1997 I went to the [Miami] drug court with a police officer, probation officer, and my medical colleagues from Public Health in Wakefield, and we went to the court and to the treatment centers. . . . And I came back a convert, and a real enthusiast for what was happening there.[2]

Upon returning to England, Barker applied for funds from the West Yorkshire Police Authority, and with the support of Keith Hellawell (who was still chief constable of the West Yorkshire Police at the time) was awarded £200,000 to start two pilot drug court programs. Barker and her colleagues were also successful in obtaining funds from private sources, including from Marks and Spencer, a British department store chain, and Euromed, a drug testing company. With this funding in place, the Wakefield drug court was launched on May 5, 1998, and the Pontefract program on July 6, 1998.

A second incarnation of drug courts in the United Kingdom was advanced in the form of DTTO (Drug Treatment and Testing Order) programs. As with the West Yorkshire courts, DTTOs were directly inspired by the U.S. drug court model. Paul Hayes, chief probation officer of the Southeast London Probation Service and a major player in British drug policy, tells how Justin Russell, another important player in U.K. drug policy, went to the United States in 1995 (the same year as did Val Barker and her colleagues) to observe drug courts:

> He [Justin Russell] was at the time a Labour Party researcher looking at the drugs policy. Very bright bloke, he is now the Home Secretary's number one advisor on this stuff. He went off to the States, and he went around looking at drug courts, and he came back with a model. He basically came back with DTTOs. . . . A few of us kicked the ideas around with him and whatever, and shaped it up.

According to Hayes, then, without the American drug court model, "We wouldn't have gotten DTTOs." In April 1998 the New Labour government issued a report, "Tackling Drugs: To Build a Better Britain," which recommended the development of DTTOs, a program that was then legislatively mandated in the 1998 Crime and Disorder Act. As directed by this legislation, three pilot programs—in Gloucestershire, Liverpool, and Croydon (South London)—were initiated in October 1998. Based on the reported initial success of these programs in the summer of 2000, the government then spent £60 million to roll out DTTOs nationally in all forty-two of Britain's probation services.

Included in this national scheme is funding for the West Yorkshire courts. Therefore, the STEP program was folded into the larger national DTTO program, though officials in Yorkshire claim that STEP will maintain its own "drug court" distinctives. Moreover, Caterina Fagg, the co-manager of STEP was commissioned to oversee the initiation of DTTOs throughout the Yorkshire County probation services, and plans to run these programs like the Wakefield and Pontefract drug courts. Therefore, the differences between the so-called British drug courts and the DTTOs (which were only rather slight to begin with) will be minimized even further by this development.

A comparison between the U.S. and the U.K. versions of the drug court are of interest for several reasons. First, as it concerns the issue of controlling drugs, the United States and Great Britain have a long history of looking to the practices and the policies of the other (Schur, 1960, 1968; Judson, 1973; Joint Committee, 1969). As Horace Judson put it back in the 1970s: "The traffic in ideas about control of narcotics has been vigorous between the two countries" (1973:123). The borrowing of legal innovations from one country to another is, of course, no unusual occurrence. As political scientist Gary Jacobsohn observes, "Changes in legal systems are often predominantly the result of borrowing from other systems" (1993:53). However, legal programs undergo significant adjustments when transported from one social context to another. As comparative law scholars make clear, "Law is a form of cultural expression and is not readily transplantable from one culture to another without going through some process of indigenization" (Glendon, Gordon, and Osakwe 1982:10). In light of this understanding, Jacobsohn cautions those involved in legal transplantations to "be aware of the relationship between law and political culture, and [to] be sensitive to those aspects of political culture that can be influenced by the law and those that can be expected to be resistant to it" (1993:53).

Peter Hassett, the director of operations of Phoenix House in Glasgow and an important player in the international drug court movement, offers a personalized illustration of the kind of awareness that Jacobsohn encourages:

In terms of the drug courts in Britain I'll share with you a salutary experience I had last year. When in the U.S. I saw this light that I really liked in a
shop and I bought it. I thought, all I have to do is change the plug over when
I got back to Britain. And I took my light home, showed it off, and was very
proud of it. I changed the plug and nothing happened. I think it blew a fuse
or something. And what I discovered was that the electrical system that the
light worked from was different, the plug was different, the bulb was different. I think that this is a useful metaphor and one which we, in the U.K.,
need to take on board in terms of looking at the transplantation of drug
courts.

As conveyed in this understanding of legal systems, law is not autonomous. It exists, indeed, it is ensconced in a particular social context. Legal change, therefore, must be sensitive to differences in culture. What
is commonsensical to one people in one locality may be nonsensical to another people in another place. As the cultural anthropologist Clifford
Geertz puts it, "The law is a distinctive manner of imagining the real"
(1983:173). That is, the law tells the story about a particular culture, a particular people. Geertz uses the metaphor of a window to illustrate this
point. Looking at the law, he says, is like looking through a window at the
cultural particularities of a certain place. The distinctives of the law, as
such, provide a glimpse into the peculiar social realities of a given society.
Law, moreover, according to Geertz is local knowledge: "local not just to
place, time, class, and variety of issue, but as to accent" (ibid.:215). The notion of accent is especially helpful as it concerns a comparison between the
United States and Great Britain. Just as the distinctive accents of our shared
language often indicate very profound cultural and regional differences,
so the varying accents of our shared common law tradition reflect significant political/legal, cultural, and historical differences. An understanding
of these differences helps to explain why a similar judicial innovation, such
as drug courts, takes on very distinct forms in different national contexts.

Thus the law is understood here as existing in a very close relationship
with culture. As Mary Ann Glendon and her colleagues put it, "Law is a
concentrated expression of the history, culture, social values and the general consciousness and perception of a given people" (Glendon et al.
1982:10).[3] Therefore, when transplantations of certain legal innovations are
attempted from one place to another it behooves us to understand, to appreciate, to be aware of the distinct cultural predilections to which legal
practices are inextricably linked. As it concerns the legal and social control
of drugs in the United States and Great Britain there are important historical, political/legal, and cultural differences. Below, I highlight some of the
significant distinctions in each of these interrelated areas, beginning with
the historical.

HISTORICAL DIFFERENCES

The institutionalization of antidrug laws at the beginning of the twentieth century was a direct consequence of international developments; efforts led mainly by the United States, but of which the United Kingdom was also a part. Both countries participated in an international conference on drugs in Shanghai in 1909, and then in three more at The Hague between 1911 and 1914. The Hague convention finally became international law when it was incorporated into the Treaty of Versailles in 1919. The purpose of these conventions was to pass international laws restricting the importation and use of drugs (primarily opium) and to encourage national laws that reflected these concerns. As a consequence of these international pressures both the United States and Great Britain passed defining drug laws in the first part of the last century. The U.S. Congress passed the Harrison Act in 1914 and the British Parliament passed the Dangerous Drugs Act in 1920. Up to this point, then, both countries followed similar paths. After 1920, however, the two countries diverged considerably.

The interpretation and application of these respective laws located the social control of drugs in distinct institutional spheres. The Harrison Act and two 1919 Supreme Court interpretations of the legislation essentially made the control of drug use a legal or law enforcement matter in the United States, whereas the Dangerous Drugs Act and the 1926 Rolleston Committee report placed the control of drugs and of the drug addict in the hands of the medical community in the United Kingdom. Not coincidentally one interpretation of the legislation was made in a legal forum, the U.S. Supreme Court, and the other by a commission made up of individuals with medical expertise. The chairman of the Rolleston Committee, Sir Humphrey Rolleston, was an eminent physician, and the other eight members of the committee all had medical qualifications. Moreover, the majority of individuals who testified before the committee were also doctors.[4]

The different findings in these two instances are instructive. On January 16, 1919, the U.S. Supreme Court handed down two decisions interpreting the Harrison Act—the *Doremus* and *Webb* cases. In the latter, the court specifically ruled that it was illegal for a physician to provide drugs to an addict for maintenance purposes. It was untenable, the court concluded, to regard prescribing drugs in this way as a legitimate medical purpose. Both decisions affirmed the prosecutorial bite of the Harrison Act, and gave the federal government the authority to indict physicians, pharmacists, and addicts who continued to prescribe, sell, and use drugs. The court essentially ruled that drug addiction was not a medical but a law enforcement issue. For the next forty years—particularly under the influential leadership of Harry Anslinger, who was commissioner of narcotics from 1930 to 1962—the law enforcement orientation of American drug policy only strengthened. For example, marijuana, which was not included in the original Harrison Act, was made illegal in 1937; Congress established stiff mandatory minimum sentences for drug offenders in the 1951 Boggs Amendment; and juries were given the option of the death penalty for the sale of drugs to minors in the 1956 Narcotics Drug Control Act.

In direct contrast, the Rolleston Committee report firmly situated the social control of drugs in Britain's medical community, and gave physicians wide discretion concerning the treatment of addicts. As stated in the report: "A prescription shall only be given by a duly qualified medical practitioner when required for purposes of medical treatment" (Bean 1974:66). In interpreting what constituted the legitimate scope of "medical treatment" the committee specifically permitted doctors to prescribe to addicts "to whom the indefinitely prolonged administration of morphine or heroin may be necessary" (Judson 1973:21). In short, whether or not to prescribe a drug for maintenance purposes was left to the doctor's discretion. Thus, the origins of the so-called British system, a system that largely remained in tact for the following four decades. This point was summarized in a 1961 statement by Rufus King, as cited in the 1969 ABA/AMA report, *Drug Addiction: Crime or Disease?*

> The key difference [between the United States and Britain] appears to be that the British medical profession is in full and virtually unchallenged control of the distribution of drugs, and this includes distribution, by prescription or administration, to addicts when necessary. The police function is to aid and protect medical control, rather than to substitute for it. (Joint Committee 1969:127)

Interestingly, while the U.S. "problem" with drug misuse grew during the four decades following passage of these defining drug laws, the drug situation in the United Kingdom remained negligible in comparison. The stark contrast led a number of scholars writing in the 1960s to recommend that the United States emulate the British example (Schur 1968; Eldridge 1967). Others, however, argued that the British approach was a consequence rather than a cause of low rates of drug use (Larimore and Brill 1960).

While greater restrictions were eventually imposed in the British system (stemming from the changing profile of the British addict and the dubious prescription practices of some physicians in the 1960s) the preeminence of the medical model still has a large influence. For example, it is still lawful for a physician to prescribe heroin in England, though this is less common than it used to be. Home Office figures showed 2,240 registered addicts receiving heroin prescriptions in 1968, but only 111 in 1996 (Bean 1974:105;

2001:86). Significantly, the reduction in heroin prescriptions is a consequence not of legal but of medical change. Doctors have moved toward a preference for methadone prescription over heroin prescription, but have retained their power to prescribe heroin should they so choose (and they have retained this power by successfully opposing international pressures to ban its manufacturing and use). As the British criminologist, Philip Bean, observes of the shift to prescribing methadone, "As far as can be seen there was no Government interference, no official directive about prescribing policy and no attempt to influence clinical decisions. The changes in prescribing practices came from the medical professionals themselves" (Bean 2001:85).

Given this historical backdrop, drug courts can be seen as a convergence of sorts, where the medical and legal models are synthesized in the context of a united program of therapeutic jurisprudence. However, the two countries arrive at the convergence from very different historical trajectories, which determines the particular shape the programs assume in each locality. For example, in the British drug court and DTTO sites I visited there was typically a medical doctor who played a significant role in the treatment. I cannot recall an instance in all the treatment sites I visited in the United States where any treatment provider was a medical doctor.[5] Joel Best says of the treatment providers in the United States today more generally that their backgrounds and credentials vary wildly, and that many of "these therapists are 'professional ex-s,' individuals with little formal training who . . . have now begun careers helping others into recovery" (Best 1999:124). This is certainly true of the treatment providers in the U.S. drug courts, where there is wide variance in levels of training, and where many treatment providers are themselves recovered (or recovering) addicts. In the United Kingdom, where the professional medical community has treated addicts for decades, levels of medical expertise are much higher, and one does not typically find "professional ex-s" in their ranks.

Relatedly, methadone (or, in some places, naltrexone) maintenance is typical in the United Kingdom. It is prescribed by a doctor who has medically assessed the drug court client. Some U.S. drug courts use methadone maintenance, but this is actually much more rare.[6] In fact, 20 percent of American drug court programs specifically prohibit the use of any pharmacological interventions (Cooper et al., 1997:83). Also reflective of Britain's medically oriented history of drug control is the emphasis on "harm reduction" as a defining quality of drug treatment. That is, reduced use rather than no use is acceptable in the United Kingdom, whereas in the United States total abstinence is the more common goal and requirement of drug courts. In the British versions of the program, harm reduction or reduced use is commonly viewed as a success. Again, this has everything to do with Britain's particular history of drug control. Recall the Rolleston

Committee's position that there are some people "to whom the indefinitely prolonged administration of morphine or heroin may be necessary." As Judson observes, "The idea of the stable addict . . . has been the most durable contribution of the Rolleston Committee to the British approach to narcotics" (1973:22).

That this medically informed perspective still colors public views of drug use was made clear in discussions with several British officials. Philip Bean, who for years has studied the U.S. drug court movement on behalf of the Home Office, makes just this case. To a group of British and American criminal justice professionals, Bean said,

> I think it's sometimes very difficult for North Americans to realize that it's still possible in Britain for heroin to be prescribed as maintenance and is often prescribed. I'm not talking about methadone; I'm talking about heroin. There isn't the culture in Britain as there is occasionally in certain parts of America to talk in terms of complete abstinence of all drug substances, including alcohol. I think that really does make a difference because the debate in Britain isn't about abstinence, it's about harm reduction.

Paul Hayes makes a similar point. He views reduced use by participants in the DTTO programs as a success. As he puts it, "the indications are that everything we hoped for in terms of reduced offending and reduced drug use is true. Across the three pilots, instead of people averaging thirty acquisitive crimes a week they are averaging three. So, in those terms it is clearly a success." And this, even though "everyone is testing positive for continued drug use." His principal concern is with reduced criminal activity, even if there are only lower levels of continued drug use. Again, such a position has historical precedence. As Hayes puts it, "The whole harm reduction philosophy has dominated U.K. drug policy for a long time."

Hayes explains further that in Britain not all drug using behavior is viewed as problematic. There are, as he puts it, gradations of drug use, including "experimental use, recreational use, problematic use, and then dependent use. "Most drug use, according to Hayes, falls in the first two categories. "People use drugs in the main because they enjoy it. And the vast majority of people in our society or yours use drugs in a non-problematic way, as the vast majority of them use alcohol in a non-problematic way. "Given this understanding it should not be surprising that the Wakefield drug court graduated participants who were still using drugs and that a recent Home Office press release called DTTOs a success, even though an average £30 per week drug habit continued among participants. As stated in the press statement issued on September 29, 2000:

> The national roll-out follows three successful pilot schemes in Croydon, Liverpool and Gloucestershire which ran from 1 October 1998 to 31 March

2000. . . . The average number of crimes committed per month by offenders on DTTOs fell dramatically from 107 to 10, while their average weekly spend on illegal drugs showed a significant reduction from £400 to £30. (Home Office 2000)

Though the medical orientation still persists in British attitudes toward drug use, drug courts and DTTOs now locate the control of drugs under the auspices of the criminal justice system. Even as recently as the 1980s, according to Paul Hayes, money for drug misusers was channeled through health agencies. But in recent years, with the perceived link between drug misuse and crime, the money is now being channeled through the criminal justice system. Hayes says, "As drug misuse is now perceived largely as a crime problem rather than a public health or individual health and welfare issue, the role of treatment has to be justified by the contribution it can make to crime reduction." Thus, drug use is no longer treated only as a medical matter, but rather as something of a mix between law and medicine, as is the case in the U.S. version of drug courts.

Both American and British court-based drug intervention schemes, therefore, offer a team-oriented approach, comprised of professionals from both medical and legal professions. As occurred in the American drug courts (Nolan 2001:61–89), adjustment to the multidisciplinary approach has sometimes been difficult for British team members. In a September 1999 meeting of representatives from the three DTTO pilot schemes, team members spoke candidly about these difficulties. Psychiatric nurses, for example, expressed concerns about "working in the criminal justice system," and wondered if it might lead to "the compromise of professional integrity." In particular they worried about "court expectations sometimes overriding treatment needs." Probation officers complained about "too much time squabbling with other disciplines," and of the "day to day difficulties concerning boundaries, philosophies, and power struggles." Representatives from the Liverpool DTTO spoke of the "cultural tensions between the agencies," and of the need for "improved clarity about the roles and relationships," of the various team members.

DTTOs, of course, are a very different environment for health professionals, who are not accustomed to enforcing treatment with a court order. As the manager of the Gloucester DTTO explained, the traditional health agenda is "done for not done to," whereas under the DTTOs, it is "done to, not done for." In other words, it is no longer voluntary treatment. Rather, in his words, "It is coerced treatment." A Liverpool probation officer emphasized the same, "The philosophy driving this is the criminal justice one. . . . It is compulsory in that you are on a court order." Adjusting to a court-based setting for treatment, again, is novel and sometimes difficult for treatment professionals. The medical doctor at the West Yorkshire drug courts spoke of her initial reservations about joining the drug court team. "Yes, it certainly puts me in a different role. For a start, I'm sort of joining the other side as you might say. I'm working in conjunction with the police and the probation service. And initially that, in my mind, produced some conflicts." Over time, however, she found that she could maintain the integrity of the doctor-patient relationship. "It's a bit of a tight rope, but by carefully walking it, you can still be someone who can coerce someone into treatment—which is one of the ways it is different—and also motivate someone into treatment, which is what you would be doing if they weren't actually on a probation order" (BBC 1999).

Thus, as in the American version of the drug courts, the British model conflates treatment and criminal justice perspectives. Unlike the United States, however, Britain arrives at this unique convergence from a history of treating drug use as more predominantly a medical matter, an orientation that still influences popular and legal perspectives on drug use. The medical doctor directing treatment at the Croydon DTTO, for example, asserted that even today "most British people would put the [issue of] drug misuse squarely in a medical framework." As we have seen, the professional presence of medical doctors, the continued emphasis on harm reduction over abstinence, and the more pervasive use of methadone are all examples of the continuing influence of the medical approach. Thus, though the British version of drug courts conflates law and medicine—and team members, like their American counterparts, experience difficulties adjusting to the multidisciplinary model—it arrives at this convergence from a very different direction than the United States, a history that still influences the way drug users are perceived and handled in the United Kingdom.

LEGAL/POLITICAL DIFFERENCES

There are also important legal distinctions. Perhaps the most obvious are the different legal structures. Most low-level drug offenses in England are handled by lay magistrate courts, which markedly differ from America's single judge criminal courts. British lay magistrate courts, the origins of which can be traced back to the fourteenth century, handle the "great bulk of minor criminal charges" (Glendon et al. 1982:177). Lay magistrates are chosen by the Lord Chancellor and typically preside over a court as a panel of three with one, selected by the panel, serving as chair. The lay magistrates are assisted by a court clerk who has formal legal training and who advises on substantive and procedural points of law. Larger cities have salaried or "stipendiary" (or "stipe" as they are often called) magistrates who, more like the American counterpart, have formal legal training and sit alone on the bench. Handling the more serious criminal cases are the more formal British Crown Courts. Lay magistrates will typically refer more serious cases to the Crown Court judge, who can impose longer sentences and stricter sanctions.

In the two West Yorkshire drug courts, twenty-four different lay magistrates (four panels for both court sites) oversee the drug court cases. Some of the DTTO clients are handled by stipendiary magistrates or Crown Court judges. But in the main both the DTTO and drug court cases are handled in lay magistrate courts. After acceptance into the program, participants will come back to court every month for what is called a "review court" session. This review court approximates the American drug court model in that it represents ongoing judicial oversight in the treatment process, and is a significant innovation for a British court. An important difference, however, is that lay magistrates simply do not have the power, authority, and discretion of a U.S. judge. As Andrew Wells, the United Nations official responsible for international drug control programs, observes, "Clearly the U.S. drug courts do have a wider range of intermediate sanctions that are not currently available under DTTO regimes." Lay magistrates, for example, cannot sanction clients to short one-day to two-week jail terms as are commonly imposed in the American drug courts. Their only real power is to revoke the probation order, which if employed effectively ends the client's involvement in the program. Thus, when participants come before the magistrates for their monthly reviews, they come before a panel that has very little actual authority.

Consider the following threat made by a magistrate to a Pontefract drug court client who had been testing dirty, not showing up for meetings, and even shoplifting to support his addiction. The magistrate said to the participant:

> You've been warned this way before, but it doesn't make a lot a difference. You are going down that path to nowhere. You are 29 years old, 29 years old. And if I hear this claptrap again, next time you come in here, and a report like this again, then [and here is the threat] I shall be having a word with my colleagues very seriously. (BBC 1999)

The contrast of an immediately imposed sanction of two weeks in jail—as might well occur in a U.S. drug court under similar circumstances—is, of course, rather glaring.

A probation officer at the Liverpool DTTO complained about the low level of direct involvement by magistrates in the lives of DTTO participants. To explain such reluctance, she proposed that judges and magistrates are too wedded to the past. As she put it, in England "there is a big tradition that sentencers don't like taking part in the operation of sentences." The manager of the Gloucestershire DTTO noted the same judicial disposition. "In this country I think we have a position where the sentencers make sentences which they then expect to be dealt with somewhere else. And they haven't got the expectation to be a part of it." Even if magistrates wished for greater involvement with clients, their power, as in the West Yorkshire drug courts, is ultimately limited. As a second Liverpool probation officer explained, "you see, the magistrates' power is still restricted on the DTTO, because we have to breach them before they can send them to prison, whereas the American judge can say to someone who is not complying, 'I'll sentence him for two weeks.'" In sum, as another added, "There are limits on what we can do in this country."

Though limited, these officers still believe an involved magistrate can have a marked effect on DTTO clients. "It has worked well," said one Liverpool probation officer. "The judge or magistrate will say, 'You've got one last chance. Get into that rehabilitation unit, or that is the end of it.' And that can really focus people's minds." Another member of the Liverpool team observed that clients respond to positive praise from the magistrates as well. "That I think does have very positive results, because they have never been to a court where they're told they're doing well. . . . The magistrate will say without anything having been said, 'Oh, I can see you look a lot better this morning.' You know, so it kind of lets them know that somebody is taking notice, that it is not just an academic exercise."

Another important structural difference between the American and British legal systems is the important role that probation plays in England. In the United Kingdom probation has more status, is more centrally organized, and has more funding. In both the DTTOs and drug courts, probation officers run the show. Thus, when those interested in the U.S. drug court have visited the annual NADCP conferences in the United States, they have been probation officers, not magistrates or judges. At a session on the English courts during the 1999 NADCP conference in Miami a questioner in attendance noted the conspicuous absence of any members from the judiciary, and conveyed a sense of incredulity that a drug court could succeed without an activist judge playing a leading role. As he put it to the members of the British panel,

> I think that for the drug court concept really to work effectively it needs not a collegial court which you've got by way of magistrates, but a one person court. And also that person needs to be there consistently. It's notable that none of your nonfundable [lay] magistrates are here. Whereas the American system seems to be court orientated and gets a great strength from that.

The strength of probation in Britain was also in evidence at the U.N. meetings in December 1999, where unlike all the other countries represented, the United Kingdom was represented by a senior probation officer.

Moreover, in preparing to start a drug court or DTTO scheme, probation officers typically provide training for the magistrates who will be involved in the program. In the United States the drug court and the drug court movement is judge led. Probation officers may play a role, but they certainly do not play a leading role in the program or the movement. As summarized in a 1992 *Federal Probation* article written by an American and a British author, "Probation in Britain is better funded, more highly trained, and more favorably regarded by justice officials" (Clear and Rumgay 1992:9). This defining orientation significantly affects the shape drug courts assume in the different countries.

Another difference as it concerns the structure of the two legal systems is the directionality of innovation. That is, in the United States the drug court movement has largely been a grassroots kind of movement. As Tim Murray, former director of the Drug Courts Program Office, put it, "It's probably the only movement in the judicial system that has bubbled up from the grassroots to the Federal government." Louisville drug court judge, Henry Weber, observes the same, asserting that apart from receiving some federal dollars, the drug court movement is "a grassroots kind of movement. It's not something where the bureaucrats in Washington tell you what to do. Each community has developed its own program for its own particular needs and they all deal with it on a local level. . . . It's totally a grassroots kind of thing."

In the United Kingdom, contrastingly, legal innovations such as drug court are more commonly initiated at the top, rather than at the local level. Jonathan Freedland made much of this point in his celebrated comparison between American and British political cultures. As he put it, where "bottom-up power" is a defining feature of American society, "in Britain power flows in the reverse direction, from the top down" (1998:19, 22). When I asked a probation officer from the Croydon program why she and her colleagues decided to implement a DTTO, her response lacked the missionary, entrepreneurial zeal typical of American drug court advocates. Instead she simply shrugged and explained that they had been told by the government to do so. In her words: "We've been basically told to get on with it. Here's the legislation. Here are the Home Office guidelines. Work with it." When I asked a medical doctor from the same program whether she anticipated that drug courts would spread in the United Kingdom, she likewise deferred to the wishes of the British government: "It will be for the government to decide. Largely we will have to move the way the government wants. . . . One of the things that is true about the British system is that we are totally dependent on government funding. . . . We are going to have do what the government says."

The top-down orientation of the British system stands in stark contrast to the grassroots orientation of the American part of the movement, where drug court professionals typically communicate a much greater sense of individual initiative and ownership of local initiatives. Judge John Schwartz, the first drug court judge of the Rochester, New York, drug court, for example, explains that the Rochester drug court came into existence because of his individual efforts and vision. "I realized that what we were doing wasn't making a dent on the drug addicted population, so it was time to try new things." Schwartz visited the Miami drug court and decided that he "liked the Miami approach. So I came back to Rochester bound and determined to do it here." Though initially unsuccessful in securing public funding for the program, Schwartz was undeterred and turned to local private sources instead. "I went out to the community, to these local foundations . . . and told them about Miami, and said that I would like to start one here, will you help out? And they did. So they funded our court for the first two years of operation." The positive publicity generated by the program eventually led to state funding of not only the Rochester drug court but several other new drug courts in New York. As Schwartz explains,

> So we were able to get the state to fund it, and they funded one in Buffalo, they funded one in Syracuse, and Suffolk County and Brooklyn. We started these before there was such a thing as federal grants. . . . So I mean, ours is truly community funded, community sponsored, and community staffed. I mean it's the true essence of what a drug court is all about.

It is the essence of what drug court is all about in the United States anyway. As we have seen, in Britain drug courts are much less locally driven. The directionality of legal change moves from the top down rather from the bottom up.

CULTURAL DIFFERENCES

Finally, consider the cultural differences that determine and shape drug courts in the respective localities. One feature of American culture that has received considerable attention over the past several decades is an increasing societal preoccupation with feelings (Rieff 1966; MacIntyre 1984; Nolan 1998; Hewitt 1988). Whether it be the political rhetoric of a president who can "feel your pain," or the daytime talk show programs where guests and audience members regularly emote about all aspects of their private and public lives, the open expression of emotion has become a defining feature of American life. As early as the mid-1970s sociologist Edwin Schur observed that in America, "Every emotion has value. . . . We must recognize all feelings, express them, open them up to the people around us" (1976:17). About the same time, Thomas Cottle noted that "our entire society seems to be leaning toward more and more divulging and exposing, and less and less confidentiality and withholding" (cited in ibid.:18).

Identification of this peculiarly American predilection continued in the 1980s, when Alasdair MacIntyre identified emotivism as a distinguishing cultural ethic. "Emotivism has become embodied in our culture. . . . We live in a specifically emotivist culture" (1984:22). Several years later, sociologist Robert Bellah and his colleagues (Bellah et al. 1985) recognized "expressive individualism" as a dominant language in American society, and political philosopher Jean Bethke Elshtain observed that, "all points seem to revolve around the individual's subjective feelings" (Elshtain 1986:92). In the past decade such analyses have only continued (Nolan 1998). Among the more recent is John Hewitt's description of the "ascendancy of feelings and emotional well-being in the culture as a whole" (Hewitt 1998:96).

Reflecting this basic cultural orientation, one finds in American drug courts and in the treatment programs associated with them a great deal of expressivism. It is not atypical for clients at the various graduation ceremonies, for example, to cry and thank the judge and others for their help. When a dozen drug court judges were asked to list the "six most important characteristics of an effective drug court judge," the most often reported response was "the ability to be empathetic or to show genuine concern" (Satel 1998:51). Such empathy is sometimes communicated through physical contact. Even hugging, particularly at graduation ceremonies, is not uncommon. In her study of drug courts published in the first issue of the *National Drug Court Institute Review*, Sally Satel observed physical contact between judge and client in fourteen of the fifteen drug courts she observed (ibid.:62–64).

Such public expressions of emotion do not play so well in British courts. Consider, for example, several comments from different magistrates on the issue of hugging. One said, "We won't hug." Another added, "That is where we draw the line." Still another, "I'm not in favor of that." He went on, "These are really criminals at the end of the day. The decency of the court must be upheld." Another: "*I* haven't gotten that close." British courts, especially Crown Courts, are much more formal than American courts. Barristers and solicitors bow when entering or exiting the courtroom, and refer to magistrates as "your worship." Crown Courts, accoutered as they are with wigs and black robes are even more formal. It is hard to imagine the kind of expressivism that characterizes many of the American drug courts being displayed in a British court. As a British Member of Parliament put it after witnessing the emotionally laden processes of one of America's drug courts, "This was impressive—indeed moving—even if, at the same time, it proved difficult to envisage such emotional events taking place in the courts in this country."

Indeed, I found British judges and magistrates clearly indisposed toward this type of behavior. In the West Yorkshire courts, probation officers provided a two-day training session for the magistrates who would be involved in the drug court program. The training included videos of U.S. drug courts in action. Of the practice of hugging clients displayed in the video, according to a West Yorkshire probation officer, the magistrates were "appalled at that concept and they still remain appalled at that concept." A medical doctor at the Croydon DTTO program likewise said of the kind of emotionalism that characterizes the American drug courts, "Well, the British magistrates just will not do it. . . . British judges are part of the British establishment. They are the British establishment. They are the last group of people who would respond to a rather more emotional morality sort of led program." According to this doctor, not only judges but everyone in the system, including clients would not be comfortable with such a style. "British drug users don't like it at all. They wouldn't like the emotional intensity of it."

Within British society, however, not everyone is so certain about the impossibility of some kind of change in this area. The highly emotional aftermath of Princess Diana's death suggests that change has already begun. As became apparent in this extraordinary event—where for better or for worse the Royals were essentially forced to emote publicly in a certain sort of way—no longer is the stiff upper lip necessarily regarded as virtuous or even desirable behavior in Britain. Indeed, such stoicism was itself pathologized in therapeutic terms. As British sociologist Frank Furedi noted, "After Princess Diana's tragic death, nobody can accuse the British of being too reserved. The unprecedented public display of grief seemed to reveal a sea change in Britain's culture" (1997). Others note a similar development. Novelist A. L. Kennedy, for example, "hailed the response to Diana's death as evidence of Britain's newfound 'emotional maturity,'" (Merck 1998:2) and Jonathan Freedland, though he thinks viewing the reaction to Diana's death as "an overnight conversion by the British to the gushy confessionalism of the U.S. . . . might be an exaggeration," concedes that the "British people *are* becoming more expressive" (Freedland 1998:189).

Correspondingly, public expressions of emotion are increasingly detectable in British political discourse. As is now well-known, Tony Blair very deliberately and successfully emulated Clinton's rhetorical style. Some have pointed to his "sharing, caring, giving" speech at the New Labour convention in 1997, his timely and emotionally correct reaction to Diana's death, and his uncanny ability to successfully emote publicly on many occasions as evidence of this.[7] At a press conference with President Clinton shortly after the Monica Lewinsky story first broke, Blair explicitly underscored the political virtue of openly and honestly communicating one's feelings. A questioner noted Blair's statements of public support for Clinton and asked the prime minister whether this was a politically risky strategy. Blair began by saying that Clinton was someone he was proud to call not just a colleague, but a friend. He went on: "And in the end, you either decide in politics you—when you are asked about people, you are going to say how you actually feel, or you're going to make a whole series of calculations. And my belief is that the right thing to say is what you feel"("Comments on the Lewinsky Allegations," washingtonpost.com, February 6, 1998).

Norman Fairclough sees Blair's ability to "to combine formality and informality, ceremony and feeling, publicness and privateness," as one of the defining and compelling features of his rhetorical style (2000:7). Blair used this style to great effect when publicly conveying his (and the country's) grief over Diana's death. Mandy Merck goes so far as to assert that in successfully tapping into the public mood as he did in this instance, Blair rather than undermining the monarchy, actually renewed its "legitimacy" (1998:5). That the public expression of emotion engenders political legitimacy, as such, signifies that important cultural change may well be under way. Frank Furedi certainly thinks so. Given these cultural currents, he argues that "public figures are [now] expected to cry and acknowledge their weakness and frailty. Emotion, once foreign and unfitting in the public realm, has become commonplace in British political life over the past decade" (1997). Perhaps, with cultural and political change, as such, British judges may become more open to public displays of emotion in the courtroom. There are signs that this is beginning to happen in some instances.

For one, it seems that the expressivism of the American drug court was in part what persuaded some British officials of the worthiness of drug courts. Val Barker, from Wakefield, for example, said of her time in the Miami drug court:

> We saw great success and great failure. And I cried and laughed and laughed and cried. And this particular day there was a Diana Ross in his court, and he [Goldstein] looked over his glasses and winked, and said "Diana Ross?" And she said, "Yes Judge." And he said, "Sing to me baby." It brought the house down. Well, I have never seen a judge behave like that. (BBC 1999)

Keith Hellawell had a very similar experience. Of Judge Goldstein's court, Hellawell observed:

> It is very much as if [Goldstein] was talking to his son or his daughter. He chastises them openly. He will reward them openly by kissing them, or putting his arm around them. He'll say, "Come up here. Come and let me see you." And he will get hold of their hands or he'll point his finger at them and say, "I'm not going to have this. You know, you are making a mess of this. You are not going to do it." And then when they get through the program there is a ceremony and they cry and everybody cheers and they give them

the certificate. And Stanley is there and he's holding them and hugging them. . . . It is the end of something great. It is very, very evangelical, almost. It really is something you have to experience to understand. (BBC 1999)

One could rightly argue, however, that just because officials were inspired by the emotional qualities of the American model does not mean these same features will easily transfer to the English courtroom. A BBC reporter raised just this issue in a question he put to Keith Hellawell: "What made you think that this alien concept of justice could be healthfully and successfully transplanted to Britain where the majority of justices of the peace, magistrates are not charismatic, huggy touchy-feeling kind of people?" To which Hellawell responded:

Because it works and because the outcome of that experience works. As far as our magistrates are concerned, some of them are extremely charismatic. I could name some in the past who've put the fear of God into me and many others, and would stamp the bench and would stand up and would be as charismatic and certainly as vocal as any judge I've seen in the United States. (BBC 1999)

As revealed in Hellawell's response, not all see the British judiciary as incapable of showing more open expressions of emotion. Caterina Fagg of the Wakefield court believes British judges and magistrates can and already have begun to move in this direction. She tells of how West Yorkshire magistrates have in some instances begun to function more like American drug court judges:

Magistrates are now asking more and being more interactive with the clients, talking about their problems, asking them to discuss their problems. We had one client, and when he withdrew from heroin he started to experience the pain of tooth decay and things like that. And this client was afraid of the dentist and he comes to the review court and it was holding up his treatment because he wasn't getting dental treatment. And I explained to the magistrates that he was afraid to go. And one of the magistrates said, "Well, do you want someone to go with you?" And he said, "Yes." And the magistrate actually met the client and took him to the dentist. We've had another magistrate who has loaned bus fares to a client. It's very new and I think that it is very much an evolving process that they will learn about.

Such an evolutionary process has even, according to Fagg, led some magistrates to agree to a sort of toned-down graduation ceremony: "The magistrates, like the judges, are very reluctant to celebrate. But what they have agreed to do in court, they have agreed that if we present a certificate, and a small gift of some type, they will endorse that procedure in the review courts." As conveyed in Fagg's description, however, this agreement represented what was really only a rather tepid endorsement, which an added caveat makes quite clear: "But they don't want to hug and they don't want to give out donuts or anything like that."

Paul Hayes conveyed a similar sort of ambivalence regarding judicial willingness to engage in a courtroom manner characteristic of the American drug courts. On the one hand he noted that "the whole context of the English courtroom is more formal than the context of a U.S. court," and that the style of the American drug court "is rather alien to the culture" of the English system. On the other hand, he conceded that "we are getting more like you, while we watch all of these terrible programs [American daytime talk shows that are broadcast in the United Kingdom] where people confess that they slept with everyone under the sun and all this. So we are getting more used to baring our souls I think." Still, according to Hayes, the British are not as far along as Americans in such behavior. As he concludes, "We still are not as good at it as you are."

Therefore, the ambivalence evident in the emerging British drug courts, to the extent that it reflects broader social tendencies, suggests a culture in flux, where stoicism and reserve may be giving way to more open and emotional forms of public communication. In the main, however, it seems judges and magistrates are still very reluctant to engage clients in a fashion that even comes close to the levels of intimacy and expressivism displayed in America's drug court programs. The manager of the Gloucestershire DTTO may have summed it up best: "The Home Office, when they saw the American judges, they loved that, and they loved the judges giving badges and giving donuts and stuff like that." As to the transferability of these practices to Britain he added, "I've heard this wonderful comment since then that American culture doesn't cross the pond easily."

Consider one final cultural matter, and this has to do specifically with British attitudes toward America. While traces of British anti-Americanism are certainly not new sentiments (Hollander 1992), in the contemporary context they seem to manifest themselves as a kind of love-hate relationship. That is, the British and others worry publicly about "American cultural imperialism," while at the same time they seem enthralled with things American.[8] Peter Hassett illustrates this paradox in a story about his efforts to introduce drug courts in Scotland.

> I was meeting with a director of social work, who has responsibility for the probation service and the second largest authority in Scotland. He says "I'll meet you in Starbucks down in Glasgow," and he came in with these Nike trainers and his Levi jeans and the rest of the American designer gear, and he said to me, "you know American ideas just don't work in Britain."

Jonathan Freedland, rather graphically, makes the same point regarding the apparently contradictory nature of British attitudes toward America:

"We simultaneously disdain and covet American culture, condemning it as junk food even as we reach for another helping—a kind of binge-and-puke social bulimia" (1998:11). He notes that given the sheer weight of cultural traffic coming across the Atlantic, the British need to be more discerning about what they import and what they do not.

CONCLUSION

As it concerns drug policy, however, the British have never imported policies and programs wholesale. They have always been rather selective. As Philip Bean opines on this matter: "What one can see is that American policies have been changed to fit British experience and made to fit British culture. . . . There is a willingness in Britain to accept some American ideas and a reluctance to accept them all. Some are worth taking on board, some not" (Bean 2001:94). Drug courts are no exception to this historical pattern. Indeed, the very different form drug courts have assumed in England makes clear that judicial programs and innovations are always located in a particular social context. The context, as such, defines the parameters and acceptability of programs, new and old. Just as the U.S.-led international efforts at the beginning of the twentieth century had very different outcomes when translated into different settings, so the court intervention schemes for drug offenders are likely to take on very different forms given the unique context within which the programs are situated.

This, because, as Clifford Geertz would put it, local knowledge—a legal culture's unique ways and particular accent—plays an important role in determining the shape, style, and scope of a legal initiative. Visible through the window of drug courts, then, are societies with distinct and still influential historical backgrounds; varying legal structures and legal habits; and very different, albeit perhaps evolving, cultural landscapes. Drugs courts, therefore, tell us as much about the fabric of differing social situations as they do about the unique distinctives of this turn-of-the-century legal innovation. George Bernard Shaw once said that "Great Britain and America are nations separated by a common language." It's also been said that "England and the United States are two countries separated by a common law" (Glendon et al. 1982:10). The uncommon legal innovation represented in the drug court movement suggests that the two statements may well depict the very same social/legal reality.

NOTES

1.   Consider several indicators of this enthusiasm: British criminologist Philip Bean noted in 1998 that "there is little doubt that Drug Courts are becom-

ing increasingly fashionable in Britain. Hardly a week goes by without someone arguing for their introduction" (Bean, 1998:101). In an address at a July 1998 drug court conference at Loughborough University, British Member of Parliament George Howarth noted that "concerns about the high level of drug-related crime have led us again to look at the American drug court concept." Brentwood Special Inspector Peter French, who has been in British law enforcement for twenty-four years, asserted at the June 1998 NADCP conference in Washington, D.C., "I am totally sold on the drug court system in America. . . . I think that now is the time for the U.K. to go along the lines that you've done. You've seen it work. I've seen it work. And I'm absolutely one hundred percent totally committed on the drug court program."

2. During the 1999/2000 academic year I visited each of the programs in Wakefield, Pontefract, Liverpool, Gloucestershire, and Croydon (South London), and interviewed probation officers, magistrates, and/or treatment providers at each site. I also visited court sites in Plymouth and Nottingham, where features of the U.S. drug court model have also been implemented or are being seriously considered. U.S./U.K. comparisons considered in this chapter draw from ethnographic observations and research on the five operational DTTOs or drug court sites in England. All citations in this chapter, unless otherwise indicated, come from interviews conducted with various probation, medical, and judicial professionals during this period, or from statements made at several conferences, including two NADCP national conferences in 1998 and 1999, where English drug court advocates participated in panel discussions; a 1999 DTTO conference; a 1998 drug court conference held at Loughborough University; and a 2000 international conference on drug courts held in Alloa, Scotland. In addition, several quotes from American drug court officials come from research conducted in the United States between 1994 and 1998 (see Nolan 2001:11–13).

3. Lawrence Friedman summarizes this understanding of the law in a similar manner: "The key concept here is legal culture: the ideas, attitudes, values, and opinions about law held by people in a society. The assumption is that these ideas and attitudes influence legal behavior. . . . Legal culture, then is a 'network of values and attitudes' . . . which determine when and why and where people turn to law or government or turn away" (1994:31–32). David Garland offers a similar view of law in his more specific discussion of penal law: "The specific culture of punishment in any society will always have its roots in the broader context of prevailing (or recently prevailing) social attitudes and traditions. . . . Penal practices exist within a specific penal culture which is itself supported and made meaningful by wider cultural forms, these, in turn being grounded in society's patterns of material life and social action" (1990:210–11).

4. See discussion of Rolleston Committee (Bean, 1974:57–70). Bean notes that thirty-four witnesses testified before the Rolleston Committee. Twenty-four were doctors, eight had connections with pharmaceutical companies, and two were from the Home Office (one was the director of prosecutions and the other was the undersecretary of state).

5. Between 1994 and 1998 I visited a total of twenty-one drug courts around the United States. A much fuller analysis of the American version of the drug court movement is found in (Nolan 2001).
6. As Canadian drug court judge Paul Bentley observes, "It is noteworthy that unlike most US drug courts, the Toronto DTC incorporates methadone maintenance as part of its treatment arsenal for heroin addicts. The abstinence model of most US courts does not permit the use of methadone."
7. Normal Fairclough, for example, observes of Blair that he "combines an everyday emotional language . . . with formal, ceremonial expressions of regret . . . in a way which brings his own emotional reaction as a 'normal person' . . . into his official task as Prime Minister." Not only did he effectively do this in his emotionally laden tribute to Diana, but he "sometimes brings personal emotion into more conventional political contexts" (2000:103).
8. Canadian drug court judge Paul Bentley made just this point in a discussion with both American and British drug court practitioners: "We have to be very careful in Canada, because although Canadians love Americans they also dislike Americans because of cultural imperialism, which we get in Canada far more than anybody else ever gets because we pick up all your stations, T.V., radio, magazines. It's unlimited."

REFERENCES

Allison, J. W. F. 1996. *A Continental Distinction in the Common Law: A Historical and Comparative Perspective on English Public Law.* Oxford: Clarendon.

Bakalar, James B. and Lester Grinspoon. 1984. *Drug Control in a Free Society.* Cambridge: Cambridge University Press.

BBC. 1999. "Drug Court USA." Presenter David Jessel, producer Susan Marling. BBC Radio 4, Summer.

Bean, Philip. 1974. *The Social Control of Drugs.* New York: Martin Robertson.

Bean, Philip. 1996. "New Developments in the U.S. Drug Courts." *Drugs: Education, Prevention and Policy* 3(2):211–13.

Bean, Philip. 1998. "Transplanting the USA's Drug Courts to Britain." *Drugs: Education, Prevention and Policy* 5(1):101–4.

Bean, Philip. 2001. "American Influence on British Drug Policy." Pp. 79–95 in *Drug War, American Style: The Internationalization of Failed Policy and Its Alternatives,* edited by Jurg Gerber and Eric L. Jensen. New York: Garland.

Bellah, Robert, Richard Madsen, William M. Sullivan, Ann Swidler, and Steven M. Tipton. 1985. *Habits of the Heart: Individualism and Commitment in American Life.* Berkeley: University of California Press.

Best, Joel. 1999. *Random Violence: How We Talk About New Crimes and New Victims.* Berkeley: University of California Press.

Clear, Todd R. and Judith Rumgay. 1992. "Divided by a Common Language: British and American Probation Cultures." *Federal Probation* (September):2–11.

Cooper, Caroline S., Shanie R. Bartlett, Michelle A. Shaw, and Kayla K. Yang. 1997. "Drug Courts: 1997 Overview of Operational Characteristics and Implementation Issues, Part Six: Drug Court Treatment Services." Drug Court Clearinghouse and Technical Assistance Project, Office of Justice Programs, U.S. Department of Justice.

Duster, Troy. 1970. *The Legislation of Morality: Law, Drugs, and Moral Judgment.* New York: Free Press.

Eldridge, William Butler. 1967. *Narcotics and the Law: A Critique of the American Experiment in Narcotic Drug Control.* Chicago: University of Chicago Press.

Elshtain, Jean Bethke. 1986. *Meditations on Modern Political Thought.* New York: Praeger.

Fairclough, Norman. 2000. *New Labour, New Language?* London: Routledge.

Freedland, Jonathan. 1998. *Bring Home the Revolution: The Case for a British Republic.* London: Fourth Estate.

Friedman, Lawrence. 1994. *Total Justice.* New York: Russell Sage.

Furedi, Frank. 1997. "A New Religion in Britain." *Wall Street Journal Europe,* 8 September.

Garland, David. 1990. *Punishment and Modern Society: A Study in Social Theory.* Chicago: University of Chicago Press.

Geertz, Clifford. 1983. *Local Knowledge: Further Essays in Interpretive Anthropology.* New York: Basic Books.

Glendon, Mary Ann, Michael W. Gordon, and Christopher Osakwe. 1982. *Comparative Legal Traditions.* St. Paul: West.

Hayes, Paul. 1998. Paper presented at seminar, "Drug Misusing Offenders and the Criminal Justice System," Strasbourg, 12–14 October.

Hewitt, John P. 1998. *The Myth of Self-Esteem: Finding Happiness and Solving Problems in America.* New York: St. Martin's .

Hollander, Paul. 1992. *Anti-Americanism: Critiques at Home and Abroad, 1965–1990.* Oxford: Oxford University Press.

Home Office. 2000. "New Powers for Courts to Help Tackle Drug Related Crime." Press release, 29 September.

Jacobsohn, Gary. 1993. *The Apple of Gold: Constitutionalism in Israel and the United States.* Princeton, NJ: Princeton University Press.

Joint Committee of the American Bar Association and the American Medical Association on Narcotic Drugs. 1969. *Drug Addiction: Crime or Disease? Interim and Final Reports of the Joint Committee of the American Bar Association and the American Medical Association on Narcotic Drugs.* Introduction by Alfred R. Lindesmith. Bloomington: Indiana University Press.

Judson, Horace Freeland. 1973. *Heroin Addiction in Britain: What Americans Can Learn from the English Experience.* New York: Harcourt Brace Jovanovich.

Larimore, Granville W. and Henry Brill. 1960. "The British Narcotic System, Report of Study." *New York State Journal of Medicine* 60(January):107.

MacIntyre, Alasdair. 1984. *After Virtue: A Study in Moral Theory.* Notre Dame, IN: University of Notre Dame Press.

Merck, Mandy. 1998. "Introduction: After Diana," *After Diane: Irreverent Elegies,* edited by Mandy Merck. London: Verso.

Nolan, James L., Jr. 1998. *The Therapeutic State: Justifying Government at Century's End.* New York: New York University Press.

Nolan, James L., Jr. 2001 *Reinventing Justice: The American Drug Court Movement.* Princeton, NJ: Princeton University Press.

Rieff, Philip. 1966. *The Triumph of the Therapeutic.* Chicago: University of Chicago Press.

Satel, Sally. 1998. "Observational Study of Courtroom Dynamics in Selected Drug Courts." *National Drug Court Institute Review* 1(1, Summer):43–72.

Schur, Edwin M. 1960. "Drug Addiction in America and England." *Commentary* 30 September:241–48.

Schur, Edwin M. 1968. *Narcotic Addiction in Britain and America: The Impact of Public Policy.* Bloomington: Indiana University Press.

Schur, Edwin M. 1976. *The Awareness Trap: Self-Absorption Instead of Social Change.* New York: Quadrangle / New York Times.

II

Theoretical Assessments

6

The Adversary System and Attorney Role in the Drug Treatment Court Movement

Richard C. Boldt

From the period between the world wars until the early 1970s, discourse about state-sponsored punishment in the United States and Great Britain was dominated by a consequentialist perspective in general, and by a focus upon rehabilitation in particular.[1] By 1980, however, striking changes had occurred in both the practice and theory of punishment. Consequentialist or utilitarian goals and justifications for punishment had been pushed into a secondary position and nonconsequentialist rationales centered on retributive notions of just deserts had gained ascendancy (Allen 1981).[2] Although the effort to build treatment into the punishment system drew critics from across the political spectrum during the late 1960s and 1970s, perhaps the most telling attacks came from the left and from liberals. A number of features central to the "rehabilitative ideal" (ibid.) that enjoyed wide support a generation ago are present to some degree in the contemporary drug treatment court. In light of these parallels, it is helpful to recall the critique of rehabilitative penal practice offered a generation ago by left-liberal commentators such as the American Friends Service Committee (American Friends Service Committee 1971; Fogel 1979).

This essay builds upon the observation of these left-liberal critics that, by blending punitive and therapeutic impulses, rehabilitative penal regimes often seek to accomplish incompatible goals. This conflict in objectives is manifested especially in the poor fit between the norms of adversary adjudication that characterize traditional criminal law practice, and the procedural informality and judicial activism common to rehabilitative undertakings. The consequences of this tension for defendants are illuminated by examining the role conflicts faced by their attorneys in drug treatment court settings.

THE ADVERSARY SYSTEM AND ATTORNEY ROLE

An adversary system of decision-making has three chief characteristics, each of which relates directly to the role of counsel. First, the parties initiate and control the process, by pursing their respective positions through affirmative presentations of evidence and argument coupled with challenges to their opponents' version of law and fact. Second, these forensic narratives and counternarratives are presented to the decision-maker according to formal procedural rules. Third, the decision-maker is charged with being neutral with respect to the conflict until such time as a decision is rendered through the application of substantive decisional rules to the parties' evidence.[3]

Given these characteristics, it should come as little surprise that most adversarial adjudications require the parties to seek the assistance of counsel. The requirement that each side's partisan account be presented according to formal procedural rules often beyond the ken of laypersons, and the requirement that these accounts be presented with an eye toward satisfying substantive rules of decision, generally will militate against *pro se* advocacy by nonlawyer litigants. Taken together, the three defining characteristics of the adversary system have been said to yield a "standard conception" (Postema 1980:73) of the lawyer's role that is reflected in the ABA's Model Code of Professional Responsibility, the ABA's Model Rules of Professional Conduct, and various standards governing criminal defense practice.[4]

Because the primary function of a lawyer in an adversary proceeding is to represent the client by seeking to accomplish the client's self-interested goals, the standard conception imposes upon the lawyer a set of mutually reinforcing duties. The first is a duty of partisanship, which recognizes that the advocate is in some senses standing in the shoes of his or her client. This duty is satisfied when the lawyer adopts the client's ends as his or her own. Additionally, the attorney is bound to avoid conflicts between the client's interests and his or her own interests or those of another client. This duty to avoid conflicts of interest is designed to insure that the lawyer's partisan zeal, his or her unity of purpose with the client, is not diluted by a competing agenda. Finally, the lawyer is forbidden from disclosing information learned in the course of the representation, unless permitted to

do so by the client. This duty of client confidentiality is intended to encourage clients to speak freely with their lawyers, again in order to safe-
guard the unity of purpose between advocate and client and to facilitate
the lawyer's partisan efforts on the client's behalf.[5]

On occasion, each of the defining features of the adversary system
comes into conflict with rehabilitative penal practice, including practice
within most drug treatment courts. As a consequence, the standard role
conception sometimes is ill-suited to the tasks facing counsel for defendants in such proceedings. In cases where the drug court defendant's express goal is to avoid all coercive measures, including rehabilitative
treatment, defense counsel may or may not be able to adopt the standard
partisan role. If the defendant's objective of avoiding therapy is well-
grounded, the adversarial model likely will hold, and the defendant's attorney will be able to pursue this outcome within the standard role
conception. If, on the other hand, the defendant's desire to avoid therapeutic measures is not well-grounded, as is often the case with defendants
whose addictive disorders include a fair degree of denial, the defense attorney will be placed in a difficult situation. According to the standard conception, the attorney should adopt the defendant's goals as his or her own,
and should pursue them with partisan zeal, despite the fact that the lawyer
may believe that it would be in the client's best interests to undergo treatment. A very different role conception for defense counsel obtains, however, in those institutional settings, including drug treatment courts, where
the express purpose of the proceeding is the provision of treatment rather
than the imposition of blame and punishment. Attorneys who adopt this
alternative role conception often view their clients as incapable of identifying appropriate goals that further their true best interests, and so impose
their own judgments regarding the objectives of the representation.[6]

This alternative role conception, which treats the defendant as impaired
in his or her capacity to make sound decisions, is incompatible with an adjudicatory model characterized by party control. It may be possible to
avoid this conclusion by locating party control in the person of defense
counsel as opposed to the defendant him- or herself, but this conceptualization only works if some sort of strong identification between the defendant and his or her lawyer can be found. In the drug treatment court
setting, however, the defense lawyer is likely to have significant links with
other ongoing participants in the process, including prosecutors, corrections officials, and judges, and to share with these actors a common set of
interests. As a result, the requisite identification between the treatment
court defendant and his or her attorney may be difficult to establish or
maintain.[7] In such circumstances, a key element of the adversarial system
will not be present.

Rehabilitative penal practices pose similar problems of fit with respect to the requirements that there be neutral, detached decision-makers and formal rules of procedure, the other key characteristics of a traditional adversarial system. In a now classic essay, Martin Shapiro explored the importance of formal decisional rules and neutral adjudication in adversarial disputing. Shapiro observed that traditional adversarial processes are essentially triadic in structure, and that this structure is inherently unstable because of its tendency to collapse into "two against one," once the decision-maker has announced a winner and a loser. In order to avoid this sort of collapse, which may undermine the legitimacy of the outcome, at least in the eyes of a nonprevailing party who may perceive there to have been an alliance between the winner and the judge, Shapiro argued that complex societies develop formal rules to govern the adjudicatory process and rely upon the office of the judge to insure that the decision-maker remains independent and professional (Shapiro 1979).[8]

The argument that triadic disputing processes rely upon detached decision-makers and formal adjudicatory rules to avoid the delegitimating consequences of a collapse into two against one is based upon the premise that decisions are more likely to be understood as fair if they are derived through a process in which both parties to the dispute have equal access to the decision-maker. In this sense, the formality of the process and the neutrality of the judge are both designed to insure that the decision-maker maintains appropriate distance from the parties in order to prevent an unfair alliance from developing with the prevailing party. By contrast, in drug treatment courts and other rehabilitative penal regimes, the stabilizing influence of procedural formality and neutrality is diminished or dispensed with entirely, precisely because the goals and interests of the parties are not understood to be in conflict. To the extent that this characterization is true, as it may be in the relationship of helping professionals and their clients, the collapse of the triadic structure may not undermine the client's confidence in the integrity and legitimacy of the system. On the other hand, when treatment is built into a system that has retained at least some of the features of traditional criminal law blaming practices, such as the power to use coercive measures, procedural informality and a lack of detachment on the part of the decision-maker can have severe negative consequences for the defendant, and can present significant conflicts for the defendant's advocate.

DRUG TREATMENT COURTS AND ATTORNEY ROLE

While treatment-based drug courts vary considerably according to each jurisdiction's statutory context, political environment, available resources, and operational goals,[9] certain core features tend to define virtually all of these undertakings. Almost without exception, these courts mute the traditional adversarial positions of prosecutor and defendant, and shift the process so that it becomes judge-driven rather than lawyer-driven. This inversion of the traditional adversary system paradigm, which ordinarily assumes that the parties' lawyers will play an active, partisan role while the judge remains passive and umpirelike, tends to be coupled with a high degree of procedural informality. Taken together, these features yield a setting in which familiar role expectations rarely serve as accurate predictors of actual practice. As one observer writes:

> [W]hat makes these drug treatment calendars unique is the nonadversarial nature of their proceedings and the active and ongoing role that the drug treatment court judge plays—generally with the support of both the prosecutor and defense counsel—in working with the treatment provider and motivating the defendant to complete the treatment program. Essentially, these "drug courts" are not courts at all, but diversion-to-treatment programs, which are supervised through regular (usually monthly) quasi-judicial status hearings at which the drug court judge enters into a dialogue with each defendant about his or her progress in the treatment / rehabilitation program. (Cooper and Trotter 1994:93)

The underlying rationale for this state of affairs recalls the thinking of the leading rehabilitationists of a generation ago (see, e.g., Wootton 1978). A key feature of the rehabilitative ideal was the conviction that antisocial or criminal conduct was the product in part or whole of some pathology operating within the offender. Given this starting point, rehabilitationist thinkers urged the criminal justice system to respond to offenders with therapeutic treatment instead of retributive punishment, either to assist the offender or, in the case of social defense theorists, to protect society from future harmful conduct. Furthermore, because rehabilitationists thought that criminal conduct was linked to individual pathology, they concentrated less on the specific facts and circumstances of completed criminal offenses and more on information about an offender's personal characteristics that were necessary for making accurate determinations with respect to diagnosis and prognosis.

Translated into the contemporary drug treatment court context, these ideas generate a powerful set of interrelated premises: Substance abuse is a disease that contributes in a substantial and direct fashion to the commission of criminal conduct. Most offenders with drug abuse problems who are prosecuted and sentenced in the traditional punishment-oriented criminal justice system do not receive treatment for their disease; therefore, upon release they resume the addictive use of drugs and associated criminal behaviors. If the offender's disease is treated, however, this linked cycle of addiction and criminality can be disrupted.[10]

Although formal notions of guilt and responsibility for past criminal conduct are not made irrelevant in the drug treatment court setting,[11] the primary focus, and therefore the design of the system, is centered upon the offender's future conduct and the characteristics of his or her disease and progress in treatment that permit useful predictions as to future criminality. This shift in focus is responsible for the push toward a relatively non-partisan, informal procedural approach on the part of drug treatment courts.[12]

In light of this redirected emphasis and procedural informality, defenders must make difficult choices in formulating an appropriate role conception. These choices fall into several broad categories. The first relates to the posture adopted by defense counsel at the moment his or her client is faced with deciding whether to enter a treatment court program or to have criminal charges resolved through the traditional adjudication system. The second category centers on counsel's decision to play either an active or a passive role in limiting the potentially severe sanctions his or her client may receive in instances of relapse. An important consideration falling within this category is the question whether defense counsel should interpose him- or herself between the defendant and the treatment court judge, or acquiesce in the common practice of permitting the judge to interact directly with defendants in open court. The final group of choices defense counsel is likely to face involves the degree to which potentially damaging or inculpating information will be shared with the court and the prosecutor.

The Decision to Participate in Drug Treatment Court

Most drug treatment courts operate either as "deferred prosecution programs" or "postdisposition programs." Treatment courts following the deferred prosecution model attempt to identify suitable defendants within days of their initial arrest, in order to capitalize on the therapeutic value of the "trauma and anxiety" associated with being taken into custody (Cooper and Trotter 1994:95).[13] If a defendant is diverted into treatment at this time, the adjudication of his or her charges will be suspended. If he or she ultimately is successful in treatment, those charges will then be dismissed.

At first blush it would appear that defendants eligible for a deferred prosecution program have everything to gain and little to lose by a decision to participate, given the opportunity to obtain treatment and avoid criminal conviction. Concomitantly, it would appear that defense lawyers, acting in their role as advisors, ought enthusiastically to recommend such participation. In fact, defense attorneys counseling clients at this threshold stage must confront several difficult issues. For many defendants, the de-

cision to participate in the treatment court process will mean that they effectively forgo the presumption of innocence and the panoply of trial rights
guaranteed by the United States Constitution.[14] In a literal sense, the defendant who opts to enter a deferred prosecution program may still con-
test his or her guilt at a full adversarial trial if he or she fails to complete
the treatment mandated by the drug court. Nevertheless, a defendant who
progresses through the entire treatment court regime and who upon "graduation" has had his or her charges dismissed ultimately may have received
"a more onerous disposition in terms of the length of time [that defendant]
is subject to court control" (Goldkamp 1994) than he or she would have received if the charges had been resolved through standard plea negotiations
or trial. Given that this "more onerous disposition" will have been imposed
without a formal adjudication of guilt, the "successful" defendant's decision to participate effectively constitutes at least a partial waiver of trial
rights.

One response to this apparent unfairness is that the treatment court's
disposition, although "more onerous" in some respects, ultimately is in the
defendant's best interest because it provides needed treatment. Moreover,
supporters are likely to point to repeated investigations that have shown
coerced addictions treatment to be even more effective than voluntary
treatment in driving this disease into remission (Satel 1998:53).[15] This response clearly frames the role conflict faced by defense counsel in this setting. If counsel's role is to facilitate the disposition that is in his or her
client's best interests, then he or she should urge the drug-addicted client
to agree to participate in treatment court. If, on the other hand, counsel
adopts the standard role conception, he or she should advise the client as
to the likely outcomes of the various choices that are available, including
the fact that rejecting the treatment court route may result in a less intrusive sanction or a sanction of shorter duration than that likely to result from
even the most successful encounter with treatment court, and should then
act zealously to effectuate the client's choice.

It will not do to argue that defense counsel can reconcile these two
alternatives by "provid[ing] thorough advice about the drug court and
let[ting] the client decide" (Judge 1997:1) because many defendants who
would benefit from treatment predictably will reject this alternative if they
understand clearly the impositions it involves. At least with respect to
those clients whose short-term preference is "to avoid or minimize loss of
liberty or other sanctions" (ibid.) counsel must choose either to be an advocate for the treatment court option or an advocate for the client's expressed goals.[16]

This conflict between zealous advocacy and membership on the treatment team is likely to be exacerbated in practice by one of the operational
elements that is said to make drug courts effective in reaching their treat-

ment goals, their capacity to "identify the drug offender and place him or her into the treatment program as soon after arrest as possible" (Brown 1997:87–88). Defense lawyers acting within the traditional role conception must attempt at least a rudimentary fact investigation, and should evaluate potential legal issues raised by available information, including possible search and seizure arguments, and questions with respect to the sufficiency of the charging document, before advising clients to enter a treatment court program. By contrast, defense counsel acting as a member of the treatment team may well conclude that the delay necessitated by adequate factual and legal evaluation of the case will undermine the therapeutic goal of instituting treatment while the defendant is still in the midst of the crisis occasioned by his or her arrest. To the extent that these goals do come into conflict in individual cases, it is no answer to urge that a balance be struck between them, unless one is willing to countenance a diminution, however slight, in the ordinary obligations of partisanship imposed by the standard role conception and the various performance standards now in place.

Defense counsel's role conflict becomes even more pronounced in a jurisdiction where the treatment court's practice is to defer prosecution only if the defendant agrees to a stipulated set of facts, or in a jurisdiction that has adopted the "postdisposition model," in which case the defendant will be required to enter a guilty plea (Cooper and Trotter 1994:96). In either of these two contexts, the lawyer's decision to facilitate his or her client's entry into the drug court program not only exposes the defendant to coercive therapeutic measures that may be more invasive and/or protracted than traditional dispositions, it also necessarily results in the waiver of factual and technical legal defenses, leaving the client "vulnerable if [he or she] ultimately fail[s] treatment" (Schreibersdorf 1997:7).

THE DEFENDER'S ROLE WITH RESPECT
TO GRADUATED SANCTIONS

The second group of issues has to do with counsel's role in limiting the potentially severe sanctions a defendant in treatment court may receive upon relapse. The fact that recovery from substance abuse often involves relapse has been taken into account in the design of most drug treatment courts, through the use of graduated sanctions rather than the all-or-nothing approach of traditional probation or parole revocation proceedings (Tauber 1994:33).[17] In some jurisdictions, these escalating sanctions are set out in contracts or clearly written policies, so that the judge has relatively little flexibility once he or she finds that the defendant has failed to adhere to one or more of the conditions of the program. In other jurisdictions, treatment court judges have greater discretion in fashioning intermediate sanctions in response to offender relapse (Satel 1998:63–64).

Here again, defense counsel faces a choice between acting as a zealous partisan according to the standard role conception or acting as part of the treatment team. In jurisdictions that permit the defendant's attorney to negotiate some of the terms of the contract, the standard conception would dictate that he or she seek inclusion of the mildest sanctions possible, entailing the smallest loss of liberty. On the other hand, a role conception that prioritizes the goal of helping the defendant to succeed in treatment over the more familiar goal of avoiding coercive measures might well lead defenders to agree to more intrusive sanctions, particularly if they believe, for example, that small doses of "shock incarceration" will help their clients to take the treatment protocol more seriously.

In jurisdictions where prenegotiated limits on sanctions are not possible, defense lawyers still face difficult choices when their clients are alleged to have violated treatment court rules. Here, the question is whether to engage in traditional forms of advocacy, such as offering evidence providing an explanation or justification for the defendant's behavior or challenging the factual basis for a finding that a violation has occurred, in order to justify a less severe sanction. In drug courts where the judge has considerable discretion, this sort of advocacy has the potential to make a significant difference in the sanctions meted out. Even in treatment courts that employ a rigid sanctioning schedule, counsel's choice either to engage in vigorous advocacy or to take a relatively passive role will be of great moment, because judicial discretion will still reside in the interstices of the graduated sanction formula and in the judge's fact-finding that a violation has taken place.[18]

The active role played by drug treatment court judges with respect to the monitoring of defendants and the imposition of intermediate sanctions conspires with the relaxed procedural approach typical of these courts to put great pressure on defense lawyers to adopt the role of "team player" instead of the zealous advocacy approach common in most criminal defense practice. Indeed, one published report describes the norm in Miami's drug court as one in which "all the justice system players are on the same team, making the same demands on the defendant and standing ready to impose the same penalties for noncompliance" (Finn and Newlyn 1993:3). To appreciate fully the extent to which the norms of formal triadic disputing are discarded, and the standard defender role conception jeopardized, it is necessary to examine in some detail how this shift toward judicial activism and procedural informality functions in the treatment court setting.

Judicial Activism, Procedural Informality, and Defender Advocacy Roles

Drug treatment courts require a shift in judicial role. Accounts consistently have reported that the conception of the judge "as someone who takes a neutral position in the resolution of conflict," has been supplanted by a new understanding in which "the judge is partisan, aiming to cure the offender of his addiction" (Bean 1996:720). To a significant extent, this revision of the traditional judicial role is due to the very design of these treatment courts, which requires the judge to play a central part in the treatment of the defendant's addiction. Before the advent of treatment-based drug courts, when judges ordered addicts into treatment as a condition of probation, they were essentially uninvolved in supervising or monitoring the course of treatment. A key feature of treatment courts, by contrast, is that the judge meets regularly with each participant in open court to review that defendant's compliance or noncompliance with the conditions of his or her treatment. The purpose of these "status hearings" is to hold the defendant publicly accountable through the use of rewards in the case of successes and graduated sanctions in the case of failures to adhere to the mandated therapeutic program.

The fact that drug court judges are directly involved in the tasks of monitoring defendants' behavior and imposing sanctions or conferring rewards is more than merely stylistic. Many substance abusers in the initial stages of recovery are most likely to be helped by a treatment regime focused on "practical problem solving and the acquisition of cognitive-behavioral relapse prevention skills" (Satel 1998:58),[19] which a judge is capable of managing. By contrast, recovering addicts are less likely to benefit from the sort of insight-oriented therapy that is the exclusive province of mental health professionals.[20] In operational terms, this means that the judge's role in sanctioning and rewarding defendants is to help them understand that their choices have consequences for which they will be held responsible, and that they control their own fate. Thus, when the judge responds promptly to a positive urine test or a missed group therapy meeting with a proportional sanction, he or she is helping to provide treatment to the defendant.

In effect, drug treatment courts seek to employ the moral authority of the judicial office, "the symbolic impact of the black robe," to drive home to defendants the seriousness with which their behavior is being taken (ibid.:47). In order for this model to work, however, the judge must be able to establish a functioning therapeutic relationship with each of the defendants he or she is supervising. The formation of this sort of a direct relationship has two significant consequences. First, it means that the judge and the defendant will come to relate to one another without the formal

distance that ordinarily characterizes traditional criminal law adjudications. This, in turn, raises the greater possibility that the judge's reactions
to an individual defendant's successes or failures may be influenced by
personal considerations or the effects of an unconscious process of counter-
transference.[21] In gross terms, the informality and immediacy of the judge's
relationship with the defendant confers a potentially ungovernable discretion not dissimilar to that which so riled critics of the rehabilitative ideal
nearly thirty years ago. As one keen observer of drug treatment court judges
has observed:

> Drug court is fertile ground for the unfolding of psychological drama. Per-
> haps, for example, the judge is a recovering alcoholic or has a loved one who
> is addicted to drugs. This could stir up inappropriately strong feelings of
> sympathy, impatience or even hostility toward a participant who happens to
> remind him of his or her former self (or his or her loved one). Consider the
> participant who casts the judge in the parental role. He or she may elicit deep
> feelings in the judge, rooted in the latter's own experience as a parent or a
> once-needed child. Or consider the participant who related to the judge in a
> provocative manner—or, more precisely, in a manner that the judge finds
> provocative—stemming from an unconscious desire to be punished or con-
> trolled or to elicit concern through censure. These kind of psychodynamic
> scenarios are more likely to get played out in a drug court, with its somewhat
> relaxed structure, than in a standard court where proceedings, expectations
> and personnel roles are clear, traditional and fairly predictable. (ibid.:54–55)

This more direct and personal relationship between the treatment court
judge and the individual participant may tend to complicate the participant's relationship with his or her own attorney. As noted earlier, ordinary
criminal proceedings rely on formal procedural rules to help maintain distance between the parties and the decision-maker, to insure that the triadic
structure does not collapse into two against one. The defense lawyer's role
in such a proceeding is to help the defendant negotiate this formal adjudication system and, in the process, to limit the arbitrary exercise of coercive
state power by safeguarding the defendant's entitlement to basic procedural rights.

In the drug treatment court setting, this conception of counsel as an in-
termediary between the lay defendant and the court is likely to be difficult
if not impossible to maintain. Indeed, given the active role assumed by the
judge in directing the defendant's course of treatment, and given the lack
of formally distancing procedural obstacles, it should come as little surprise that observers of these courts report that "some judges discourage
the presence of the attorneys" at status hearings and other similar proceedings (ibid.:67). In those courts where defense attorneys typically are
present at hearings, questions with respect to their appropriate role are, if

anything, even more difficult. As one experienced drug treatment court attorney has described it:

> The judge has become so accustomed to this "team approach," that in a recent letter to me, she specifically stated that "the automatic nature of the sanction scheme necessarily transforms to some degree the role of defense attorneys from adversary to counselor. . . ." Indeed, she appeared to suggest that defender advocacy on points of law may have no place in her court at all. (Schreibersdorf 1997:7)

This notion, that the proper approach for defense attorneys is to avoid intervening between the judge and the defendant in order to allow a therapeutic relationship to develop, makes good sense from the perspective of a judge who understands his or her role to be entirely consistent with the best interests of the defendant. From the perspective of a given defendant, however, even the most well-intentioned interventions on the part of a treatment court judge may be experienced as belittling, punitive, or unfair. The conundrum for defenders is how to mediate this clash of perspectives: should they proceed principally as members of the treatment team and seek to persuade their clients that the court's position has integrity, or should they adopt the point of view of at least some defendants and seek to undermine the judge's efforts by raising potentially available points of law? Moreover, if rehabilitative impulses have a tendency to become debased into punitive responses, as the left-liberal critics of the rehabilitative ideal suggested over twenty-five years ago, and if individual treatment court judges may on occasion be moved to act out of personal pique or unconscious reactions to an individual defendant, should defense lawyers conceptualize their role as that of a vigilant advocate, even if this sort of advocacy has the tendency to undermine the therapeutic power of an otherwise direct relationship between treatment court judges and the defendants with whom they are working, or should they act to reinforce that relationship in the hopes that it will prove to be in their clients' interest in the long run?

One response to these questions is that they do not lend themselves to resolution in the abstract, but rather require individual defense attorneys to make careful choices in the rich context of a given treatment court and a particular case.[22] The difficulty with this approach is that it assumes defenders will be capable of identifying each moment of decision when it arises, and will be able to act without undue pressure from the very institutions that have created the role tension in the first place.[23] In addition, many of these choices effectively will come down to questions with respect to the disclosure of information in the sole possession of the defendant. If the defendant is engaged by the judge in a colloquy in open court, without the benefit of formal rules of procedure or the opportunity to prepare a measured response, it is likely that damaging concessions or other harmful statements will be made before counsel has had the opportunity to review their legal and practical consequences with his or her client. Thus, even if the lawyer is able to discern that a critical decisional moment is at hand, he or she may not be able to intervene in order to preserve the choice or share its significance with the defendant.

These concerns about the untoward disclosure of sensitive information implicate both the partisanship and confidentiality duties that are central to the standard attorney role conception. Once again, this tension between zealous advocacy and cooperation derives in significant part from the blending of punitive and therapeutic functions in drug treatment courts. Clearly, the open and frank acknowledgment by defendants of their past or continuing abuse of alcohol or illegal substances, their attitudes toward treatment, their involvement in criminal activity, and other like information is an important component of the process of recovery. At the same time, much of this information is likely to be relevant to the investigation, prosecution, or sentencing of defendants either for the charges that are the basis of their involvement in the treatment court or for other crimes. Defense lawyers practicing in treatment courts necessarily face a host of difficult choices with respect to this information, and these decisions form the final group of role conflicts mentioned earlier.

Confidentiality and the Defense Lawyer's Role

If treatment court judges' direct conversations with participants during status hearings have an important therapeutic function, there is good reason for defense attorneys who understand themselves to be members of the treatment team either to encourage or permit their clients to proceed in an unguarded fashion. It is plain, however, that some participants will acknowledge their involvement in criminal offenses while interacting with the judge. According to a recent survey of defenders who practice in drug courts, conducted by the National Legal Aid and Defender Association, only half the respondents reported that their clients are given immunity for anything said in open court, "in the event of subsequent prosecution."[24] For defendants who do not obtain immunity, these "therapeutic" statements can have severe negative consequences, and defenders who adhere to the standard role conception therefore may feel obliged to depart from the cooperative norms associated with a treatment orientation. In deferred prosecution programs, admissions made by defendants with respect to the facts and circumstances of their pending charges may serve as the basis for a later conviction if they prove to be unsuccessful in treatment.

Even in jurisdictions that employ a postdisposition model, statements made by defendants without immunity may be used in determining their sentences or may be used to institute or support charges for other offenses in a new or separate prosecution.

Perhaps the most difficult confidentiality problems for defense attorneys to manage result from the close cooperative relationship typically established between treatment court judges, prosecutors, and treatment providers. In order to carry out the evaluation and prognosis functions inherent in a rehabilitative approach, the criminal justice members of the treatment team require considerable information from drug counselors and others regarding defendants' participation and progress in treatment. Often, however, clients reveal "sensitive personal and family information or incidents of relapse and drug activity during therapy sessions" (Ward 1997:4). Ordinarily, in the United States this sort of information would be protected by federal laws and regulations governing the confidentiality of substance abuse treatment records, precisely because its disclosure and use to investigate or prosecute patients would be likely to have a deleterious effect on treatment providers' ability to create the atmosphere of trust and safety required for effective therapy.[25] Nevertheless, this very information sometimes is made available to the court and prosecutor pursuant to broadly worded patient consent forms routinely executed by defendants at the inception of their participation in the treatment court program. Although such waivers of confidentiality rights are voluntary in the sense that defendants can refuse altogether to grant permission for disclosures to be made, the consequence of such a decision is likely to be their exclusion from the treatment court program.

In the final analysis, the waiver of some confidentiality protections may be a fair trade-off for a great many defendants, but difficulties remain for defense counsel with respect to the scope and wording of the written consent their clients are asked to give. Defense attorneys who seek to negotiate narrowly worded consent forms that strictly limit the information to be shared to objective data relating to attendance, participation in treatment, and the results of urine tests may find the court or prosecutor unwilling to circumscribe the information they receive. In fact, many treatment courts employ standardized confidentiality waiver forms that contain few if any limitations on the kinds and amount of information that treatment providers will be obligated to share with the criminal justice officials involved in the case. In these instances, defenders will be forced to make difficult choices, as will their clients, without any necessary assurance that the information will be used solely to further the goals of treatment that the state officials share with the defendant, rather than the ends of punishment that they do not hold in common.

RESPONSIBLE ADVOCACY IN DRUG TREATMENT COURT:
A VISION OF PRACTICE FOR DEFENDERS

Many of the left-liberal critics of rehabilitative penal practice in the late 1960s and 1970s based their analysis on the premise that punishment is "morally problematic," and therefore requires normative justification (Duff and Garland 1994:2). In their view, all state-sponsored penal practices implicate the core values held to be central in the liberal theory of the state. Liberals place individual freedom at the top of this list of core values, and see the citizen's relationship to the state as properly governed by a system of individual rights that constrain the uses of official power in ways that limit individual autonomy, privacy, and choice (Boldt 1995:2358–59; Handler 1988:1018). Because state-sponsored punishment by definition limits the sanctioned individual's freedom and autonomy, the need for moral justification is established. Even given this conception of the normative requirements for legitimate coercive state practices, liberal theory recognizes that punishment may be justified to the extent that its use protects the right of other citizens to be free from crime. However, because of the background commitments mandated by this perspective, the state "must punish no more than is necessary to secure the proper aims of punishment, and its penal institutions must not intrude too far on individual privacy and freedom" (Duff and Garland 1994:3).

The left-liberal critics of rehabilitation argued that penal practices in the mid-twentieth century often failed this test of moral justification. Their claims can be organized into three related categories. The first group of considerations bore upon the principle that the state should seek to accomplish its legitimate penal purposes employing the least invasive means possible. The critics argued that the criminal system, including its adjunct mental health experts, was incapable of performing the accurate and effective diagnosis, evaluation, and prognosis of offenders. Advocates of the rehabilitative ideal conceived of criminal behavior as a symptom of individual pathology, but the classification of any individual offender's "disorder," and the formulation of an appropriate treatment protocol, often was beyond the ability of the experts. As a consequence of this inherent vagueness of diagnosis and lack of clarity about proper treatment, argued the liberal critics, the scope of the state's power over individuals was dangerously enlarged (American Friends Service Committee 1971). As Francis Allen has explained, an important source of restraint on governmental power is the principle of relevance. When vague notions of "illness" and "treatment" are permitted to define the ambit of authority that corrections officials may employ with respect to an offender, they are put at liberty to impose measures directed not just toward affecting his or her behavior, but also his or her "'soul': his [or her] motives, his [or her] history, his [or her] social environment" (Allen 1981:47, quoting Michel Foucault).

The liberal critics coupled this argument with respect to the vagueness of the state's goals and the resulting expansion of state power, with the further claim that the natural tendency of a rehabilitative enterprise is to collapse into punishment, and the "natural progress of any program of coercion is one of escalation" (American Friends Service Committee 1971:25). Their conclusion was that, without regard to the good intentions of corrections reformers, rehabilitative regimes necessarily expand and become debased into serving other than therapeutic ends (Allen 1981:50–53).[26]

If expansion and debasement were the first items on the left-liberal critics' bill of particulars, they were equally concerned about protecting the dignity interests of defendants in rehabilitative regimes. They argued that coercive therapy is paternalistic and thereby suspect in light of the commitments of liberal theory to individual autonomy and freedom of choice. In addition, they argued that a program of involuntary treatment undermines human dignity because it treats the recipients of therapy as objects and not as responsible moral agents. In the words of C. S. Lewis, an early and forceful proponent of the liberal critique:

> To be "cured" against one's will and cured of states which we may not regard as disease is to be put on a level with those who never will: to be classified with infants, imbeciles, and domestic animals. But to be punished, however severely, because we have deserved it, because we "ought to have known better," is to be treated as a human person made in God's image. (Lewis 1953)

Although the critics held open the possibility of bad motives on the part of judges, prosecutors, and corrections officials, their essential complaint applied even in the face of the best of official intentions. This concern was framed in terms of the power of perspective. From the perspective of the corrections establishment, if the imposition of therapeutic measures was accomplished for the purely benign purpose of helping offenders overcome individual pathology, then it was neither punitive nor in conflict with the interests of the recipients of those services. From the perspective of the acted-upon offenders, however, the very fact that treatment was involuntary rendered it punitive, particularly if it involved institutionalization, the loss of privacy, or additional restrictions in other areas ordinarily left to the autonomous choice of individuals. Such a perspectival divergence between the state and the individual offender was deeply disturbing to the critics, especially given liberal theory's axiomatic view that state power must be cabined by clearly delineated individual rights if individual liberties are to be protected.

Each of these elements of the left-liberal critique of rehabilitative penal practice applies to some degree to contemporary drug treatment courts. To ascertain the basic outlines of a responsible vision of practice in these courts, defenders must formulate adequate responses to these concerns.

Protecting Defendants' Dignity Interests

Paradoxically, the argument that involuntary treatment undermines human dignity because it fails to treat the recipients of therapy as responsible moral agents, appears to be inapposite to the sort of substance abuse treatment involved in drug courts. This is because the very purpose of this therapeutic approach is to assist the defendant in learning how to take responsibility for his or her conduct. In this regard, a setting in which addicted defendants are given genuine choices, are helped to understand the likely consequences of competing alternatives, and are held responsible in a predictable and rational fashion for the decisions they make, is likely to serve both a therapeutic function and a dignity enhancing purpose.

For this fortuitous coincidence of purpose to occur, however, defense attorneys must act to insure that their clients are afforded the opportunity to exercise genuine choice in making the decision to enter a treatment court program. This notion of genuine choice is not meant to suggest that such a decision will be unconstrained, or that the defendant's participation will be fully voluntary. Often, defendants on the threshold of drug treatment court face a set of alternatives in which each choice carries undesired consequences. Rather, a defendant's choice will be genuine, and hence consistent with basic notions of human dignity, if it is made with some significant understanding of the costs and benefits of each available alternative, and if the defendant is permitted to choose based upon his or her own calculation of the relative weights of these costs and benefits.

There are at least three potential impediments to this sort of responsible decision-making on the part of drug court defendants. The first is that many treatment courts pace the initial steps of the program to insure that defendants will begin their participation while still experiencing a sense of crisis occasioned by their arrest. This may require the defendant to act, sometimes by entering a guilty plea, before his or her attorney has had an opportunity to conduct meaningful factual or legal investigation of the case. If this push to initiate treatment quickly prevents defense counsel from making an adequate evaluation of the defendant's chances of avoiding conviction in the traditional adjudication system, a decision on the defendant's part to enter drug treatment court cannot be said to rest upon a full consideration of the likely consequences of each available alternative.

Second, even if the goal of substance abuse treatment is to help an individual learn to take responsibility for conduct by anticipating consequences and exercising impulse control in response to predictable outcomes, it is clear that addicts at the start of the process are likely to have significant denial regarding their substance-abusing behavior and their need for treatment. Thus, many defendants, if given a thorough briefing by counsel on the choice either to enter drug treatment court or to have criminal charges resolved through the traditional system, will opt to avoid treatment court, even though their lawyers, acting in their best interests, would have decided otherwise. Ironically then, in order to gain the assent of those eligible defendants whose denial would otherwise lead them to reject treatment, the process pushes defense counsel to advocate for the treatment court option on the grounds that participation in therapy ultimately will permit the client to assume the status of a responsible moral agent.

The third impediment to genuine choice grows out of a potential lack of transparency in the information defendants are provided regarding the confidentiality consequences that are likely to flow from their agreement to participate in a treatment court program. Because court authorities need some modicum of information about the defendant's attendance and participation in treatment in order to perform their supervisory functions, the federal confidentiality laws and regulations permit judicial and prosecutorial actors to condition a defendant's entry into treatment upon his or her agreement to waive some or all of his or her rights to confidentiality.

By definition, if the choice to enter the program is to be genuine, defendants must be helped to understand the potential costs and benefits involved, including the potentially harmful consequences that can result from the disclosure to judicial or prosecutorial authorities of personal— sometimes incriminating—information gained in the course of substance abuse treatment, as well as the considerable benefits in terms of confidentiality to which defendants are entitled if they enter treatment on their own and without mandate from the criminal justice system. A genuine choice with respect to the waiver of confidentiality, in other words, requires that the defendant first be informed of the unusually generous privacy protections already in place, which his or her consent will extinguish.[27] If defendants simply are presented with a standardized waiver form and told little beyond the fact that their signature is required in order to enter the treatment court program, it is unlikely that they will appreciate the full legal or practical significance of their decision to execute the form or to undertake the treatment court regime.

A drug treatment court defender who wishes to be responsive to the dignity concerns of the critics must address each of these impediments. With respect to the first, a vision of practice centered upon protecting the moral agency of the defendant cannot afford to trade the client's opportunity to consult with an attorney before deciding to participate, in favor of a generalized goal of expedited disposition. The defender must resist all efforts to force a decision from his or her client until such time as counsel has adequately examined the case and can provide his or her client with a good assessment of the likely outcome of each available option, including trial. Even if this insistence on having sufficient time means that the therapeutic benefits derived from starting treatment while the defendant is in crisis will be lost, and even if the client's eligibility to participate in drug court will be withdrawn altogether, it is still incumbent upon counsel to demand that his or her client be given adequate time to make a fully informed, and therefore genuine choice.

As to the second impediment, this vision of practice demands that defenders engage in a process of consultation with their clients in which each available option is described in detail, and the consequences of each choice explained in dispassionate terms, so that clients will be able to exercise control over their own cases. In some instances, the result of this counseling may well be that a defendant who would benefit from treatment will choose not to enter the drug court program. This may be a poor choice, when viewed from the point of view of the defendant's long-range well-being. Nevertheless, this vision of practice demands that the defendant's dignity interests be accorded substantial weight in the formulation of an appropriate defender role conception, in order to prevent the defendant from being treated as an object rather than a responsible agent.

Finally, this vision of practice calls upon treatment court defense lawyers to insure that clients who execute confidentiality waiver forms grant consent that is truly informed. This requirement is directly related to a frequently identified goal of the drug treatment court model, which is to give defendants sufficient control over their participation that they can justly be held accountable for their conduct. Persons with substance abuse problems often experience very little control in their daily lives. Before they can develop a sense of responsibility for their actions, therefore, they must be helped to identify those features within their environment over which they can and should begin to exercise control. With respect to the waiver of confidentiality protections, this set of ideas requires that defendants be told clearly that they possess legal rights that give them virtually exclusive control over a broad array of personal information that may be developed in the course of treatment. Further, defendants must understand that it is their choice alone whether to permit some or all of this information to be shared with criminal justice officials. In addition, they must realize that each of the alternatives open to them is likely to carry certain predictable consequences, and they must be prepared to take responsibility for whatever choice they make. If defense lawyers insure that each of these elements of informed consent is in place before their clients either sign consent forms or refuse to waive their confidentiality rights, the goal of preserving genuine choice, which is central to maintaining basic notions of dignity, will be furthered.[28] If, on the other hand, consent is obtained as a mere bureaucratic formality, with little or no attention given to ascertaining whether defendants actually understand the significance of their decision, then the process will have failed to accomplish this basic requirement.

Representing Defendants' Perspectives and Guarding against the Debasement of Treatment into Punishment

Closely related to the critics' concerns over protecting defendants' dignity interests was their observation that rehabilitative penal regimes tend to submerge the perspectives of individual offenders within the claims of benevolent therapeutic purpose that characterize the enterprise. As discussed earlier, rehabilitative practices, including drug treatment courts, involve the merger of two ordinarily distinct state functions, treatment and punishment. When these functions become intertwined, a risk is created that the absence of any overt conflict of interest between the state and the individual participant, which may characterize therapeutic state activities, will tend to mask the conflict that is inherent when the state seeks to blame and punish individual defendants. Attending to this danger, by seeking to give voice to the individual defendant's experience of the process as potentially coercive and punitive, is a critical task for defenders in rehabilitative penal institutions, including drug treatment courts.

Ordinarily, the conflict between the state's penal interests and the individual defendant's liberty interests is managed through the application of formal procedural protections implemented within a stable adversarial system. This due process model is at the core of liberal legal theory, which seeks to restrain state power by granting citizens basic procedural rights. As the critics noted a generation ago, these essential procedural rights may be placed in jeopardy by the tendency of rehabilitative penal regimes to employ an alternative approach, characterized by informality, indeterminacy, and broad discretionary decision-making, which is thought better suited to the goal of providing treatment to offenders (American Friends Service Committee 1971; Fogel 1979).

The occasion for any individual defendant's participation in drug treatment court, however, is the state's decision to lodge criminal charges against him or her. Moreover, under any variation of the treatment court model, the defendant necessarily progresses through the mandated treatment regime under threat of criminal sanction. Indeed, the defendant's participation in each of the various therapeutic activities that constitute this treatment regime is in some sense coerced conduct. The individual participant, in short, is first and foremost a criminal defendant subject to a loss of liberty as a direct result of the state's exercise of its prosecutorial power. Drug treatment court defenders should therefore seek to preserve the basic features of ordinary criminal proceedings, in order to emphasize their clients' status as criminal defendants. These features of adversary disputing, including formal procedures, clearly defined decisional rules, and detached, neutral decision-makers, constitute the fundamental mechanisms by which persons accused of crimes are guaranteed a fair opportunity to be heard. In their absence, defendants' voices are not structurally protected, and their perspectives are likely to be lost within the often sincere claims of the state to be acting in their best interests.

In order to represent their clients' perspectives effectively, defenders cannot undertake to perform other roles that require the adoption of competing perspectives. In particular, they must resist invitations to join the treatment team, or to form structural alliances with other repeat players within the treatment court environment, because to do so would deny the essential conflict of interest that exists between those other criminal justice officials and the individual defendant whom the defender represents.

In addition to forming a singular identification with the defendant and his or her perspective, defense counsel also should force an appropriately formal distance between the treatment court judge and the parties. At a minimum, the defender should insist upon playing a mediating role in any initial proceedings before the judge and in subsequent status hearings. There may be occasions when it is appropriate for the defendant to interact directly with the court, but the decision to proceed in this fashion should be the result of a careful evaluation by counsel with respect to the client's ability to give voice to his or her experience of the process.[29] In any event, the lawyer should always be present in court for proceedings involving his or her client, and should be prepared to address the court on the client's behalf whenever the perspective of his or her client diverges from that of other criminal justice officials involved in the case. While it is difficult to say in advance what specific interventions might be called for at any given moment, it is clear that even the small rhetorical details of the setting may demand the defender's advocacy. So, for example, counsel may be obligated to raise objections to the practice in some treatment courts of referring to graduated sanctions, including periods of incarceration, as "adjustments" rather than punishments or sanctions (McColl 1996:502). Or, counsel may appropriately insist that the judge refrain from awarding T-shirts to defendants who have been successful in treatment (Bean 1996:719), or from sponsoring picnics and other out-of-court activities (Satel 1998:69).

At root, the perspectival critique is a reminder that the legitimacy of the criminal justice system, and its ultimate effectiveness as an institution for the inculcation of basic societal values, depends upon the rigor with which its formal triadic structure is maintained and a collapse into two against one is avoided. The therapeutic goals of a drug treatment court should not be permitted to disrupt the fundamental elements of a procedurally just process, by, for example, undermining the unambiguous loyalty of defense counsel or the neutrality of the judge. The core commitments of liberal theory demand that coercive state practices be justified by reference to legitimate collective interests. At the least, the individuals whose liberty is to be restrained should be afforded a meaningful opportunity to be heard, and their perspectives should be evaluated fairly along with the state's expressed purposes. Finally, this evaluation should be undertaken by a decision-maker who is neither a partisan nor an active participant in the state's coercive enterprise.[30] To be sure, these requirements may make it more difficult to institute a process of therapy in any given case. All the same, they are essential because they serve instrumental interests in preventing unnecessary restrictions on individual liberty, as well as larger ideological goals with respect to maintaining the integrity of the community's official blaming practices.

ACKNOWLEDGMENTS

This essay is derived from a longer article analyzing the drug treatment court movement that was published in the *Washington University Law Quarterly* (Boldt 1998).

NOTES

1. As used in text, the phrase "consequentialist perspective" is intended to describe a utilitarian approach to punishment. In this sense, a consequentialist account "justif[ies] punishment by its contingent, instrumental, contribution to some independently identifiable good. That is to say, the good that punishment is to promote—whether this is happiness, dominion, autonomy, welfare, or crime prevention—can be identified without reference to punishment itself" (Duff and Garland 1994:6).
2. Francis Allen points to a shift in statutory sentencing provisions in California in the mid-1970s as a prime example of this decline of the rehabilitative ideal in practice:

   The California sentencing act of 1976 serves as a useful indicator. The 1976 act repealed older sentencing provisions whose overriding purposes, according to a California court, were to "maximize rehabilitary efforts." The new law states in accents not heard a decade earlier: "The Legislature finds and declares that the purpose of imprisonment for crime is punishment. This purpose is best served by terms proportionate to the seriousness of the offense with provision for uniformity in the sentences of offenders committing the same offense under similar circumstances"

(Allen 1981:7–8, quoting *Holder v. Superior Court*, 269 Cal. App.2d 314, 74 Cal. Reptr. 853, 855 [1969], and DERING'S CALIFORNIA CODE ANN Section 1170[a][1][1977])

A similar shift in the academic literature also occurred during the decade of the 1970s. In particular, this shift in the theory of punishment was marked by the work of Andrew von Hirsch and others who pressed the notion of "just deserts" as the proper retributive basis for sentencing practice (von Hirsch 1976, 1981).

3. For a classic account of these characteristics of the adversary system, see (Fuller 71).

4. See especially American Bar Association, Model Code of Professional Responsibility, Canon 7 (1983); American Bar Association, Model Rules of Professional Conduct, Rules 1.2, 1.6, 1.7, 3.1 (1996); American Bar Association, Standards For Criminal Justice Defense Function, Standards 4-3.8, 4-5.1, 4-5.2, 4-6.2 (3d ed., 1993).

5. There is an extensive literature on the institutional and ideological foundations of defense counsel's advocacy role. For a general discussion of advocacy roles, see (Luban 1988:52; Simon 1978:36–37). For a more detailed analysis of and debate about the limits of criminal defense counsel's partisan role, see (Luban 1993:1729; Mitchell 1987:339; Simon 1993:1703).

6. This alternative role conception clearly implicates the notion of paternalism, which has been defined as "the imposing of constraints on an individual's liberty for the purpose of promoting his or her own good" (Thompson 1980:246; see also Luban 1981).

7. In the drug treatment court setting, for example, we are told that the defendant's attorney must operate as a member of the treatment "team" (Judge 1997:1). Membership on this team may serve to undermine the ability of the defender to maintain a strong identification with his or her client. One experienced defense lawyer has explained this process within the context of the Brooklyn, New York, treatment court as follows:

> One attorney is assigned full time to the Treatment Court to handle all Legal Aid cases in that court. . . . This one attorney attends the same training programs as the district attorney, the judge and the court personnel, including a recent training trip to Los Angeles. The obvious risk is the erosion of zealous defense advocacy as the three participants—judge, prosecutor and defense attorney—begin to consider themselves "teammates." (Schreibersdorf 1997:7)

8. Shapiro argued that "the most fundamental device for maintaining the triad is [the] consent [of the disputants]" (Shapiro 1979:285), but that complex societies tend to substitute law and office for the particular consent of the parties (ibid.:285–86).

9. One observer has written that drug treatment courts "range . . . from crowded dockets in huge courtrooms where participants are managed in a brisk, assembly-line fashion, to more intimate courts where the atmosphere resembles a fellowship meeting" (Satel 1998:50).

10. This set of related assertions is drawn especially from Cooper and Trotter (1994) and McColl (1996:500).

11. One could argue, however, that blame and responsibility for particular illegal acts are rendered irrelevant in deferred prosecution programs, where coercive measures are implemented without any formal adjudication of guilt (Cooper and Trotter 1994:95).

12. This is true in part because fact-finding with respect to diagnosis and prognosis arguably does not lend itself to "trial-by-battle" (Handler 1965: 26). Moreover, the typical posture assumed by defendants in the traditional adversary system, in which responsibility for the alleged criminal conduct is denied and the state is put to its proof at trial, is thought to undermine the basic therapeutic goal of helping the offender to overcome his or her denial (Allen 1981:17; McColl 1996:490). Finally, an adversarial approach founded upon formal procedural rights designed to protect defendants against the coercive authority of the state is judged to be unsuitable for the sort of cooperative venture contemplated by a treatment court, in which the prosecution and defendant are assumed to have shared or common interests in diagnosing the problem and monitoring the course of treatment (Cooper and Trotter 1994: 96).

13. The notion here is that being in "crisis" may help to motivate an addict to enter treatment even if his or her denial would ordinarily result in his or her resisting treatment.

14. At a minimum, this list includes the right to a jury trial, U.S. CONST. Art. III, section 2, clause 3; U.S. CONST. Amend. VI, the right not to be compelled to be a witness against oneself; U.S. CONST. Amend. VI, the right to a speedy and public trial; U.S. CONST. Amend. VI, the right to confront witness and to have the use of compulsory process for obtaining witnesses; U.S. CONST. Amend. VI, the right to have the effective assistance of counsel; U.S. CONST. Amend. VI, and the right to be free of conviction unless the state proves each element of the offense beyond a reasonable doubt, *in re Winship*, 397 U.S. 358 (1970).

15. This description of the treatment regime as "coerced" is not meant to suggest that treatment court participants are denied the opportunity either to grant or withhold their consent before entering the program. Instead, the reference is intended to make clear that that consent is given under circumstances that greatly constrain the defendant's range of choice. "Many drug court participants have no desire to be in treatment; it was chosen on the basis of expediency. They are resistant to treatment. Nevertheless, they remain in treatment because of the threat of sanctions and/or jail, and while they are literally captive in the program, they acquire genuine, internal motivation" (Satel 1998:59).

16. Indeed, the drug treatment court model has been described as requiring "a breakdown in the traditional adversarial roles assumed by defense attorneys and prosecutors as it relies heavily on the defense attorneys *convincing offenders* of the advantages of treatment and *steering them* away from accepting a more traditional plea involving minimal, or no, supervised treatment" (Smith, Davis, and Lurigio 1994:vii, emphasis added).

17. Graduated sanctions have been defined by one leader of the drug treatment court movement as "the measured application of a spectrum of sanc-

tions, whose intensity increases incrementally with the number and seriousness of program failures" (Tauber 1994:33).

18. Indeed, one study found that "under one Denver Drug Court judge, 66% of participants got 'good and passable reviews' and 14% were sent to jail over the course of a year. Under his successor, only 40% received 'good and passable reviews' and 40% went to jail. This drug court program was stable over the years examined, save for the switching of judges" (Satel 1998:50).

19. For addicts—as well as some other individuals whose behavior is self-destructive—insight can follow change, and need not precede it as conventional psychodynamic theory has it. Thus formal exploration of deep-seated psychological conflicts is contraindicated. To put it another way, it often takes a period of abstinence for the addict to understand why he or she needed drugs in the first place (Satel 1998:58–59).

20. Although the drug treatment court model appears to be structured around this conception of treatment, it is not clear that it is universally the case that behavior-based therapies must always precede insight-oriented treatment in order to be most effective. It is probably the case that some treatment modalities work better for a given individual than do others, depending upon a range of factors including the patient's age, social functioning, and treatment history. For a treatment court program to be fully effective, therefore, a broad range of diagnostic and therapeutic tools designed to individualize the program to meet the needs of each participant would be required.

21. "The Freudian concept of transference refers to the patient's 'transferring' tightly held attitudes (beliefs) and emotional dispositions forged in childhood onto new individuals in their lives. . . . Counter-transference is the inverse of transference; it describes the therapist's reaction to the patient. In the context of drug court, 'judicial' countertransference would thus refer to the personal reactions that are invoking in the judge by the participant (in the clinical setting, by analogy, it would refer to the therapist's response to the patient). Classically, these reactions are unconscious—that is, outside the awareness of the judge (or therapist)—but are manifested in ideas, feelings or behaviors that are inappropriately intense (in the positive or negative direction) or somehow not fully rational" (Satel 1998:53–54).

   For more on countertransference in psychotherapy, see (Goldstein 1984: 200–1).

22. This response finds support in some relatively recent scholarship, which urges the use of contextualized reasoning as a way to solve problems. Katharine Bartlett, for example, has explained that such

   practical reasoning approaches problems not as dichotomized conflicts, but as dilemmas with multiple perspectives, contradictions, and inconsistencies. These dilemmas, ideally, do not call for the choice of one principle over another, but rather "imaginative integrations and reconciliations," which require attention to particular context. (Bartlett 1990:851)(citation omitted)

23. Scholars working in the juvenile court area have made a similar observation. For example, "defense lawyers who routinely practice in juvenile court face tremendous institutional pressure to cooperate in maintaining a smoothly functioning court system" (Ainsworth 1991:1128); "the zealous lawyer also could expect some pressure from the bench to conform to the nonadversarial and informal nature of juvenile proceedings" (Federle 1996:1673).

24. *Defenders Largely Satisfied with Drug Court Experience,* Indigent Defense (National Legal Aid and Defender Association), Nov.–Dec. 1997, at 8.

25. *See* section 408 of the Drug Abuse Office and Treatment Act of 1972, Pub. L. No 92-255, 86 Stat. 65, 79 (codified as amended at 42 U.S.C. section 290dd-2 (Supp. IV 1992). This law and its implementing regulations, Public Health Services, Department of Health and Human Services, Confidentiality of Alcohol and Drug Abuse Patient Records, 42 C.F.R. sections 2.1 to 2.67 (1987), apply to virtually all treatment providers likely to be utilized by drug treatment courts. For a fuller discussion of this confidentiality scheme, see (Boldt 1995:2330–34).

26. The critics argued that debasement is inherent given the "conceptual weakness of the rehabilitative ideal. Vagueness and ambiguity shroud its most basic suppositions"(Allen 1981:51). In addition, they pointed out that "equally serious is the vagueness that surrounds the means to effect rehabilitation" (ibid.:52) and the fact that "correctional institutions and programs must serve punitive, deterrent, and incapacitative ends" in addition to therapeutic goals (ibid.:53). Finally, they argued that the ready availability of coercive solutions necessarily reduces the likelihood that "more creative but more difficult and problematic voluntary alternatives" will be attempted (American Friends Service Committee 1971:25).

   Such a collapse of purpose is bad enough on its own terms, but the critics argued that the consequences of systematic debasement in this arena were especially pernicious because of the gaping distances that emerged between the claims of the penal reformers and the realities of their practice.

   > In one place or another solitary confinement has been called "constructive meditation" and a cell for such confinement "the quiet room." Incarceration without treatment of any kind is seen as "milieu therapy" and a detention facility is labeled "Cloud Nine." Disciplinary measures such as the use of cattle prods on inmates become "aversion therapy" and the playing of a powerful fire hose on the backs of recalcitrant adolescents "hydrotherapy." Cell blocks are hospitals, dormitories are wards, latrine cleaning "work therapy." The catalog is almost endless. (Allen 1981:51)

27. The confidentiality regulations recognize the importance of educating patients about their rights in this regard. In fact, they require that patients be given a written summary of the federal law and regulations. See 42 C.F.R. section 2.22(a) (1994). Notwithstanding this injunction, it is unlikely that treatment court defendants will appreciate the full extent of the protections they are waiving unless substantial individual counseling occurs.

28. This conclusion may be overly optimistic for several reasons. First, it is at least suspect whether consent obtained from one who is incarcerated or otherwise under state control can ever really be regarded as an expression of that person's autonomous judgment (see Burt 1979). In addition, the very notion of consent, which is "derived from liberal political values" (Allen 1981:45), rests upon a set of assumptions about the self-interested nature of individual choice that simply may not hold for everyone in society. For example, Robin West has argued that a fundamental assumption of liberal theory, "that human beings consent to transactions in order to maximize their welfare," may be false with respect to the consent granted by many women (West 1987:91). For an elaboration of West's hypothesis, and an application of it to the consent provisions within confidentiality law, see (Boldt 1995:2363–67).

29. In particular, counsel should be attentive to the danger that power imbalances between participants in informal decisional processes can subvert those processes' outcomes (Lerman 1984; Abel 1985).

30. Although, as Shapiro points out:

> Even in those few societies that seek to insulate the judge from the rest of government, he is expected to administer the criminal law, that is, to impose the will of the regime on a party being prosecuted by the regime. With extremely great care to the various rituals of independence and impartiality, some criminal courts may succeed in maintaining the appearance of thirdness. However, few of the defendants in contemporary Western criminal courts are likely to perceive their judges as anything other than officers of the regime seeking to control them. (Shapiro 1979:287)

Nevertheless, the mere fact that the structure of the triad, and hence the perception of the tribunal as fair, is weakened by virtue of the criminal court judge's membership in government is no reason to give up entirely on larger efforts to prevent a complete collapse into two against one.

REFERENCES

Abel, Richard. 1985. "Informalism: A Tactical Equivalent to Law?" *Clearinghouse Review* 19:375.

Ainsworth, Janet E. 1991. "Re-Imagining Childhood and Reconstructing The Legal Order: The Case for Abolishing the Juvenile Court." *North Carolina Law Review* 69:1083.

Allen, Francis A. 1981. *The Decline of the Rehabilitative Ideal.* New Haven, CT: Yale University Press.

American Friends Service Committee. 1971. *Struggle For Justice: A Report on Crime and Punishment in America.* New York: Hill & Wang.

Bartlett, Katharine T. 1990. "Feminist Legal Methods." *Harvard Law Review* 103:829.

Bean, Philip. 1996. "Current Topic: America's Drug Courts: A New Development in Criminal Justice." *Criminal Law Review* 1996:718.

Boldt, Richard C. 1995. "A Study In Regulatory Method, Local Political Cultures, and Jurisprudential Voice: The Application of Federal Confidentiality Law To Project Head Start." *Michigan Law Review* 93:2325.

Boldt, Richard C. 1998. "Rehabilitative Punishment and the Drug Treatment Court Movement." *Washington University Law Quarterly* 76:1205.

Brown, James R. 1997. "Drug Diversion Courts: Are They Needed and Will They Succeed in Breaking the Cycle of Drug-Related Crime?" *New England Law on Criminal and Civil Confinement*. 23:63.

Burt, Robert. 1979. *Taking Care of Others: The Role of Law in Doctor-Patient Relations*. New York: Free Press.

Cooper, Caroline S. and Joseph A. Trotter, Jr. 1994. "Recent Developments in Drug Case Management: Re-engineering the Judicial Process." *Justice System Journal* 17:83.

Duff, R. A. and David Garland. 1994. *A Reader On Punishment*. Oxford and New York: Oxford University Press.

Federle, Katherine Hunt. 1996. "The Ethics of Empowerment: Rethinking the Role of Lawyers in Interviewing and Counseling the Child Client." *Fordham Law Review* 64:1655.

Finn, Peter and Andrea K. Newlyn. 1993. *Miami's "Drug Court": A Different Approach*. Washington, DC: United States Department of Justice.

Fogel, David. 1979. *We Are The Living Proof: The Justice Model for Corrections*. Cincinnati: W. H. Anderson.

Fuller, Lon L. 1971. "The Advesary System." Talks on America Law 34 (Harold J. Berman ed., 2nd ed).

Goldkamp, John S. 1994. *Justice and Treatment Innovation: The Drug Court Movement*. Washington, DC: United States Department of Justice.

Goldstein, Eda G. 1984. *Ego Psychology and Social Work Practice*. New York: Free Press.

Handler, Joel F. 1965. "The Juvenile Court and the Adversary System: Problems of Function and Form." *Wisconsin Law Review* 1965:7.

Handler, Joel F. 1988. "Dependent People, the State, and the Modern/Postmodern Search for the Dialogic Community." *University of California Law Review* 35:999.

Judge, Michael P. 1997. "Critical Issues for Defenders in the Design and Operation of a Drug Court." *Indigent Defense* (National Legal Aid and Defender Association), Nov.–Dec., at 1.

Lerman, Lisa G. 1984. "Mediation of Wife Abuse Cases: The Adverse Impact of Informal Dispute Resolution on Women." *Harvard Women's Law Journal* 7:57.

Lewis, C. S. 1953. "The Humanitarian Theory of Punishment." *Res Judicatae* 6:224.

Luban, David. 1981. "Paternalism and the Legal Profession." *Wisconsin Law Review* 1981: 454.

Luban, David. 1988. *Lawyers and Justice: An Ethical Study*. Princeton, NJ: Princeton University Press.

Luban, David. 1993. "Are Criminal Defenders Different?" *Michigan Law Review* 91:1729.

McColl, William D. 1996. "Baltimore City's Drug Treatment Court: Theory and Practice in an Emerging Field." *Maryland Law Review* 55:467.

Mitchell, John B. 1987. "Reasonable Doubts Are Where You Find Them: A Response to Professor Subin's Position on the Criminal Lawyer's "Different Mission." *Georgetown Journal of Law and Ethics* 1:339.

Postema, Gerald J. 1980. "Moral Responsibility in Professional Ethics." *New York University Law Review* 55:63.

Satel, Sally L. 1998. "Observational Study of Courtroom Dynamics in Selected Drug Courts." *National Drug Court Institute Review* 1:43.

Schreibersdorf, Lisa. 1997. "The Pitfalls of Defenders as "Team Players." *Indigent Defense* (National Legal Aid and Defender Association), Nov.–Dec., at 7.

Shapiro, Martin. 1979. "The Logic of the Triad." Pp. 284–86 in *The Structure Of Procedure,* edited by Robert M. Cover and Owen M. Fiss. New York: Foundation.

Simon, William H. 1978. "The Ideology of Advocacy: Procedural Justice and Professional Ethics." *Wisconsin Law Review* 1978:29.

Simon, William H. 1993. "The Ethics Of Criminal Defense." *Michigan Law Review* 91:1703.

Smith, Barbara E., Robert C. Davis, and Arthur J. Lurigio. 1994. "Introduction to Special Issue, Swift and Effective Justice: New Approaches to Drug Cases in the States." *Justice System Journal* 17:vii.

Tauber, Jeffrey S. 1994. "Drug Courts: Treating Drug-using Offenders Through Sanctions, Incentives." *Corrections Today* 56:28.

Thompson, Dennis F. 1980. "Paternalism in Medicine, Law, and Public Policy." P. 246 in *Ethics Teaching In Higher Education,* edited by Daniel Callahan and Sissela Bok. New York: Plenum.

von Hirsch, Andrew. 1976. *Doing Justice: The Choice of Punishments.* New York: Hill & Wang.

von Hirsch, Andrew. 1981. "Desert and Previous Convictions in Sentencing." *Minnesota Law Review* 65:591.

Ward, Robert L. 1997. "Confidentiality and Drug Treatment Courts." *Indigent Defense* (National Legal Aid and Defender Association), Nov.–Dec., at 4.

West, Robin L. 1987. "The Difference in Women's Hedonic Lives: A Phenomenological Critique of Feminist Legal Theory." *Wisconsin Women's Law Journal* 3:81.

Wootton, Barbara. 1978. *Crime and Penal Policy: Reflections on Fifty Years' Experience.* London and Boston: G. Allen & Unwin.

7

Therapeutic Jurisprudence and Drug Treatment Courts: Integrating Law and Science

John Terrence A. Rosenthal

INTRODUCTION

The rapid spread of Drug Treatment Courts (DTCs) to jurisdictions across the country indicates a new direction for the nation in terms of solving the problems of drug use and drug-related crime (Dorf and Sabel 2000; Belenko 2000; Gelben 2000). The creation of DTCs reflects the recognition on the part of communities and community leaders that drug addiction can be effectively treated, and that treatment is the most cost-effective means of reducing drug use and drug-related crime (Alvarez 2001).

Concerns about the expansion of DTCs have been voiced both by those who see DTCs as a return to the rehabilitative ideal of the fifties, sixties, and early seventies (Boldt 1998; Hoffman 2000; *Harvard Law Review* 1998) and by those who fear that DTCs are "soft on crime." Critics also argue against DTCs, claiming that they are invasive of a defendant's life, violate a defendant's Constitutional rights, or cause ethical conflicts for defense counsel (Boldt 1998; Quinn 2000).

This chapter will demonstrate that these fears are either exaggerated or unfounded. DTCs represent a rational and effective means of breaking the vicious cycle of drug use and drug-related crime. First, DTCs are set up and function in ways that can and do reconcile and advance all four of the traditional moral justifications for criminal punishment. In addition, for preadjudication purposes, DTCs regimes are constructed to strengthen community safety and to support the regulatory goals of preventing drug use during the pretrial period. Second, DTCs accomplish the various goals of punishment and pretrial detention regimes by instituting procedures that address an offender's drug addiction through the use of treatment protocols that lead to drug abstinence. Third, DTCs use therapeutic jurisprudence concepts to analyze, create, implement, and adjust their orientation, structure, processes, and procedures to account for the very unique aspects of drug addiction. Fourth, the procedures used in DTCs are not overly invasive nor do they violate an offender's rights. As a result, DTCs not only break the cycle of drug use and drug-related crime, they simultaneously promote and enhance long-term public safety.

JUSTIFICATIONS FOR CRIMINAL PUNISHMENT

A Punishment, is an Evill inflicted by publique Authority, on him that hath done, or omitted that which is Judged by the same Authority to be a Transgression of the Law; to the end that the Will of men may thereby the better be disposed to obedience.

—Thomas Hobbes, *Leviathan*

Criminal punishment of an individual by government for a crime usually involves the infliction of pain on an individual, or deprivation of a person's liberty, or both (Kadish and Schulhofer 1995). Due to the seriousness of these consequences, societies generally require that government vindicate its application of punishment. There are four traditional, moral justifications for government-inflicted criminal punishment: (1) retribution, (2) deterrence, (3) rehabilitation, and (4) incapacitation (Greenawalt 1983; Packer 1968, 1972). The reasonableness and validity of any of these rationales for state-sanctioned criminal punishment depends on at least three things: (1) the theory's basic assumptions about human nature, (2) the existence and accessibility of useful and necessary information that support or refute the assumptions, and (3) the ability of society to use the appropriate information effectively to implement the punishment (Grupp 1971).

The procedures or methods used to punish an offender only make sense if they dovetail with the assumptions about human nature underlying the given theory of punishment. If the underlying assumptions supporting a certain theory of punishment and the actual facts about the offender, or class of offenders, are incongruous, this situation can lead to an incoherent, ineffective, and even unjustified application of punishment. Such a situation calls into question the underlying moral rationale supporting the application of that type of punishment.

The following sections describe the rationales and assumptions that define the traditional moral justifications for government-sponsored criminal punishment.

Retribution

Retributivism is the view that punishment is justified by the moral culpability of those who receive it. A retributivist punishes because, and only because, the offender deserves it.

—M. S. Moore, "The Moral Worth of Retribution"

Under the theory of retribution, society should punish a wrongdoer simply because he or she committed a crime (Packer 1968, 1972). Retribution can be seen as either an expression of revenge or a method of expiation (Packer 1968). The former is the application of punishment to a wrongdoer in order to express the moral condemnation of the community and the latter ensures that the individual repays the debt he or she incurred to society by committing the wrongful act. According to some retributive theorists, "Punishment is essentially a matter of removing from wrongdoers a kind of advantage they gained, precisely in preferring their own will to the requirements authoritatively specified for that community's common good" (Finnis 1998). Under versions of retributivist theory, when an individual acts in contravention of the law, he or she expresses, through action, a preference for his or her own desires at the expense of the well-being of others, and therefore the common good of the entire community (Morris 1976).

This deliberate assertion of one's self-preference by breaking the law is wrong if one assumes that all human beings are created equal and that no person should be reduced to a means for another's gratification (Pope Pius XII 1972). To restore balance to the community, the appropriate authorities within the community judge the individual accused of wrongdoing, and if found guilty through the adjudicative process, he or she is punished. Punishment, under a retributive theory, is a way of bringing the moral scale of a community back into balance by negating the advantage of the wrongdoer vis-à-vis the community (Kant 1972).

Although the retributive theory of justice is often equated with the concept of lex talionis (*Black's Law Dictionary* 1990)—an eye for an eye—retributive theory does not specify this idea as the requisite process or method of implementing punishment (Moore 1987). According to some retributivists, punishment should negate the advantage gained by the offender by breaking the law. This can mean that punishment should be proportional to the offense, that an offender should suffer consequences that bear a direct relationship to his or her crime (Locke 1973).

In addition to the idea of proportionality, some retributivists have also expressed the idea that "in any state of affairs capable of being improved by it, punishment's justifying point is to make an improvement" (Finnis 1998). That means that punishment can satisfy other social goals as long as the primary justification for punishment is the guilt of the offender.

Underlying the theory of retribution is the basic assumption that individuals are rational beings and as such an individual's acts represent deliberate choices (Packer 1968, 1972; Hegel 1972). Thus, according to retributivists, punishment for an individual who chooses to act in contravention of the law is appropriate when society, through its laws, evaluates a given act as wrong and determines that a given person has committed that wrong. Therefore, punishment, according to retributivists, is justified only if the person is rational when he or she chooses to commit the wrong.

Unlike the other justifications for punishment, for most retributive theorists, retribution is justified strictly by past events without regard for repercussions that may result from the punishment. Retributivists do not look at the future behavior of the criminal that results from the punishment, nor how others react to the fact or potential of punishment.

Although seemingly straightforward in its application, retributivism is not without its shortcomings. One of the most obvious is the theory's built-in assumption that a given system of criminal adjudication is infallible: somehow ensuring that only the guilty receive fines, supervision, or imprisonment. Recent events around the country, including the moratorium on the death penalty in Illinois and questions surrounding convictions in Oklahoma, demonstrate the fallacy of this assumption (e.g., Associated Press 2001; Loscombe 2001). More importantly, though, the retributivist theory gives an inadequate answer concerning the appropriate punishment for "apparently"[1] victimless crimes like drug use. Although retributivists argue that the desires of the criminal's victims are irrelevant to the question of whether the criminal should be punished (Moore 1987), the retributive theory fails to prescribe what kind of punishment is proportionate for a crime in which the direct harm from the crime is inflicted only on the criminal. Finally, the theory of retribution cannot be applied in any preadjudicative setting since the very essence of the theory rests on the notion of moral culpability as determined by some sort of adjudicative body.

Deterrence

The general objective which all laws have, or ought to have, in common, is to augment the total happiness of the community; and therefore, in the first place, to exclude, as far as may be, every thing that tends to subtract from that happiness; in other words, to exclude mischief. But all punishment is mischief: all punishment in itself is evil. Upon the principle of utility, if it ought at all be admitted, it ought only to be admitted in as far as it promises to exclude some greater evil.

—Jeremy Bentham, "Principles of Penal Law"

The deterrence theory of criminal punishment is based on the utilitarian principle that the moral justification for any action should depend on whether or not that action increases total human happiness more than it subtracts from that happiness. The application of punishment to a person involves pain and/or deprivation of some sort. Given that punishment involves a decrease in happiness, under the theory of deterrence, the government can only morally justify the use of punishment if the benefits of the punishment outweigh the harm it produces (Beccaria 1872; Andenaes 1974).

The key to the utilitarian theory is the assumption that individuals are rational. Rational individuals make choices about their actions and they will choose happiness over unhappiness (Bentham 1996). Since punishment involves pain and/or deprivation, and thus unhappiness, individuals will act so as not to incur punishment. Thus, punishment deters wrongdoing and increases happiness.

In order to be an effective deterrent, punishment must be sufficiently swift, sure, and severe that a rational individual will choose not to commit a wrong (G. R. Blakey, discussions conducted at University of Notre Dame Law School August 1996–April 1997; Bentham 1838–1843). This follows from the assumption that rational individuals will act in order to avoid pain or deprivation. If a potential offender is not sufficiently certain he or she will actually be apprehended, found guilty in an adjudicative process, and punished, and that the punishment will outweigh the gain derived from the crime, punishment will fail as a deterrent (Beccaria 1971).

Deterrence is generally broken down into two categories: general deterrence and specific deterrence (Packer 1968, 1972). General deterrence results when persons in the community shun committing crimes to avoid the consequence of punishment (ibid.). Specific deterrence occurs when the punished individual refrains from committing future wrongs to avoid future punishment (Blackstone 1979). The effectiveness of both general and specific deterrence depends on the punishment being proportional to the offense. If citizens view a potential punishment as capricious disproportional, or unjust, punishment loses its deterrent effect. In such circumstances citizens either will not or often cannot comply with the law (Packer 1972; Taylor 1997).

As with retributive theory, the theory of deterrence does not specify a mode or type of punishment. The deterrence theory only requires that the type of punishment chosen must increase overall happiness, be that via the individual, the community, or both, rather than decreasing total happiness.

Of course, nonutilitarians can also have deterrence as a goal of punishment (Moore 1987). The difference between utilitarians and nonutilitarians is that the former group believes that deterrence must be the primary justification for punishment. In contrast, retributivists believe that society should only mete out punishment if such punishment is morally justified, the moral justification being the guilt of the offender.

Deterrence as moral justification for punishment has its flaws. Since punishment is justified if it deters future criminal acts, and thereby increases happiness, punishing an innocent individual is a logically sound conclusion if it provides increased deterrence. This follows from the fact that deterrence, in contrast to retribution, focuses exclusively on the results of the punishment.

The deterrence theory also does not provide society with a certain means for measuring the resulting levels of happiness and unhappiness, i.e., the utility of the punishment. A given society may be able to measure the marginal deterrent effect of a given punishment as a proxy for some aspects of the increase in happiness that results from punishment. Yet, measuring marginal deterrence has proven to be extremely difficult. The deterrence theory will, in addition, never provide society with a sure means of measuring or evaluating all of the resultant effects of a given regime of punishment on a given offender: how does one go about measuring the unhappiness of an individual who received the death penalty against the happiness of the person's potential or actual victims or the community?

Rehabilitation

> *The rehabilitative ideal, then, not only is projected as the most efficient way to protect society against the likelihood of later relapses into crime, but also motivated by humanitarianism, a belief in the worth and dignity of every human being and a willingness to expend effort to reclaim him for his own sake and not merely to keep him from again harming us.*
>
> —H. Weihoffen, "Punishment and Treatment"

The theory of rehabilitation as a moral justification for punishment, like that of deterrence, can also be categorized as utilitarian: reduction of unhappiness or increase in happiness. The rehabilitative theory works on the assumption that the criminal has committed a crime due to some underlying pathology like a mental or physical illness, or from learned antisocial behavior. Contrary to deterrence and retribution, the rehabilitative theory does not necessarily posit a rational individual as defined by the community. Rather, criminal conduct, according to some rehabilitation proponents, may have its roots in any number of things, e.g., the person's socioeconomic background, or mental illness. Thus, under the rehabilitative theory, reformation of the individual offender and the ability to reform him or her is the moral justification for punishment.

In the rehabilitative theory, because the individual may have limited control over the circumstances that led him or her to commit the crime, the act of a crime, alone, is not a sufficient moral justification for punishment. Instead, under the rehabilitative theory, punishment is justified because it can and should cause an offender to reform and to overcome his or her predisposition to the criminal behavior. Since, using the rehabilitative ideal, an individual's criminal conduct results from a "disease," a mental or physical illness, or from learned antisocial behavior that is generally curable/treatable, the implementation of proper therapies/treatment can avert an individual's future criminal conduct.

Rehabilitation focuses on the individual and his or her reform to produce an increase in the happiness of the community. By reforming the individual through punishment, the rehabilitative theory increases community happiness by preventing future criminal activity by that individual (Moore 1984). Rehabilitation can also increase the happiness of the individual through his or her "successful treatment." Either or both of these results are construed as moral justification for the rehabilitative theory of punishment. Thus, the rehabilitative justification for punishment is that the offender is "sick" or maladapted and punishment is justified to "cure" or "reform" the offender.

The rehabilitative ideal also has its share of problems. Of primary concern to many is the fact that the ideal leaves open the option of indeterminate sentencing: an offender should not be released until he or she is "reformed" (Packer 1968). Recent state laws enacted to keep pedophiles or repeat sex offenders in a custodial setting even after the expiration of their criminal sentences are examples of logically defensible actions according to the rehabilitative ideal. This idea, however, seems counter to the ideal encapsulated in the creation of codes: that sentences for similarly situated offenders should be the same in order to avoid the potential for capricious and arbitrary sentencing by overzealous judges.

The rehabilitative ideal also can be based on the notion the offender is not "rational" when he or she manifests criminal behavior, thus leading to the conclusion that criminal behavior should be treated as a "disease." The "medicalization" of criminal behavior has some critics worried that all sorts of allegedly antisocial behavior could be criminalized and that various civil liberties may be lost as "criminals" are "reformed." Others concerned about being soft on crime, or being perceived as such, worry that expanding the definition of "disease" may allow "dangerous" criminals to get out of long arduous sentences.

The rehabilitative theory lost much of its initial persuasive power in the 1970s possibly as a backlash against the counterculture movement of the late 1960s (Allen 1981). Opponents of the ideal viewed it as either soft on crime or leaving too much discretion in the hands of judges, as noted above. It is of interest to note that several scholars have recently observed that certain classes of offenders may be amenable to reformation (Martinson 1979; Vitiello 1991).

Incapacitation

Unlike the first three rationales, incapacitation is not based upon the assumption that human persons are rational and free or sick and determined. The only basic presumption is that the individual [punished] is likely to act in an undesirable manner if not [punished].

—K. P. Blakey, "The Indefinite Civil Commitment of Dangerous Sex Offenders Is an Appropriate Legal Compromise between 'Mad' and 'Bad'—A Study of Minnesota's Sexual Psychopathic Personality Statute"

The theory of incapacitation rests on the assumption that the individual is a danger to himself or to others. Therefore, the basic goal of incapacitation is the prevention of future criminal conduct and/or injury to self or to others in the community through the imposed restraint of the potential offender. Generally, incapacitation is accomplished by removing the individual from society. Advocates of incapacitation often draw a distinction between collective incapacitation and selective incapacitation (Cohen 1983). The collective strategy entails all persons convicted of the same offense getting the same sentence regardless of circumstances. The selective incapacitation strategy requires giving individualized sentences to offenders based on predictions about the likelihood that the offender will commit crimes at a higher rate if not incarcerated.

Incapacitation as a moral justification for punishment also has problems. Incapacitation as a principle can lead to the conclusion that offenders should be locked up until after the age of forty, since statistics show that criminal behavior has a tendency to decrease in individuals forty or older (G. R. Blakey, discussions conducted at University of Notre Dame Law School August 1996–April 1997). The theory also lends itself to indeterminate sentencing. Collective incapacitation might lead to the substantial overcrowding of prisons and many would argue that present drug laws are doing exactly that. Finally, incapacitation appears to be based on predictions of future criminal activity and therefore may violate the tenet that persons should only be punished for crimes they actually committed and not for crimes they *might* commit in the future. Another note of interest with regard to incapacitation and drug use is the prevalence of drugs inside our present-day prisons and jails. If the goal is to prevent further drug use, and drug users are able to satisfy their addictions in jail, are jails really suited for incapacitation with respect to drugs?

In addition to the ethical and moral problems presented by the theory of incapacitation, there are informational considerations. "The gulf between what is known about incapacitation and what is claimed for it has never been greater than in the early 90's. Policy debates on incapacitation are infected with impossible claims" (Zimring and Hawkins 1995). The inconclusive nature of data regarding the effectiveness of incapacitation should be cause for hesitation before this particular moral justification for punishment is accepted.

Preadjudication Drug Testing Regime[2]

The general foundation of the traditional moral justifications for criminal punishment is the belief that punishment should only be meted out after an individual has been found guilty of a crime through a process of adjudication. Yet, with increasing frequency, persons are held by law enforcement prior to trial in order to prevent their flight or to protect the community. Because such detention is not the result of an adjudication of guilt, any sort of pretrial detention regime should not "impose" punishment on an individual. Although no court has dealt specifically with the mandatory drug testing and drug treatment regimes of the nation's DTCs, several courts have ruled on the constitutionality of pretrial detention, and mandatory pretrial drug testing and have held that they pass constitutional muster (Witte and Bailey 1998).

In *United States v. Salerno*, 481 U.S. 739 (1987), a case challenging the constitutionality of the Bail Reform Act's pretrial detention regime under both the Fifth and Eighth Amendments, the Supreme Court reiterated that under the Fifth Amendment "the mere fact that a person is detained does not inexorably lead to the conclusion that the government has imposed punishment." To determine whether or not a "restriction on liberty constitutes impermissible punishment or permissible regulation," the court looked to the intent of the government to establish whether the particular restriction is punitive or regulatory. If the government can demonstrate that the restriction has a rationally related purpose, and that restriction is not excessive in relation to its purpose, then the pretrial restriction does not violate the Fifth Amendment. As stated by the Court, "Preventing danger to the community is a legitimate regulatory goal," and "The Government's regulatory interest in community safety can, in appropriate circumstances, outweigh an individual's liberty interest."

In addition to *Salerno*, at least three other courts have dealt specifically with drug testing, and all have upheld such testing against various statutory and constitutional challenges: *In re* York, 9 Cal. 4th 1133 (1995); *Oliver v. United States*, 682 A.2d 186 (D.C. Ct. App. 1996); *Terry v. Superior Court*, 73 Cal. App. 4th 661 (1999). Thus, mandatory and random drug testing is not necessarily unconstitutional, and such regimes can be required of an individual in a preadjudicative period.

Therapeutic Jurisprudence

Therapeutic jurisprudence is the study of the role of the law as a therapeutic agent.

—D. B. Wexler and B. J. Winick, *Law in a Therapeutic Key*

In contrast to the previously discussed rationales for punishment, or pretrial detention, therapeutic jurisprudence (TJ) need not only be used to answer the question of "why punish?"[3] Instead, therapeutic jurisprudence can also assist society in answering the questions of "how to punish" or "how to regulate or detain." Therapeutic jurisprudence suggests that society uses "social science to study the extent to which a legal rule or practice promotes the psychological or physical well-being of the people it affects" (Slobogin 1995). Through the use of various social and medical sciences, therapeutic jurisprudence illuminates how laws, legal processes, and agents within the legal system either support or undermine the public policy reasons for instituting those laws and legal processes when viewed from a psychological or physical perspective.

Therapeutic jurisprudence reasoning and analysis need not predominate over other societal values or priorities. The goal of therapeutic jurisprudence analysis, according to its creators, is not to "trump other considerations" (Wexler and Winick 1996) but to ensure that those considerations are placed in the proper context (Wexler and Schopp 1992). This jurisprudence suggests only that society examine the psychological and mental health aspects of laws and legal processes to determine how well a law or legal process supports and/or advances its underlying public policy goal. "Therapeutic jurisprudence does not resolve conflicts among competing values. Rather, it seeks information needed to promote certain goals and to inform the normative dispute regarding the legitimacy or priority of competing values" (Wexler and Winick 1996). Through therapeutic jurisprudence analysis, policymakers, legislators, and judges can acquire facts that will either bolster or weaken the reasoning for implementing or continuing the laws or legal process in question (Hora, Schma, and Rosenthal 1999).

Because therapeutic jurisprudence is also normative in nature it can be used as an analytical tool to support or attack the validity of certain policies and their underlying values. Therapeutic jurisprudence can assist the analytic process of academicians, legislators, and policy advocates in the following ways:

> First, therapeutic jurisprudence analysis that achieves convergence among all relevant values provide strong support for the recommended conclusion. If the values justify existing law, the analysis supports the *status quo*. But if the values oppose the *status quo*, then the therapeutic analysis provides a strong justification for legal reform. Second, although, as a discipline, therapeutic jurisprudence need make no substantial commitments to particular moral or political theories, individual advocates of therapeutic jurisprudence will and should argue for law reform on the basis of therapeutic jurisprudential analysis, bolstered by their own normative visions. . . . Most importantly, therapeutic analysis will sometimes change one's views of the import, recommendation, or weight of some value. . . . [T]he [therapeutic] analysis, in combination with background moral and political principles, may change one's perspective about weight of particular values. . . . In short, therapeutic analysis can change one's view as to the proper legal rule, procedure, or outcome. In rare cases, an analysis could suggest revamping the entire legal system. These reasons alone amply justify the therapeutic jurisprudential program. (Kress 1999)

The normative aspect of TJ implies that its practitioners need not "reach the same answers" (ibid.) about a given subject. "As a program, therapeutic jurisprudence is only committed to the claim that therapeutic effects matter morally and legally and thus that, all else equal, a law or regime with better therapeutic effects is preferable" (ibid.). Therefore, the fact that TJ proponents may fall on different sides of an issue does not invalidate TJ as a jurisprudential philosophy.

Given the nature of therapeutic jurisprudence, whether the results of therapeutic jurisprudence analysis are accepted or rejected, the questions posed and issues raised by therapeutic jurisprudence analysis must be asked and answered. The analysis must take place because lawyers, judges, the law, and legal processes all function therapeutically or antitherapeutically regardless of whether laws and legal agents account for these consequences. The focus of the theory on consequences, on empirically verifiable results based on various social sciences, is one of the aspects of therapeutic jurisprudence that sets it apart from other jurisprudence philosophies (Winick 1996). Therapeutic jurisprudence allows legislators, judges, and legal practitioners to make policy decisions based on empirical studies and not uninformed hunches or the criminal justice shibboleth of the moment.

Because society can use therapeutic jurisprudence to focus on the "how" aspects of punishment and various detention regimes, and not necessarily the "why," therapeutic jurisprudence is compatible with any of the various justifications for punishment, or pretrial detention regimes. Following the reasoning of some retributivists, therapeutic jurisprudence can explain which types of punishment are proportional, and which will improve the good of the community (Finnis 1998). Although the concept of proportionality is largely a value judgment, TJ can assist a community in evaluating what is proportionate by allowing authorities to assess an offender's moral culpability based on the person's mental state. From the standpoint of deterrence, therapeutic jurisprudence can clarify whether or not a given punishment or legal process is likely to succeed or is succeeding in deterring future criminal conduct, either specifically or generally. Under a rehabilitative ideal, therapeutic jurisprudence can help determine whether or not an individual's actions are based on a "disease" or learned antisocial behavior, or if the person's actions are motivated by some other consideration. Therapeutic jurisprudence can also assist judges, legislators, policy advocates, and community leaders in ascertaining what kinds of punishments will incapacitate various types of offenders, and what types of detention regimes are rationally related to their stated regulatory objectives.

In contrast to the unyielding contours of the traditional justifications for criminal punishment, therapeutic jurisprudence provides a pragmatic method for analyzing and assessing the rational for a given punishment or detention regime. With its reliance on the theories and conclusions of social and medical sciences (Slobogin 1995), and its inherent normative flexibility, therapeutic jurisprudence allows society to choose not only the appropriate type of punishment for a given category of offender, and detention regime, it also aids individuals in evaluating how to best implement that punishment or detention regime to optimize the desired results.

Used properly, therapeutic jurisprudence can help answer the three critical questions regarding punishment posed at the beginning of the chapter. First, therapeutic jurisprudence allows policymakers to analyze critically whether or not the basic assumptions underlying the traditional rationales for punishment and those of detention regimes are accurate (ibid.). Second, therapeutic jurisprudence requires one to look at the various academic fields to see if the sciences have investigated and found research answers relevant to particular areas of law. Finally, therapeutic jurisprudence can assist decision-makers in analyzing whether the information culled from academic research can be employed to solve particular problems.

DTCs use therapeutic jurisprudence principles to answer these three important questions about punishment and pretrial detention programs as they relate to drug-addicted criminal offenders. First, many DTC practitioners identify the basic fact that drug-addicted offenders do not act in a rational way when it comes to drug use. These practitioners derive this conclusion from the evidence produced by the medical and social sciences indicating that addiction is a "brain disease" (Leshner 1998; Massing 2000). Second, even if not all DTC advocates subscribe to the disease model of addiction (Wise and Kelsey 1998; Massing 2000), all advocates accept the idea that drug addiction is treatable, and the proper treatment regime can help the addicted individual achieve abstinence from drug use. Finally, DTCs use the information about drug addiction produced by the medical and social sciences to shape the court's procedures to reinforce the goals of reducing recidivism and decreasing the load on the criminal justice system by producing drug abstinence in the court's participants.

Drug treatment courts represent the application of therapeutic jurisprudence at both the macro- and microlevels of the criminal justice system. At the macrolevel, communities establish and form drug treatment courts with the understanding that treatment can realistically prevent drug-addicted offenders from future drug use and from committing future drug-related crimes. At the microlevel, therapeutic jurisprudence arms DTC practitioners with information about what may enhance or detract from the effectiveness of a procedure or given course of treatment for DTC participants. Through this analysis, DTC practitioners can modify the courts and their procedures to increase the effectiveness of DTCs.

DRUG TREATMENT COURTS: THERAPEUTIC JURISPRUDENCE IN ACTION

DTCs represent a new phase in the fight against drugs and drug-related crime. Other methods of fighting drug addiction and drug-related crimes have often failed because they have not effectively addressed the underlying problem: the offender's drug addiction. Both the retributive and deterrent theories of punishment may fail because their common assumption, that humans always act rationally, may not be applicable to people in the grip of drug addiction. Those with an addiction use drugs despite the known negative physical and social ramifications of such drug use. Yet, even if drug-addicted individuals are considered rational for purposes of punishment, DTCs use treatment regimes that take the behavior patterns of addicted individuals into account to produce abstinence.

Unlike the rehabilitative theory of punishment, DTCs do not punish primarily because the drug offender has a "disease" or can be "reformed." Rather, DTCs are aimed at a reduction in recidivism and a concomitant decrease in the caseload of the particular court system. DTCs are structured so that the method of punishment facilitates the treatment process. DTCs

also accomplish real incapacitation, not through generally ineffective confinement, but through court-imposed treatment regimes; treatment regimes
that reduce drug use and increase abstinence, thereby decreasing other
criminal conduct usually associated with drug use. Finally, DTCs use pretrial detention regimes that are rationally related to the goals of abstinence
and crime reduction.

This section will discuss the history of DTCs, one theory of addiction,
and the justifications for the orientation, structure, and procedures of DTCs.
It will also show how DTCs use therapeutic jurisprudence ideals to analyze and shape the court's orientation, structure, and procedures. In using
therapeutic jurisprudence as an analytic tool, DTC practitioners recognize
that drug addiction, whether recognized as a disease or some form of maladapted behavior, causes addicts to exhibit certain behavior patterns. In
recognizing addiction as a treatable disease or a correctable behavior pattern, DTCs use judicially imposed treatment protocols to facilitate a drug-
offender's abstinence from drug use.

Even if DTC critics, and some supporters, choose not to characterize addiction as a disease, despite current public policy and overwhelming evidence to the contrary, evidence shows that DTCs are still an effective means
of reducing drug use and drug-related crimes.

The History of Drug Treatment Courts

Drug Treatment Courts find their roots in the "War on Drugs" policies instituted by the federal government and various state governments in the
late 1980s (Inciardi, McBride, and Rivers 1996; Carlson 1998). These policies were the result of what citizens of this country perceived as a large and
insidious influx of cocaine, in both powder and the base form known as
"crack," into the country. Through various laws, the federal government
and various state governments expanded the number of criminal drug offenses, and instituted mandatory minimum sentences for those found
guilty of these drug offenses.

Legislatures intended for these laws to stem the flow of drugs entering
the country by increasing both the incapacitation and deterrence effects
(Caulkins, Schwabe, and Chiessa 1997). As law enforcement agencies began to implement these laws, a flood of drug cases pushed its way into both
state and federal criminal justices systems (Belenko 1998). In 1985 alone,
647,411 people were arrested for drug-related crimes. By 1991, the number
of individuals incarcerated for drug offenses exceeded one million.

Statistics collected from twenty-three cities nationwide indicate that between 50 and 80 percent of all male arrestees tested positive for drugs, and
that female arrestee numbers are similar to those of males. These statistics

suggest that increasing the number of drug crimes and the penalties for those crimes are not necessarily effective methods of deterring future drug use or drug-related crime. Studies also show that although drug use has decreased slightly in recent years, the number of chronic users has remained steady despite the significant punishments for those convicted of drug possession or drug-related crimes. "Addiction, and not a predisposition to criminal behavior, would explain why a large group of core drug users persevere in their behavior despite tougher sanctions" (Hora, Schma, and Rosenthal 1999).

Just looking at the number of cases dealing with drug possession offenses may understate the real gravity of the societal problems that stem from drug addiction. A study in Miami demonstrated how drugs are intertwined with other crimes. The study found that in a one-year period, 573 substance abusers "committed 6,000 robberies and assaults, . . . 900 auto thefts, 25,000 acts of shoplifting, and 46,000 other larcenies or frauds" (Finn and Newlyn 1993; Rosenthal 1993).

The tremendous number of drug-related cases entering the various state criminal justice systems seemed on the verge of overwhelming these systems, causing them to falter under their own weight. The report from one jurisdiction suggests the fallacy of assuming that increased penalties would significantly reduce drug use.

> The appalling fact is that because the system fails through lack of resources or resolve to effectively treat the problem of drug abuse when the offender first encounters the system, the same individuals return over and over again. To simply house these offenders at great expense is a short-sighted and ultimately a prohibitively expensive and self-defeating approach to the problem. To perpetuate an underfunded, ineffective, hurried, and, on occasion, unfair criminal justice system for which those subject to the system have no respect is little better than having no system at all (Russell Committee 1990).

State criminal justice systems responded to this pressure by consolidating drug offender cases. One of these consolidated formats is the Drug Treatment Court. DTCs differ from traditional court systems in significant ways. Unlike traditional courts, DTCs do not assume that probation, prison, or parole produces effective deterrence or incapacitation effects on drug-addicted offenders. Instead, many DTCs work under the basic assumptions that addiction is a biopsychosocial disease that can be successfully treated through various types of treatment regimes. Even those DTC practitioners who view addiction from a behavioral standpoint believe that addiction is treatable. The DTC format simply recognizes that "once addicted, it is almost impossible for most people to stop the spiraling cycle of addiction on their own without treatment" (Leshner 1999). DTCs attack the problems of drug use and drug-related crime by attacking the actual source of these problems: the offender's drug addiction.

Addiction

Although there is disagreement about how to define addiction, the American Society of Addiction Medicine recognizes addiction as a "disease process characterized by the continued use of a specific psychoactive substance despite physical, psychological or social harm" (Steindler 1994). Addiction encompasses three major behavioral characteristics: (1) obsession with the acquisition of the drug, (2) compulsive use of the drug, and (3) relapse, which is defined as addiction behavior in a person who has previously attained abstinence for a meaningful period of time (ibid.).

Once viewed primarily by our society as a moral failing or the manifestation of an individual's flawed character, advances in science have shown that addiction should be seen as a brain disease (Brust 1999; Leshner 1999). Addiction does start as the voluntary taking of a drug by an individual [O'Brien and McLellan 1998; *Robinson v. California*, 370 U.S. 660, 670-78 (1962) (Douglas, J. concurring)]. This voluntary act can quickly change into an involuntary act, resulting from a chemically produced compulsive craving for the drug once the person crosses the line from casual drug use to addiction. The compulsive craving for the drug is probably the result of dramatic physiological changes in the brain: an actual altering of brain chemistry and a resulting change in behavior.

This understanding of addiction has led to a change in the philosophies regarding drug treatment. In the mid-1970s, many treatment providers thought so-called coerced treatment was an ineffective method of dealing with addiction (Lipton 1995). With a greater understanding of the nature of addiction, treatment professionals have changed their opinions regarding coerced treatment and the need for an individual to "hit bottom" before recovery can begin. Treatment professionals now believe that the single greatest predictor of treatment success is not how an individual arrives in a treatment program, but how long a person stays in treatment (Anglin 1998). Whether a person enters a treatment program in prison, as part of a court-imposed sanction, or "voluntarily" due to threats or pressure from a spouse or employer, or because of the health consequences of continued drug use, it is the individual's length of stay in treatment that matters most for drug treatment success.

Studies support the idea that treatment is a cost-effective method of decreasing drug use. One recent comprehensive study suggested that every dollar spent on treatment could result in as much as seven dollars in savings (Gerstein et al. 1994). The savings were derived from a reduction in work-related and medical service-related costs incurred due to drug use and drug-related activities.

DTCs provide a unique opportunity for communities to break the cycle of drug use and crime that ensnares many drug addicts. Through court-imposed and supervised treatment programs, DTCs combine the coercive power of the courts with advances in addiction treatment to help drug-addicted offenders overcome their addiction. With an eye to reshaping the offender's behavior, DTCs shape their orientation, structure, and procedures to account for the nature of addiction, thereby maximizing the chances for continued drug abstinence by the offender.

DTCs: Orientation and Procedures

The basic premise of all DTCs is that the traditional criminal justice methods of parole, probation, and imprisonment do little to prevent recidivism in drug-addicted offenders (Belenko 2000; Wilson 2000).

> Many features of the [traditional] court system actually contribute to . . . [drug] abuse instead of curbing it: Traditional defense counsel functions and court procedures often reinforce the offender's denial of . . . [a drug] problem. . . . Moreover, the criminal justice system is often an unwitting enabler of continu[ed] drug use because few immediate consequences for continued use are imposed. (Drug Courts Program Office 1997)

DTCs exemplify the coherent application of the recent advances in the sciences of addiction and addiction treatment to the problems of drug addiction and drug-related crimes. Therapeutic jurisprudence provides the analytic tools necessary for DTC practitioners to fashion effective strategies for promoting drug abstinence in addicted offenders.

Orientation.   The recognition of addiction as a biopsychosocial disease or maladapted behavior forces DTCs to adopt a new orientation to drug use and drug-related crimes. DTC practitioners view drug use of an addicted offender not as a necessarily willful act, but rather as a likely symptom of a treatable disease or behavioral disorder—addiction. This paradigm shift allows DTCs to be considered as a means to an end rather than as ends in themselves. DTC practitioners regard the role of the court as facilitating drug abstinence through treatment.

With the goal of producing drug abstinence in drug-addicted offenders, DTCs foster a collaborative environment between prosecutor, defense counsel, probation officer, judge, and treatment providers. These traditionally partisan players come together to formulate the basic guidelines for the DTC participants. This nonadversarial approach facilitates the offender's treatment because "the team's focus is on the participant's recovery and law abiding behavior—not on the merits of the pending case" (Drug Courts Program Office 1997).

DTCs incorporate the policy requirements of both the defense counsel and the prosecutor to protect the offender's due process rights while also guaranteeing an appropriate level of public safety. The defense attorney is responsible for determining that the case against the offender is solid enough to warrant an alternative to trial. The altered role of the defense attorney in DTCs has raised concerns regarding a defendant's access to effective counsel, due process, and other constitutional rights (Quinn 2000; Reisig 2001; Judge 1997). Potential constitutional and/or ethical problems as they concern these issues, however, can be addressed by including defense counsel, along with all other "stake-holders," in processes of setting up a drug court program (Judge 1997; Burke 1997; Reisig 2001). Equal representation of defense counsel in the planning and initiation of DTCs should prevent violations of defendants' rights, as such. The prosecutor's office sets out the criteria for the type of offenders that may be eligible to participate in the DTC program. This determination is based on an assessment of the drug problems facing the community, and the resources available to deal with those problems. Generally, DTC participants are nonviolent drug offenders who pose little threat of future physical violence to members of the community. However, each DTC's entrance criteria vary to fit the particulars of the local legal culture and the needs of the community it serves.

This new orientation of DTCs is not inconsistent with the traditional moral justifications for punishment, or pretrial detention regimes, nor does it mean that DTCs do not hold drug offenders accountable for their actions. To the contrary, DTCs adopt the position taken by drug treatment professionals, that although addicts may not be responsible for their disease, they are responsible for their recovery (Steinberg 1998). DTCs require the offender to attend court regularly, submit to frequent urinalysis testing, and undergo various types of drug treatment therapies. The offender must demonstrate progress or suffer certain court-mandated sanctions. In pre-plea, preadjudication DTCs, sanctions may include termination from diversion after which the defendant is processed in the normal criminal justice system.

With the shift in orientation comes a fundamental and important shift in the way DTC practitioners view "relapse." Relapse, as differentiated from a "use episode," is the "recurrence of psychoactive substance-dependence behavior in an individual who has previously achieved and maintained abstinence for a significant period of time" (Steindler 1994). Rather than seeing relapse as a lack of willingness of the offender to participate in the program, relapse is viewed as a normal occurrence, and a DTC judge will administer "smart" punishment, i.e., punishment that facilitates the treatment process (Marlowe and Kirby 1999).

Procedures.   In recognizing and addressing the compulsive behavior of drug-addicted offenders, DTCs create and implement procedures specifically designed to interrupt the offender's addictive habits. Potential DTC candidates are quickly screened and can find themselves in front of a DTC judge within forty-eight hours after the original arrest. Often, offenders are taken to their first treatment session the day they first appear at the DTC in order to take advantage of the impact of the "crisis" that confronts them.

To bolster the treatment effort, DTC practitioners design the courtroom process in a particular way. For example, DTCs handle program graduates first in order to show newer participants positive examples of successful recovery and to instruct them regarding program expectations. The court then devotes time to those DTC participants who may enter the court in custody. This practice is designed to convey the serious nature of the court and treatment process. It also emphasizes that while drug use per se may not result in expulsion from the DTC, it does carry penalties. Finally, the court handles the newcomers who are entering the DTC program. All of these procedures are founded on the notion that every aspect of a DTC can and does have a powerful impact on the success of the defendant's treatment. Thus, at their core, these practices are viewed through a therapeutic jurisprudence lens to achieve the best abstinence outcomes.

The Use of Social and Medical Science

The use of these types of procedures exemplifies the best practices in treatment for addiction based on recent research. Protocols outlined in the Center for Substance Abuse Treatment's "Treatment for Stimulant Use Disorders" support this assertion. The document is a Treatment Improvement Protocol (TIP) representing the best practice guidelines for cocaine and methamphetamine addiction. TIPs are developed by national expert researchers and practitioners in the field and are subject to peer review. An analysis of TIP #33 on stimulant use shows just how effective DTCs can be when acting therapeutically.

Contingency Management or Contingency Contracting is recommended for those with stimulant use disorders. The TIP declares that to get the desired behavior the treatment provider (or court in the DTC context) must give immediate consequences, either to reinforce or punish participant behavior. Examples of this principle at work in a DTC may include the opportunity to reduce fees through volunteer work at a participant's children's school or immediate jail time for a positive urine test. The behaviors—testing clean and reestablishing parenting skills—are reinforced by punishment or reinforcement, the traditional carrot and stick approach.

The TIP also addresses the issue of the addict's possible ambivalence or skepticism about treatment. This condition is reduced in a DTC. The "choice" to enter treatment is coerced by the criminal justice system. The consequences of nonparticipation are perceived as greater than the resistance to initiate treatment. DTCs are also more helpful to clinicians, who are frequently frustrated by stimulant users' lack of enthusiasm about the goals and methods of treatment. Addiction doctors and other treatment providers are quick to admit that judges in a DTC have more power over their patients' treatment than they do and that keeping a patient in treatment is aided by the court. The TIP also suggests practitioners "maximize treatment engagement." DTCs require full-time employment/job seeking/schooling or substantial volunteer work to combat idle time. Thus, the boredom and lack of daytime activities, which may lead to drug use, are minimized in DTCs.

TIP urges an integrated approach to stimulant use treatment. It also recommends providing support for treatment participation. DTC coordinators/case managers address clients' concrete needs including transportation, childcare, temporary shelter, Temporary Aid to Needy Families (TANF)—the new "welfare," and Social Security and Unemployment Insurance benefits. They help with paperwork, develop resumes, set up appointments, make "reminder" calls, and provide daily support to DTC participants who are experiencing a myriad of problems and issues.

Successful treatment responds quickly and positively to initial inquiries. This necessity is echoed in Drug Court Key Component #3: "Eligible participants are identified early and placed promptly in the drug court program." The TIP recommends assessment procedures to enhance treatment engagement such as keeping the assessment brief, identifying clients' expectations, providing a clear orientation, offering options, and involving significant others. Each and every part of this recommendation is met by DTCs. The TIP also recognizes that treatment staff behaviors may enhance treatment engagement. The same may be said of DTC judges and other professionals in the courtroom. Clients/participants must be treated respectfully, in a warm, friendly, and courteous manner. Staff must convey an empathetic concern and be straightforward and nonjudgmental, the demeanor required of a DTC judge. These therapeutically oriented behaviors, as manifested in DTCs, increase treatment success.

Among the strategies included in TIP #33 are specific treatment goals. In a DTC such goals are found expressly in a written behavioral contract with specific minimum requirements. The contract recommends frequent contacts, which is a benchmark of a DTC. The use of positive incentives to reinforce treatment participation is also important. Some DTCs have weekly prize "drawings" as a reward for those who are doing well in the program. The analysis of this TIP suggests that DTCs follow the treatment regimes and ideas recommended by drug treatment providers and thereby reinforce the goal of treatment—drug abstinence.

The Results

Although critics may argue about the underlying jurisprudence rationale of the DTC movement—retribution, deterrence, rehabilitation, or incapacitation—one thing remains clear: DTCs reduce recidivism. The most recent, long-term studies of the recidivism rates of DTC participants shows that DTC participants are at least 10 to 15 percent less likely to be rearrested after three years as compared to non-DTC drug offenders (Shaw and Robinson 1999; Deschenes 1999a, 1999b; Belenko 1998; Johnson and Latess 2000).

These same studies also support the assertion that DTCs are more cost effective than the traditional modes of punishment. DTCs cost about three to five thousand dollars per participant per year, while incarceration costs the community twenty-five to thirty thousand dollars per inmate per year. In addition to the savings from reduced incarceration, DTCs lower the costs of drug use to the community through reduced health care and law enforcement costs. Finally, by promoting drug abstinence, DTCs reduce the costs of future criminal behavior and the costs associated with stolen property. All of these results suggest that DTCs are a rational, cost-effective approach to solving the problems of drug use and drug-related crime in this country.

CONCLUSION

DTCs have spread to jurisdictions throughout the country. Federal, state, and tribal governments have embraced DTCs as an effective means of breaking the cycle of drug use and the resulting drug-related crime. The principles and practices of DTCs are being used in child neglect and abuse cases, in mental health courts dealing with offenders who have co-occurring mental health disorders (addiction plus another mental health problem), with juveniles, and with domestic violence perpetrators. DTCs use therapeutic jurisprudence concepts to analyze the various facts about drug addiction and to effectively implement judicially supervised drug treatment programs. The use of therapeutic jurisprudence by DTCs does not contravene the four traditional moral justifications for punishment: retribution, deterrence, rehabilitation, and incapacitation. Rather, DTCs employ therapeutic jurisprudence analysis to magnify and enhance aspects of each of these traditional justifications in the context of how the criminal justice system deals with drug use and drug-related crime. Preadjudicative DTCs also use TJ in order to implement detention regimes that bear a rational relationship to their underlying regulatory goals.

DTCs implement proportional punishments for drug offenders, thereby following the theory of retribution. The punishment mandated by DTCs is participation in judicially supervised treatment. Studies show that treatment is the most effective method of deterring individuals from future drug use. These same studies show that decreased drug use leads to decreases in drug-related criminal activity. Thus, these findings indicate that DTCs are consistent with the deterrence model for punishment.

In understanding the medical nature and disease and behavioral models of addiction, DTCs use a punishment process that treats and addresses the offender's disease or behavioral problems of addiction. This basic understanding is compatible with the rehabilitative justification for punishment. Because studies show that treatment is the most effective way of preventing drug use, DTCs provide for the "incapacitation" of drug users though treatment. Finally, by using various drug treatment regimes, pre-adjudication DTCs implement procedures and processes that are rationally related to their regulatory goals of drug abstinence, reduction in pretrial criminal behavior, and decreasing the burden on the court system.

Whether by design or by absolute blind luck, we now know that DTCs are the best way to address addiction from both a treatment perspective and from a therapeutic jurisprudence perspective. Using an analysis that leads to solutions to the problems caused by criminal behavior, that is, a treatment orientation, DTCs represent not only the best practices from a treatment perspective but from the criminal justice system's perspective as well. Policy options such as decriminalization, legalization, and harm reduction are not addressed by DTCs. However, so long as laws prohibit drug use, and the criminal justice system must deal with drug-addicted offenders, DTCs represent the best practices we know of to address this type of criminal problem.

ACKNOWLEDGMENTS

I wish to thank Professors Michael Dorf and David Wexler for their helpful comments on the early drafts of this chapter.

NOTES

1. The word *apparently* is used to qualify the idea of drug use as a victimless crime because studies have indicated that there are collateral victims in os-

tensibly victimless crimes: people who live in the neighborhoods in which drugs are sold and used and the business owners who operate businesses in these areas. All of these individuals suffer when drug use, drug sales, and drug-related crimes degrade the community.

2. Contrary to the argument advanced by some, simply because drug testing can take place during both the pretrial phase and the punishment does not necessarily mean that the two are equivalent. Were this not the case, there could never be pretrial detention of any sort because such detention always involves deprivation of liberty, the same deprivation that results from punishment through incarceration.

3. The question Why punish? has already been answered by legislatures, both state and federal, and the issue of legalization of drug use will not be debated in this chapter. While the United States Supreme Court in *Robinson v. California*, 370 U.S. 660, 660–668 (1962), held that a statute making it a misdemeanor to be an addict violated the Eight Amendment's prohibition against cruel and unusual punishment as applied to the states through the Fourteenth Amendment, the Court declined to address the issue of whether a statute prohibiting public drunkenness similarly violated those same Amendments. See *Budd v. California*, 385 U.S. 909 (1966) (Fortas, J. dissenting) (asserting that alcoholism is a disease and that individuals exhibiting the symptoms of such a disease should be precluded from punishment under the Eighth Amendment). Implicit in the decision of the Court to deny a writ of certiorari in *Budd* is the idea that states are perfectly within their domain to legislate against activities that result from drug or alcohol use while not being able to criminalize the fact and status of being an addict or alcoholic. Were this not the case, alcoholics who kill people while driving drunk, pedophiles who molest children, serial rapists, and those who commit property crimes or crimes like prostitution while under the influence of drugs or as a result of drug use could not be prosecuted for their offenses if their condition were considered a disease or the result of a disease over which they have little or no control. Although the wisdom of criminalizing drug use is debatable if one accepts that addiction is, in fact, a brain disease, that issue is not the point of this chapter, nor is the idea that drug use mitigates the culpability of individuals who commit other crimes due to their drug use.

REFERENCES

Allen, F. A. 1981. The Decline of the Rehabilitative Ideal—Penal Policy and Social Policy. New Haven, CT: Yale University Press.

Alvarez, L. 2001. "An Enforcer Who Sees the Human Side of Drug Battles. *New York Times*, 3 September, p. A10.

Andeneas, J. 1974. *Punishment and Deterrence*. Ann Arbor: University of Michigan Press.

Anglin, M. D. 1998. "The Efficacy of Civil Commitment in Treating Narcotic Addiction." In *Compulsory Treatment of Drug Abuse: Research and Clinical Practice*, edited by C. G. Leukefeld and F. M. Tims. Rockville, MD: National Institute on Drug Abuse.

Associated Press. 2001. "Police Chemist Accused of Shoddy Work Is Fired." *New York Times*, 26 September, p. A16.

Beccaria, C. 1872. *An Essay on Crimes and Punishments*. Albany, NY: W. C. Little.

Beccaria, C. 1971. "On Crimes and Punishments." In *Theories on Punishment*, edited by S. E. Grupp. Bloomington: Indiana University Press.

Belenko, S. 1998. *Research on Drug Courts: A Critical Review*. New York: National Center on Addiction and Substance Abuse.

Belenko, S. 2000. "The Challenges of Integrating Drug Treatment into the Criminal Justice Process." *Albany Law Review, 63*, 833–76.

Belenko, S. and Peugh, J. 1999. *Behind Bars: Substance Abuse and America's Prison Population*. New York: National Center on Addiction and Substance Abuse.

Bentham, J. 1838–1843. "Principles of Penal Law." In *The Works of Jeremy Bentham*, edited by J. Bowring. Edinburgh: W. Tait.

Bentham, J. 1996. "An Introduction to the Principles of Morals and Legislation." In *The Collected Works of Jeremy Bentham*, edited by J. H. Burns and H. L. A. Hart. Oxford: Clarendon.

Black's Law Dictionary. 1990. 2nd ed. Minnesota: West Group.

Blackstone, W. 1979. Commentaries on the Laws of England: A Facsimile of the First Edition of 1765–69. Chicago: University of Chicago Press.

Blakey, K. P. 1996. "The Indefinite Civil Commitment of Dangerous Sex Offenders Is an Appropriate Legal Compromise Between 'Mad' and 'Bad'—A Study of Minnesota's Sexual Psychopathic Personality Statute." *Notre Dame Journal of Ethics and Public Policy* 10:227–315.

Boldt, R. C. 1998. "Rehabilitative Punishment and the Drug Treatment Court Movement." *Washington University Law Quarterly* 76:1205–1306.

Brust, J. C. M. 1999. "Substance Abuse, Neurobiology, and Ideology." *Journal of the American Medical Association* 56:1528–37.

Carlson, B. 1998. "Addiction and Treatment in the Criminal Justice System." In *Principles of Addiction Medicine*, 2nd ed., edited by A. W. Graham and T. K. Schultz. Chevy Chase, MD: American Society of Addiction Medicine.

Caulkins, J. P., Schwabe, W. L., and Chiessa, J. 1997. *Mandatory Minimum Drug Sentences, Throwing Away the Key or the Taxpayers' Money*. Santa Monica, CA: Rand Corporation.

Cohen, J. 1983. *Incapacitating Criminals: Recent Research Findings*. Washington, DC: U.S. Government Printing Office.

Department of Health and Human Services. 1999. *Treatment Improvement Protocol 33*, Publication Number 99-3296. Washington, DC: U.S. Government Printing Office.

Deschenes, E. P. 1999a. *Evaluation of Los Angeles County Drug Courts*. Los Angeles County, CA; California State University Long Beach. Department of Criminal Justice.

Deschenes, E. P. 1999b. *Evaluation of Orange County Drug Courts*. Los Angeles County, CA; California State University Long Beach. Department of Criminal Justice.

Dorf, M. A. and Sabel, C. F. 2000. "Drug Treatment Courts and Emergent Experimentalist Government." *Vanderbilt Law Review* 53:831–83.

Drug Courts Program Office, U.S. Department of Justice. 1997. *Defining Drug Courts: the Key Components*. Washington, DC: U.S. Government Printing Office.

Elkins, D. 2000. "Chief Justice Touts 'Therapeutic Justice.'" *Virginia Lawyers Weekly*, May.

Finn, P. and Newlyn, A. K. 1993. *Miami's "Drug Court": A Different Approach*. Washington, DC: U.S. Government Printing Office.

Finnis, J. 1998. *Aquinas: Moral, Political and Legal Theory*. Oxford: Oxford University Press.

Gelben, R. S. 2000, May. "The Rebirth of Rehabilitation: Promise and Perils of Drug Courts." *Sentencing and Crime* 6.

Gerstein, D. R., Harwood, H., Fountain, D., Suter, N., and Malloy, K. 1994. *Evaluating Recovery Services: The California Drug and Alcohol Treatment Assessment*. Washington, DC: National Opinion Research Center.

Greenawalt, K. 1983. "Punishment." In *Encyclopedia of Crime and Justice*, edited by S. H. Kadish. New York: Macmillan Library Reference.

Grupp, S. E. 1971. "Introduction." *Theories of Punishment*. Bloomington: Indiana University Press.

Harvard Law Review (1998). "Developments in the Law: Alternatives to Incarceration." *Harvard Law Review* 111:1863–1990

Hegel, G. W. F. 1972. "The Philosophy of Right." In *Philosophical Perspectives on Punishment*, edited by G. Ezorsky. Albany, NY: State University of New York Press.

Hobbes, T. 1972. *Leviathan*. In *Philosophical Perspectives on Punishment*, edited by G. Ezorsky. Albany, NY: State University of New York Press.

Hoffman, M. B. 2000. "The Drug Court Scandal." *North Carolina Law Review* 78: 1437–1534.

Hora, P. F., Schma, W., and Rosenthal, J. T. A. 1999. "Therapeutic Jurisprudence and the Drug Treatment Court Movement: Revolutionizing the Criminal Justice System's Response to Drug Abuse and Crime in America." *Notre Dame Law Review* 74:439–537.

Incardi, J., Mcbride, D. C., and Rivers, J. E. 1996. *Drug Control and the Courts*. Thousand Oaks, CA: Sage.

Kadish, S. H. and Schulhofer, S. J. 1995. *Criminal Law and its Processes: Cases and Materials*, 6th ed. New York: Panel.

Kant, I. 1972. *Justice and Punishment*. In *Philosophical Perspectives on Punishment*, edited by G. Ezorsky. Albany, NY: State University of New York Press.

Kress, K. 1999. "Therapeutic Jurisprudence and the Resolution of Value Conflicts: What We Can Realistically Expect, in Practice, from Theory." *Behavioral Science and the Law* 17:555–88.

Luscombe, B. 2001. "When the Evidence Lies." *Time Magazine*, 13 May.

Leshner, A. I. 1998. "What We Know: Drug Addiction Is a Brain Disease." In *Principles of Addiction Medicine*, 2nd ed., edited by A. W. Graham and T. K. Schultz. Chevy Chase, MD: American Society of Addiction Medicine.

Leshner, A. I. 1999. "Science-based Views of Drug Addiction and its Treatment." *Journal of the American Medical Association* 282:1314–24.

Lipton, D. S. 1995. The Effectiveness of Treatment for Drug Abusers under Criminal Justice Supervision. Rockville, MD: National Institute of Justice.

Locke, J. 1993. *Two Treatises on Government*, edited by Mark Goldie. Boston: Tuttle.

Marlowe, D. B. and Kirby, K. C. 1999. Effective Use of Sanctions in Drug Courts: Lessons from Behavioral Research. Washington, DC: National Drug Court Institute.

Martinson, R. 1979. "New Findings, New Views: A Note of Caution Regarding Sentencing Reform." *Hofstra Law Review* 7:243–58.

Massing, M. 2000. "Seeing Drugs as a Choice or as a Brain Disease." *New York Times*, 24 June, p. A17

Mccoll, W. D. 1996. "Baltimore City's Drug Treatment Court: Theory and Practice in an Emerging Field." *Maryland Law Review* 55:467–518.

Mill, J. S. 1970. "On Liberty." In *Essential Works of John Stuart Mill*, edited by M. Lerner. New York: Bantam.

Moore, M. S. 1984. *Law and Psychiatry*. Cambridge: Cambridge University Press.

Moore, M. S. 1987. "The Moral Worth of Retribution." In *Responsibility, Character and Emotions*, edited by F. Shoeman. Cambridge: Cambridge University Press.

Morris, H. 1976. *On Guilt and Innocence*. Berkeley: University of California Press.

National Institutes of Health. 1992. "The Economic Costs of Alcohol and Drugs in the United States—1992." Http://www.nida.nih.gov/economiccosts.html.

National Legal Aid and Defender Association. 1999. *The Case for Treatment v. Incarceration*. Http://www.nlada.org/indg/nd97/casefor.htm.

O'Brien, C. P. and McLellan, A. T. 1998. "Myths about the Treatment of Addiction." In *Principles of Addiction Medicine*, 2nd ed., edited by A. W. Graham and T. K. Schultz. Chevy Chase, MD: American Society of Addiction Medicine.

Packer, H. L. 1972. "The Practical Limits of Deterrence." in *Contemporary Punishment: Views, Explanations, and Justifications*, edited by R. J. Gerber and P. D. Mcanany. Notre Dame, IN: Notre Dame University Press.

Pope Pius XII. 1972. "Crime and Punishment." In *Contemporary Punishment: Views, Explanations, and Justifications*, edited by R. J. Gerber and P. D. Mcanany. Notre Dame, IN: Notre Dame University Press.

Quinn, M. L. 2000. "Whose Team Am I on Anyway? Musings of a Public Defender about Drug Treatment Court Practice." *New York University Review of Law and Social Change* 26:37–75.

Rawls, J. 1955. "Two Concepts of Rules." *Philosophical Review* 1:3–22.

Rosenthal, M. S. 1993. "The Logic of Legalization: A Matter of Perspective." In *Searching for Alternatives: Drug Control Policy in the United States*, edited by M. B. Krauss and E. P. Lazear. Stanford, CA: Hoover Institute Press.

Russell Committee. 1990. The Drug Crisis and Underfunding of the Justice System in Baltimore City, Report of the Russell Committee. Baltimore, MD: Bar Association of Baltimore City.

Shaw, M. and Robinson, K. 1999. *Effective Use of Sanctions in Drug Courts: Lessons from Behavioral Research*. Alexandria, VA: National Drug Court Institute.

Slobogin, C. 1995. "Therapeutic Jurisprudence: Five Dilemmas to Ponder." *Journal of Psychology, Public Policy, and Law* 1:193–219.

Steinberg, J. 1998. "Medical Strategy: Interventions." In *Addiction Intervention:*

Strategies to Motivate Treatment-seeking Behavior, edited by R. K. White and D. G. Wright. Binghamton, NY: Haworth.

Steindler, E. M. 1994. "Addiction Terminology." In *Principles of Addiction Medicine*, edited by N. S. Miller. Chevy Chase, MD: American Society of Addiction Medicine.

Taylor, T. 1997. "The Cultural Defense and its Irrelevancy in Child Protection Law." *Boston College Third World Law Journal* 17:331–64.

Vitiello, M. 1991. "Reconsidering Rehabilitation." *Tulane Law Review* 65:1011–54.

Ward, R. L. 1999. "Confidentiality and Drug Treatment Courts." Http://www.nlada.org/indg/nd97/confid.htm.

Weihoffen, H. 1971. "Punishment and Treatment." In *Theories of Punishment*, edited by S. E. Grupp. Bloomington: Indiana University Press.

Wexler, D. B. and Schopp, R. F. 1992. "Therapeutic Jurisprudence: A New Approach to Mental Health Law." In *Handbook of Psychology and Law*, edited by D. S. Kagehiro and W. S. Laufer. New York: Springer-Verlag.

Wexler, D. B. and Winick, B. J. (eds.). 1996. *Law in a Therapeutic Key* Durham, NC: Carolina Academic Press.

Wilson, D. J. 2000. *Drug Use, Testing, and Treatment in Jails*. Washington, DC: Bureau of Justice Statistics.

Winick, B. J. 1996. "The Jurisprudence of Therapeutic Jurisprudence." *Journal of Psychology, Public Policy, and Law* 3:184–206.

Wise, R. A. and Kelsey, J. E. 1998. "Behavioral Models of Addiction." In *Principles of Addiction Medicine*, 2nd ed., edited by A. W. Graham and T. K. Schultz. Chevy Chase, MD: American Society of Addiction Medicine.

Witte, M. and Bailey, L. M. 1998. "Pre-adjudication Intervention in Alcohol-related Cases." *Judges' Journal* Summer:32–36.

Zimring, F. E. and Hawkins, G. 1995. *Incapacitation: Penal Confinement and the Restraint of Crime*. Oxford: Oxford University Press.

8

Drug Treatment Courts: A Traditional Perspective

Susan Meld Shell

The therapeutic drug court movement raises a number of important issues from the perspective of traditional philosophic and moral views of punishment and justice. Philosophers since the time of Plato have reflected on the paradoxical character of human evil. In the famous formulation of Socrates: since we always do what we think good, all vice is ignorance, and all virtue wisdom about the true nature of the good. The implications of this radical view for ordinary moral and political practice are sweeping, as Plato and Socrates well knew. For one thing, retribution in the ordinary sense (and the moral indignation that typically accompanies it) becomes entirely misplaced. The proper response to wrongdoing is not the infliction of compensatory harm upon those doing wrong (as if they had gotten away with something) but removal of the disorder in the wrongdoers' soul—disorder associated with a lack of knowledge of what is genuinely desirable. The best kind of punishment, and perhaps the only kind that is really just, would be indistinguishable from therapy, achieving in the wrongdoer's soul what medicine achieves in a disordered body.

Much of Plato's *Gorgias* is devoted to rehearsing this argument before an audience imperfectly equipped to understand it. As Socrates teasingly tells an indignant Polus: one should hasten to be punished for one's wrongdoing (just as a sick man hastens to a doctor); and, for the same reason, one should do all one can to help one's enemies escape being punished (Plato 1961:264). The absurdity of this final point, which simultaneously questions and assumes the reasonableness of "getting even"—should alert us,

however, to the partiality of the view just represented, and to the inade-
quacy of the "ideal" view of punishment for ordinary social and political
life. If punishment were identical to ordinary therapy, the obvious association of punishment with pain would remain a mystery. Socrates' comparison of punishment to painful yet beneficial medical procedures such
as surgery only serves the more eloquently to highlight their difference:
where pain in medicine is an unfortunate contingency, the painfulness of
punishment is (or is regarded as) essential.

The necessary yet problematic relation of punishment to therapy is raised
in a different way in this volume's previous chapter "Therapeutic Jurisprudence and Drug Treatment Courts: Integrating Law and Science." While
John Rosenthal defends what may well be a reasonable response to the
problem of drug-related crime, his way of doing so is defective insofar as
it fails adequately to address the aforementioned issue. Drug Treatment
Courts, that is to say, may (or may not) be a prudent compromise, given
current circumstances, between traditional jurisprudential notions of guilt
and innocence, and traditional medical models of health and sickness. But
that compromise becomes a dangerous one, when, as in Rosenthal's essay,
the difficulty underlying that compromise is itself forgotten or ignored. To
state that difficulty most briefly: to the extent that drug-taking is an illness,
it cannot also be (in any common sense of the word) a crime.

Rosenthal attempts to parry this concern by claiming to be neutral on
the question of what punishment is ultimately for. Whatever one's "theory" of punishment, drug treatment courts are, in his view, both an attractive response to the problem of drug-related crime, and a promising
embodiment of the principles of "therapeutic jurisprudence." Therapeutic
jurisprudence, it is claimed, furthers the goals of all (reasonable) theories,
and this, precisely because, like all good science, it is essentially neutral as
to goals. Therapeutic jurisprudence—here defined as "the study of the role
of law as a therapeutic agent"—is not restricted to asking the question,
Why punish? but instead assists society in answering the question, How
to punish? (Rosenthal, this volume:154). Therapeutic jurisprudence measures the effects, for good or ill, that various judicial procedures have upon
criminals and the populace at large, the better to bring about the various
goals that criminal justice has traditionally aimed at.[1] More specifically, it
uses "social science" to ascertain the effects of criminal justice on people's
"psychological" and "physical" well-being.

One could well wonder, however, at this point, why such a "scientific"
approach should be peculiarly identified with the medical sciences, as opposed to more obviously "social" sciences, such as economics and political science.[2] Might not these disciplines be of equal, or even greater, help
in answering the question, How punish? If the goal of therapeutic jurisprudence is merely a reasonable attentiveness to what can be learned by

courts and legislators from the results of systematic scientific inquiry, why narrow one's focus so unreasonably? Or are economic jurisprudence, sociological jurisprudence, etc., to be of equal standing? "Therapeutic jurisprudential reasoning and analysis need not predominate," the author insists, "over other societal priorities" (ibid.:154). But might not the isolation of therapeutic inquiry from other modes of social and political analysis distort our understanding of what is and is not genuinely beneficial? And how do we know, without delving into questions touching on religion and philosophy, what truly counts as an improvement? "Therapeutic jurisprudence," proponents assure us, "does not resolve conflicts among competing values. Rather, it seeks information needed to promote certain goals and to inform the normative dispute regarding the legitimacy or priority of competing values." The goal is not to "trump other considerations" but to place them "in the proper context" (ibid.).

The author's seemingly modest admission that therapeutic jurisprudence should not predominate over other "societal values" thus masks a deeper assumption that the approach he favors yields uniquely objective insight into matters of the deepest moral and political concern. What privileges therapeutic jurisprudence over other modes of inquiry in defining the "proper context" is, it seems, its presumed reliance on "empirically verifiable results," allowing for "policy decisions based on empirical studies" rather than on "uninformed hunches" (ibid.:155). (The alternative of the informed hunch is not one Rosenthal pauses to consider, even though it may better characterize good policy than does his own crudely Weberian understanding of values chosen in the light of facts.) And yet the history of such empirical studies should raise doubts about the sufficiency of such reliance in establishing the context in which basic political and moral questions are to be resolved. The currently contested status of psychiatry altogether makes one's reservations all the greater.

The author's fallback argument is that drug treatment courts, understood as an extension of the principles of therapeutic jurisprudence, are "compatible with" and useful to any of the "traditional moral justifications of punishment"—be it retribution, deterrence, rehabilitation, or incapacitation. Proponents of each have something to gain and hence nothing to fear from it (ibid.:145, 166). These claims will be considered in reverse order, following a brief summary and discussion of the history and nature of drug treatment courts as presented in his chapter.

Drug treatment courts, according to Rosenthal, are a response to the vast increase in drug-related criminal cases due to the toughening of drug laws in the mid-1980s. Faced with a deluge of cases, and the peculiarities of drug crimes as such, courts in a number of jurisdictions looked for ways to improve and expedite their handling of such cases. Drug treatment courts represent both an explicit and an implicit melding of traditional criminal justice concerns with efforts to address drug addiction from the standpoint of public health. Eligible defendants (typically, nonviolent drug offenders) who opt to participate in such courts waive many ordinary rights to due process in exchange for removal to an explicitly therapeutic setting, whose point is not punishment but cure. In effect, the defendant pleads "guilty" and in so doing becomes a "client" rather than a criminal.[3] Treatment staff are enjoined to treat the "client/participant" in a "friendly and courteous manner" and to convey "empathetic concern." Even the judge is "non-judgmental" inasmuch as drug taking for an addict is understood to be "nonwillful" (ibid.:164). Participation in such a program is voluntary in the sense that the defendant chooses to participate and retains the option of returning to the ordinary criminal justice system, where he/she may be subject to incarceration and other ordinary penalties. The client who is persistently noncompliant runs the risk of being returned against his/her will. This threat is intended to encourage him/her to succeed in breaking his/her addiction, and allows one to call such treatment "forced" rather than strictly voluntary.

REHABILITATION

In the case of rehabilitation (and incapacitation), the issue of "compatibility" is relatively straightforward, inasmuch as drug treatment courts are clearly rehabilitative in their primary intention. If we assume that the meaning of "rehabilitation" (or health) is obvious, the question of compatibility will depend on the actual effects of drug treatment courts on their offender-clients, i.e., on whether such courts make people better. That these effects may, in fact, be hard to measure will here be left aside, as will the fact that some reports as to favorable results have been seriously contested.[4] It seems reasonable to assume that drug treatment courts, if effective, could meet most, but not necessarily all, the concerns of strict rehabilitationists.

For some proponents of rehabilitation, the *limitation* of "forced" treatment (if this is, in fact, what works best) to criminals might seem an invidious denial of services to others equally needy. Why should one have to commit a crime to become eligible for the most effective treatment? And yet the very existence of DTCs would seem to make a policy of involuntary treatment of noncriminal addicts all the less likely.

A further difficulty is raised by the prospect of significant advances in treatment over those currently favored. Current treatment protocols treat the "forced" character of drug treatment as an advantage. Moreover, current treatment stresses the "responsibility" of clients—a partial compromise, it seems, with more traditional understandings of drug abstinence as a matter of moral character. The addict may not be held responsible for his illness by current treatment protocols; he *is* held responsible "for his own recovery" (ibid.:162). In short, the therapies favored by drug treatment courts seem to reflect the current popularity of AA "twelve step" and related recovery programs more generally. Further research into chemical addiction may, however, yield methods as little related to personal responsibility and moral character as are current methods of treating cancer and heart disease. If the best cure for addiction should turn out to be a medicinal agent, administered in a pleasant liquid form, under country club conditions, would drug treatment courts adopt the new protocol? If so, claims that treatment holds criminals "accountable" would be seriously weakened. If not, rehabilitationists could rightly complain that criminal addicts were not receiving the most effective treatment.

DETERRENCE

Drug treatment courts (and therapeutic jurisprudence generally) raise a more obvious series of questions for proponents of "special" and "general" deterrence. While drug treatment courts—assuming that their treatments work—reduce recidivism, and thus achieve the aims of "special" deterrence, their "general" deterrent impact, both positive and negative, on the community at large seems more difficult to gage. Rosenthal maintains that ordinary deterrence is ineffective against addicts, inasmuch as addicts, being addicts, are unable to respond to normal negative incentives. But the author ignores the fact that drug addicts do not start out as addicts. Lessening the harshness of penalties runs a risk of lessening incentives against drug taking by those not yet addicted. We may never know how many individuals desist from drug taking in the first instance, and thus avoid addiction, owing to their fear of punitive consequences. It is reasonable to assume that such fears have *some* impact, though it is hard to say how much, or how much the prospect of a therapeutic alternative to criminal penalties such as incarceration lessens that fear. Thus, it is hard to say how much drug treatment courts contribute to the overall deterrent goal of preventing crime.[5]

A different sort of difficulty arises from the peculiarity of drug taking as a "victimless" crime. Unlike murder or theft, taking drugs involves no direct or immediate harm to others. And many harms related to drug taking are arguably the result of the illegal traffic in drugs rather than drug taking itself. Finally, we do not typically criminalize behaviors (such as smoking) deemed harmful mainly to the agent. There is thus a serious question as to whether drug use should be a crime at all. Drug treatment courts treat drug use as a crime to be prevented, whereas more effective "prevention" of the harms to which drug use gives rise may well lie in legalization. Thus, from a strictly utilitarian perspective, drug treatment courts might be too soft (inasmuch as they erode incentives against initial drug use) or, alternatively, too harsh (inasmuch as they present a distracting alternative to the more effective policy of legalization).[6]

Finally, someone strictly concerned with the prevention of societal harms might object that drug treatment courts have a generally disturbing effect upon the moral fiber of society, by contributing to an increasing blurring, in popular consciousness, between questions of guilt and punishment and those of illness and recovery. As thinkers such as Christopher Lasch (1978) and James L. Nolan, Jr. (1998) have argued, these are difficult and serious matters, about which it is hard to draw ready conclusions. It seems likely that habits of mind reinforced by such explicit assimilation of punitive and therapeutic language and goals have important consequences for the larger political and moral culture. However efficacious in a narrow sense, the wider effect of the drug treatment court movement, along with therapeutic jurisprudence generally, must be duly weighed before any general judgment can be rendered as to its compatibility with the larger objectives of deterrence.

RETRIBUTION

Surely the most troubling aspect of drug treatment courts, from a traditional philosophic perspective, lies in their uneasy relation to retribution. (This difficulty is all the greater, insofar as drug treatment courts are treated as embodying principles of therapeutic jurisprudence generally.) An early sign of Rosenthal's unwillingness to take retributive goals seriously is his signal reliance on Hobbes to summarize the goals of punishment *tout court*: "A Punishment," says Hobbes, "is an Evil inflicted by publique Authority, on him that hath done, or omitted that which is Judged by the same Authority to be a Transgression of the Law; to the end that the Will of men may thereby be the better disposed to obedience" (Rosenthal, this volume:146; see also Hobbes 1994:215) But Hobbes is also famous for saying "the aim of punishment is not a revenge but terror." Indeed, there are few political thinkers who strive more rigorously to expunge from the political and psychological vocabulary of punishment any notion that inflicting harm on a wrongdoer might be desirable in itself. Such "backward looking" aims are, for Hobbes, the very definition of unreasonableness (and Locke [1960:312], who speaks of "retribution," but redefines it in terms any Hobbesian could approve, hardly differs on this score).[7]

A second difficulty with the author's argument follows from his fuzzy account of retribution. A retributive theory of punishment is said to be the view that punishment is justified by moral culpability alone: punishment, he says, is in this view warranted because, and only because, it is *deserved*. But what makes an act deserving of punishment? The author here runs together a variety of views, from a more traditional approach, which links culpability to rebellion against duly constituted (and perhaps ultimately divine) authority, with a familiarly "Kantian" one, which links it to infringement of the equal rights and dignity of others. Thus, on the one hand, culpability is said to arise from a "preference for one's own will" to the "authoritatively specified" good of society; and, on the other, from an "unfair" advantage arising from treating others as "mere means" (Rosenthal, this volume:147). From a traditional Christian standpoint, on the other hand, the crime involved is also, and primarily, a sin—a misuse of God-given powers that is an affront to God's authority. From this standpoint, drug taking, like gluttony and other forms of self-abuse, is intrinsically deserving of requital, whether or not the human law prohibits it, and not primarily because it "reduces others to a means." The author also identifies the "retributive" theory with the view that punishable actions must be "rationally" chosen, and that punishment must "fit" the crime. At the same time, he specifically repudiates the view that retribution implies *lex talionis*, without suggesting an alternative measure of requital. It is thus difficult to see what sort of "fit" Rosenthal has in mind.[8]

Now, drug use might be viewed retributively from either a traditional or a liberal perspective. From a Kantian point of view, illegal drug use ought primarily to be punished, not because it harms the drug user or the larger interests of society, but because it violates a law duly enacted to achieve an appropriate public purpose. (That purpose could, for example, be public safety, given the violence that tends to accompany the drug trade.) Punishment in this case would aim, primarily, at upholding the equal dignity of citizens (e.g., by canceling the unfair advantage that law breakers otherwise enjoy vis-à-vis the law abiding). From a more traditional point of view, the emphasis would be on the intrinsic evil of the action, whether or not it constituted an affront to others.[9] In either case the primary object of punishment would not be to improve the criminal or provide other social benefits but to secure justice through requital of blameworthy evil.[10]

It is difficult to see, however, how drug treatment courts are consistent with the "goals of retribution" as understood from either point of view. Drug treatment courts transform a crime calling for requital into a "condition" meriting treatment. To be sure, they do so in a criminal justice setting. In effect, the offender is permitted to relinquish something of his or her status as a legal adult, for whom terms of guilt and innocence are applicable. Instead, he or she enters voluntarily into a kind of temporary wardship. In this new setting, the goal is no longer punishment but cure. Whatever "penalties" such treatment involves essentially aim at helping the offender deal with his or her addiction. When clients are "punished" for failures of compliance, the "penalty" is not intended as a just response to evil but as an alternative technique (where ready compliance fails) of treating their psychological and/or neurochemical disturbance. The goal for all concerned, in short, is not requiting the offence (to God or man) but overcoming the addiction. This is so much the case, indeed, that "backsliding"—far from being morally reviled—is accepted as a necessary aspect of recovery.[11]

According to the authors, this therapeutic turn is as it should be: drug users, once addicted, are virtually powerless to avoid their drug use.[12] Although addiction was "once viewed primarily by our society as a moral failing or the manifestation of an individual's flawed character," advances in science have shown that it should instead "be seen as a brain disease" (ibid.:160). In a word, the addict cannot help it. One might conclude that an addicted drug user should not be punished at all, for the same reason that we do not punish the certifiably insane. The crucial distinction for courts would then be that between the nonaddicted illegal drug user, who is punishable, and the addict, who is not (but who might, like the insane, be subject to involuntary commitment and/or treatment).

This is not, however, the tack taken by the author, who would not so much exempt addicts from responsibility for their drug use as hold them "responsible" in a new way. Drug treatment courts "adopt the position taken by drug treatment professionals, that although addicts may not be responsible for their disease, they are responsible for their recovery." Hence, "the new orientation" represented by such courts is "not inconsistent with traditional moral justifications of punishment," nor does it mean that offenders are not "held accountable for their actions" (ibid.:162). To be sure, it is not his or her illegal action for which the offender is held "accountable" but "his willingness to participate" in his own program of recovery.

And yet it is highly doubtful that "accountability" in this special sense could satisfy a defender of retributive punishment as the author himself earlier defines it. Far from subjecting clients to unpleasantness just "because they deserve it," the techniques in question pursue the singular goal of helping them get better. "Accountability" here does not signal a return to the ordinary moral realm of innocence and guilt, but merely the use of one tool (among others) to encourage compliance and thus aid treatment. A drug treatment court judge, we are told, "will administer 'smart' punishment; punishment that facilitates the treatment process" (ibid.:162–63). Thus the "accountability" of offenders (as in "accountability for one's recovery") is not linked to moral culpability in the ordinary sense. (Indeed, judge and staff are specifically enjoined to be "nonjudgmental.") As we have seen, drug treatment courts view relapse not "as a lack of willingness of the offender to participate," but as a normal aspect of treatment. The offender, in other words, is not really expected to comply, at least not initially, and never with wholehearted confidence. Without recovery, addicts are not morally responsible for their drug use; with it, they are no longer addicts. While it may be good therapy to subject offenders to progressive penalties for noncompliance, just as it may be good parenting to subject young children to progressive penalties for misbehavior, neither satisfies the morally robust demands of true retributive justice.

It is for this reason, perhaps, that the author finally rests his argument as to the compatibility of retribution and drug treatment courts solely on the fact that the treatment in question is "proportional" to the offense, and in this (narrow) sense consistent with retributive aims. As he himself summarily concludes:

> The use of therapeutic jurisprudence by DTCs does not contravene the four traditional . . . justifications for punishment: retribution, deterrence, rehabilitation and incapacitation. . . . DTCs implement proportional punishments for drug offenders, thereby following the theory of retribution. The "punishment" mandated by DTCs is participation in judicially supervised treatment. (Rosenthal, this volume:165–66)

And yet even this narrowed claim cannot stand, given the author's understanding of illegal drug use as the product of addiction. For what exactly is retributively proportional about forced treatment for offenses that the perpetrator is ostensibly powerless to avoid? If the penalty here "fits" the crime, it is only in the sense that treatment can be said to "fit" an illness or "condition," not in the usual sense (demanded by retributive justice) of matching the harm done to criminals with their degree of culpability—a culpability that their status as "addicts" implicitly removes. (Hence the author's own strained reference to the "punishment" thereby inflicted.)

In sum, Rosenthal fails to sustain his claim as to the compatibility of drug treatment courts and the ordinary goals of punishment—a failure that is, as we have seen, especially marked insofar as punishment is deemed retributive, or essentially concerned with moral and legal culpability.

AN ALTERNATIVE DEFENSE OF DRUG TREATMENT COURTS

There might, however, be justification of drug treatment courts more satisfactory from a traditional moral standpoint. That approach would hold addicts responsible, not only (in the manner of today's "professionals") for their recovery, but also, and primarily, for their addiction. In what sense, then, are addicts blameworthy for actions over which they are unable, *ex hypothesi*, to exercise the normal sort of control? Most addicts become addicts through their own free choice, i.e., by voluntarily and deliberately engaging in (illegal) activities they know (or ought to know) may seriously impair their future power of choice. Unlike an ordinary disease, that is to say, addiction arises from acts (themselves illegal) that reasonable human beings are properly expected to avoid. Thus even if, as the author insists, "advances in science have shown that addiction should be seen as a brain disease," it does not follow that addiction is not also "a moral failing or the manifestation of an individual's flawed character" (ibid.:160). On the contrary, the commonsense understanding of habitual drug use as a function of bad character, an understanding they explicitly reject, may provide drug treatment courts more adequate support than the "professional" defense they offer—even, and perhaps especially, given the advances that lead us to view drug use as chemically addictive, making it a temptation that the user is virtually powerless to resist on his or her own.

To be sure, chemical addiction per se is not part of the traditional or commonsense account of moral life, an account arguably presented in its fullest and most compelling form by Aristotle. Aristotle does speak of evils, however, that are in some respects analogous to drug addiction. To cite one example from the *Nichomachean Ethics:* drunkenness may render a person's actions "involuntary," and yet the person remains responsible for the actions leading to that state of drunkenness. Indeed, as Aristotle notes, this liability is so great that crimes committed while a person is drunk often receive double punishment (though, as he also indicates, this may in part be with a view to matters other than strict moral culpability) (Aristotle 1926:147). Even more pertinently, *all* wrongdoers are, in a certain sense, in the position of the actual or potential addict, inasmuch as moral disposition is the result of habits voluntarily acquired. We are all, in a way, responsible for our own character (for otherwise, as Aristotle notes, the very possibility of blameworthiness would be threatened) (ibid.:145, but cf. 121, 79). Each of us chooses to perform the good or evil deeds that, repeated over time, imperceptibly determine our moral constitution.[13] It may be true that the man of evil character is no longer able to resist committing evils. And yet he himself chose to perform those evil deeds which have become habitual. Thus "men are themselves responsible for having become careless through living carelessly, as they are for being unjust or profligate if they do wrong or pass their time in drinking and dissipation. They acquire a particular quality by constantly acting in a particular way" (ibid.: 147). Indeed, Aristotle explicitly compares the culpability of the habitual evildoer, or person of bad character, with that of one who has through his own fault made himself irreversibly ill. An unjust man can no more make himself just by wishing to be so, than a sick man can make himself well by wishing to be so; and yet illness, too, can result from morally culpable acts (e.g., intemperate living):

> At the outset [such a one] . . . might have avoided the illness, but once he has let himself go he can do so no longer. . . . Similarly, the unjust and profligate might at the outset have avoided becoming so, and therefore they are so voluntarily, although when they have become unjust and profligate it is no longer open to them not to be so. (Aristotle 1926:149)

We are all, in a way, responsible for our own character, even though that character, once acquired, is, for all practical purposes, fixed. Although punishment ought to be like "medicine," it actually functions this way mainly in the young. Aristotle harbors few illusions as to the capacity of punishment to improve the souls of hardened criminals. Indeed, if there is a difference between chemical addiction and ordinary bad character, it is in the greater power the addict may retain to overcome a bad habit. From an Aristotelian point of view, in other words, the addict is not more determined (than the man of evil character) to perform harmful and wrongful deeds but less so. Thus, if there is reason, from an Aristotelian point of view, to treat addicted illegal drug users differently than ordinary criminals, it is not owing to their lesser culpability for the condition in which they find themselves, but to greater prospects for reversing it.

One might counter that, however blameworthy drug addicts may be for their past behavior, their present legal culpability remains problematic. It is current illegality that they are charged with—not the activity, perhaps years past, which led to their addiction.

Additionally, persons are not ordinarily held legally accountable—not, at least, in a liberal regime like our own—for behavior that mainly harms themselves. If addicts are morally culpable only in the way that the intemperate are morally culpable for their ruined health, theirs is not a lapse we normally deem criminal. Even Aristotle, who treats moral evils such as intemperance as of immediate concern to lawmakers, does not suggest that those who eat or exercise improperly (and thus bring illness on themselves) should be subject to legal penalties.

Finally, there is surely something peculiar about addiction that distinguishes it from ordinary bad character. The addict (*ex hypothesi*) need not have given up the ordinary decencies in the same way or to the same degree. Addicts find themselves in the grip of a craving that they themselves may recognize to be irrational, and hence acts, in some sense, against their own will and better judgment. Their condition is closer to insanity (in some of its forms) than to corruption of character in the usual sense. Addicts, in short, are not habituated to (in the sense of taking direct pleasure in) doing harm to others. We are thus justified in regarding their compulsion as somehow mitigating. It is for this reason, above all, that we hold out hopes for their recovery. Relieved of the addiction, if not of the propensities that led them to acquire it, we believe they can return, in a way hardened criminals cannot, to a reasonably normal civil and moral life.

How might such an analysis play out vis-à-vis drug treatment courts as currently constituted? If, in fact, addiction can be treated (and there is at least limited evidence that this is so),[14] we have good reason, from both an Aristotelian and a common sense perspective, to provide addicts with such treatment. It should be done, however, in a way least likely to conflict with ordinary moral understanding. If drug treatment courts allow addicts to avoid a plea of guilt or innocence, and to place themselves under a kind of limited wardship, it is owing not to their lack of moral culpability for their addiction, but to the peculiar character of their present condition. In this heightened susceptibility to the dictates of pleasure and pain, the addict resembles both what Aristotle calls the man of defective self-restraint (who acts from desire but not from choice (ibid.:129, cf. 65) and Aristotle's depiction of the very young child: both profligates and children "live at the prompting of desire," the appetite for pleasure being strongest in childhood (Aristotle 1926:185).[15] And yet, unlike young children, addicts know they are responsible for their condition and are, at least potentially, ashamed of it. Whereas children are disciplined to obedience through pain, the adult addict is in full possession of a spiritedness that renders such direct "pruning" of the appetites difficult if not impossible. This spiritedness may take the form either of self-reproach or resentment of the authority of others. In either form, it blocks the normal channel by which young children, on an Aristotelian understanding, gradually learn to discipline themselves. The therapeutic impulse to exonerate the addict, as earlier described, is thus understandable, if not altogether wise. It is understandable, because it attempts to restore the addict to a more childlike state; it is unwise, because the moral judgment of the addict (along with the developed spiritedness on which that judgment partly depends) cannot be slighted or ignored without weakening the capacity for full moral "recovery."

And yet something like drug treatment courts could be readily defended, from an Aristotelian point of view, with only slight amendments. The Aristotelian judge would encourage addicted offenders' present efforts at reform without exonerating them from blame for the behavior that has made those efforts necessary. That encouragement would stress, instead, the offenders' reasonable hope of returning to a normal life, given their own efforts and the additional support of immediate, court-imposed rewards and penalties. The strong, but limited, analogy between addiction and childhood lends credibility to the practice of allowing addicted offenders the option of a kind of voluntary wardship. The therapeutic need not supplant the retributively punitive, under such arrangements, so long as offenders continued to pay (and to regard themselves as paying) for their wrong-doing through a loss of freedom. Such payment would assure, in turn, that treatment not altogether mitigate deterrence of the not yet ad-dicted—no small worry for an Aristotelian. Most importantly of all, by paying due attention to the moral culpability of the addicted offender, such an approach would minimize the larger difficulties, both for society at large and for the addict's own moral recovery, to which drug treatment of the sort encompassed here seems likely otherwise to lead. In short, the political and therapeutic goals favored by Rosenthal seems more likely to succeed through policies that encourage addicted offenders to confront and deal with their own moral failings, than through policies premised on their nonexistence.

NOTES

1. But compare Hora et al. (1999:439–537). The authors there stress the affin-ity of therapeutic jurisprudence with other "consequentialist" heirs to the school of legal realism as propounded by Oliver Wendell Holmes and Ros-coe Pound (ibid.:446).
2. Although the authors include "social science" as among the resources of "therapeutic jurisprudence," they implicitly limit that science to the nar-rowly (and psychologically) "behavioral" (compare, for example, pages 151 and 156–57 of Rosenthal's essay in this volume).
3. That this is said to occur as part of a "preadjudication treatment regime" only serves to further blur the question of whether the process involved is essentially disciplinary or medical. Moreover, the author's strong reliance on *United States v. Salerno*, which turns on the fact that predetention drug testing is "regulatory" rather than "punitive," weakens his later claim that mandated treatment as he understands it is "punishment" in a sense that a retributivist would accept. Compare (Hora et al. 1999:11–12, 27).
4. For a thoughtful review of such data, see Nolan (2001:128–32).
5. Although Rosenthal notes the difficulty of measuring deterrent effects as a function of overall social utility (Rosenthal, this volume:150), he fails to apply this conclusion to his own argument; thus, he treats the declines in recidivism attributed to drug treatment courts as a net social gain, and does so on implicitly preventive grounds, without considering whether or not such reductions come at the expense of an increase in future crime or other social ills.
6. Rosenthal raises the issue of decriminalization, but does not consider whether drug treatment courts are more likely to facilitate or to impede it.
7. "And thus in the State of Nature, *one man comes by power over another;* but yet not Absolute or Arbitrary Power, to use a Criminal when he has got him into his hands, according to the passionate heats, or boundless extrava-gancy of his own Will, but only to retribute him, so far as calm reason and

conscience dictates, what is proportionate to his Transgression, which is so much as may serve for Reparation and Restraint." What Locke calls "retribution" is equivalent to what Hobbes calls "terror," i.e., a "proportionality" determined by consequentialist (rather than retributive) ends. (But compare pp. 147–48, 149–50, and 165 of Rosenthal's essay in this volume. The author consistently elides proportionality as a function of deterrence and proportionality as function of culpability [or blameworthiness] per se.)

8. Cf. Aristotle's critical discussion of strict reciprocity as a standard of requital. According to Aristotle, punishment should be "proportionally" reciprocal, so that (to cite his example) a man who wrongly strikes an officer deserves a greater punishment than being struck in turn. Retributively speaking, to strike an officer deserves a harsher penalty than would striking an ordinary citizen because the moral evil done is proportionally greater (Aristotle 1926:281).

9. On this view, any difficulties arising from retributive punishment of so-called "victimless" crimes become mute. (Compare pp. 147–48 of Rosenthal's essay in this volume.)

10. For a fuller consideration of the importance of blameworthiness in the criminal law, see Kadish (1987).

11. In the author's words: "Clients/participants must be treated respectfully and in a warm, friendly and courteous manner. Staff must convey empathetic concern and be straightforward and nonjudgmental, the demeanor expressed by a DTC judge" (Rosenthal, this volume:164).

12. The voluntary act of drug use can "quickly change into an involuntary act, resulting from a chemically produced compulsive craving" (ibid.:160).

13. "Our dispositions are not voluntary in the same way as our actions. Our actions we can control from beginning to end, and we are conscious of them at each stage. With our dispositions on the other hand, though we can control their beginnings, each separate addition to them is imperceptible, as is the case with the growth of a disease" (Aristotle 1926:153).

14. For a fuller discussion, see (Hora et al. 1999:529–35). But compare Nolan (1998:103–12). On alternative approaches to mandatory drug treatment, compare Kleiman (1992:192–99).

15. As the Loeb editors note, the very term for profligacy (*akolasia*), which also means naughtiness (as in the naughtiness of children), literally means "the result of not being punished."

REFERENCES

Aristotle. 1926. *Nichomachean Ethics* (Loeb Edition), edited by H. Rackham. Cambridge, MA: Harvard University Press.

Hobbes, Thomas. 1994. *Leviathan*, edited by Richard Tuck. Cambridge: Cambridge University Press.

Hora, Peggy Fulton, Schma, William G. and John T. A. Rosenthal. 1999. "Therapeutic Jurisprudence and the Drug Treatment Court Movement: Revolutionizing the Criminal Justice System's Response to Drug Abuse and Crime in America." *Notre Dame Law Review* 74(2):439–537.

Kadish, Sanford H. 1987. *Blame and Punishment: Essays in the Criminal Law*. New York: Macmillan.

Kleiman, Mark A. R. 1992. *Against Excess: Drug Policy for Results*. New York: Basic Books.

Lasch, Christopher. 1978. *The Culture of Narcissism*. New York: Norton.

Locke, John. 1960. *Two Treatises of Government*, edited by Peter Laslett. Cambridge: Cambridge University Press.

Nolan, James L., Jr. 1998. *The Therapeutic State: Justifying Government at Century's End*. New York: New York University Press.

Nolan, James L., Jr. 2001. *Reinventing Justice: The American Drug Court Movement*. Princeton, NJ: Princeton University Press.

Plato. 1961. *The Collected Dialogues of Plato*, edited by Edith Hamilton and Huntington Cairns. Princeton, NJ: Princeton University Press.

9

The Drug Court Movement:
An Analysis of Tacit Assumptions

James J. Chriss

INTRODUCTION

Over the last decade a tremendous amount of legislative and scholarly energy has been directed toward the conceptualization, implementation, and institutionalization of drug (or drug treatment) courts in the United States. From the drug court perspective, persons who are brought before the court for drug and/or alcohol related charges are to be dealt with as "clients" who will be provided rehabilitative treatment by court personnel and associated health and treatment professionals. This fundamental transformation of the court from an adversarial to a nonadversarial context, whereby judges and attorneys are now part of a therapeutic "team" instead of playing their traditional roles as objective, dispassionate agents of the criminal justice system, follows the ideals of therapeutic jurisprudence. In order to understand more fully the nature of therapeutic jurisprudence and the drug court, it is necessary to examine not only what is stated overtly in legislative records, court briefs, scholarly writings, and the popular press, but also what remains unstated or tacitly assumed. Alvin W. Gouldner (1970, 1976, 1980) has provided such a program of reflexivity and critique for examining and uncovering the tacit domain assumptions underlying any public project or policy. I suggest that certain implicit, largely unexamined assumptions—such as the broad acceptance of the medical model of disease—within the drug court context contradict a number of public policies or initiatives simultaneously pursued and enforced within the system. This systematic examination of the crucial points at which the infrastructural level of the drug court policy is at odds with its technical level (that is, with what is stated overtly) is essential for informing and improving drug policy and initiatives.

The first part of the chapter will be devoted to summarizing Gouldner's program of critique. The second part will examine several key public documents related to the drug court movement. These publications, authored by drug court proponents, make assertions about the success of the program or the necessity of its continuance or expansion. Other documents are legislative records or federal policy initiatives on the creation, funding, implementation, or expansion of drug courts across various jurisdictions. In the final sections, following Gouldner's guidelines, I present a critical hermeneutic examination of the texts discussed in the second part of the chapter, as well as several policy recommendations for the operation and conceptualization of drug courts.

GOULDNER'S PROGRAM OF CRITIQUE

In order to utilize Gouldner's (1970, 1980) program of critique, one must first understand the distinction he makes between the technical and the infrastructural levels of social theory. The *technical* level of theory refers to the actual theoretical system itself, that is, the interrelated set of postulates or statements that purport to explain or predict something about the empirical social world. Besides the overt articulation of some public project or plan of action, the technical level also involves the actual construction of the theory, including the specification of the particular analytical strategies employed (e.g., deductive vs. inductive, functionalist vs. historicist, descriptive vs. explanatory).

The *infrastructural* level of theory refers to the (often) unstated ideological presuppositions (Alexander 1982) or domain assumptions lying behind and undergirding the actual theory. These tacit assumptions reflect taken-for-granted attitudes toward, or positions on, knowledge (epistemology), values (axiology), and reality (ontology). Members of particular theory groups share the same or similar set of background assumptions about the world, and hence the working consensus they hold about the world is rarely opened to scrutiny or reflected upon. Importantly, the infrastructure of theory provides an internal sentiment structure, a source of solidarity, out of which a group of like-minded individuals comes to accept the world as "natural" or "given."

Gouldner argues that it is not sufficient simply to analyze or test the

technical level of theory, that is, what is stated overtly. Besides textual ex-
egesis, whereby texts are studied as cultural objects in an attempt to interpret and specify what a theory is overtly stating, the critic must also look
for and explore the systematic silences (the glosses) in a text or theory. In
order to fully understand or test theories as public projects, one must examine those things which the theory or theorist takes as unproblematic and
not worthy of articulation. In essence, theories are public projects that attempt to change or intervene in the world in some way (Gouldner 1974).
Gouldner refers to these publicly avowed aspects of the theory as "good
news," while "bad news"—anomalies and contradictions residing at the
infrastructural level of theory—tends to be systematically repressed, muted,
or glossed (Gouldner 1976). The task, then, is to foreground these otherwise tacit elements of a theoretical system (or public project), which usually remain hidden in its infrastructure (Chriss 1999a).

Rather than merely demystifying, denuding, or disempowering theory,
Gouldner's primary aim is to articulate the ways in which bad news is repressed. As Gouldner states:

> It is intrinsic, then, to the critique practiced here to reject an account of his-
> tory that is essentially polyannalike, and to help persons bear bad news con-
> cerning their most cherished projects, neither overestimating their own
> chances nor underestimating the projects of their adversaries. The critique in
> practice is stripped of the myth of inevitable progress. (1980:18)

And further,

> The rule I follow says that, if there is something systematically silenced in an
> area of discussion, it is the analyst's responsibility to bring it into focus. In
> this analytic, then, it is a critical theorist's special task to speak the bad news.
> (ibid.)

The social critic must also be prepared to critically examine public projects that seem for the moment to have the backing and blessings of numerous constituencies in society. This is certainly the case with the drug
treatment court, which is widely hailed as a resounding success by lawyers, treatment professionals, legislators and politicians, law enforcement
and corrections agencies, intellectuals and scholars, community leaders
and organizations, news media, as well as the general public. Indeed, there
are more than one thousand drug courts in various stages of planning or
operation in the United States today, and they are beginning to appear in
other countries such as Canada, Australia, England, Ireland, and Scotland
(Nolan 2001:43). I now turn to the evidence of this support as contained in
various publications and legislative records.

VIEWS ON THE DRUG TREATMENT COURT

In his "Message From the President" addressed to the Congress of the United States, President Clinton provided a brief summary and overview of his 1995 *National Drug Control Strategy*. In a passage worth noting, the president stated:

> Most importantly, the *Strategy* responds to the need for a new covenant between the American people and their government—one that matches more opportunity with more responsibility. This *Strategy* gives those who have fallen prey to drugs the opportunity to change their behavior, and it gives these youths who are at risk for starting to use drugs positive alternatives. (Office of National Drug Control Policy 1995: 3)

This notion of giving persons who use drugs and/or alcohol and who subsequently run afoul of the law an "opportunity to change their behavior" is the guiding logic or ethos of the drug court. Instead of "punishing" these persons by throwing them into an ever-expanding prison population with its attendant high rates of recidivism, drug courts are set up so as to offer persons a "second chance" and an opportunity to "clean up their act," as it were. In coalition with treatment professionals,[1] the drug court judge develops a treatment strategy suited to the needs of each particular client, and strong incentives are in place to ensure that these persons take full advantage of their "opportunity" (Cohen 1999).

How and why has federal drug policy changed so dramatically between the early 1980s—represented by President Reagan's crime control approach dubbed the "war on drugs"[2]—and the overtly therapeutic approach of the drug court beginning in the late 1980s? Briefly, the story is that the appearance of crack cocaine in the late 1970s ushered in a new and never before seen wave of drug use and abuse and a concomitant increase in violent street crime associated with its distribution and sale. Being a "law and order" president, Mr. Reagan's reaction was simply to step up enforcement of current drug laws and establish new initiatives to combat the perceived menace, including tougher and longer sentences not only for drug trafficking but also for casual use.

The story continues that Reagan's "war on drugs" was a failure insofar as lots of people were being thrown into jail—many for relatively minor drug violations—thereby creating an unprecedented growth of the prison population and a terrible backlog of drug cases within our court system, while at the same time doing little to reduce drug use or drug-related crime. Since the traditional "punish and control" approach (Danziger and Kuhn 1999:167) to the drug problem did not appear to be working, many observers within policy, legislative, and scholarly circles felt it was time to try something else.

The first drug treatment court was established in Miami in 1989, which happened to be a hotbed of drug-related, violent street crime.[3] Speaking at the 1999 annual convention of the American Bar Association in Atlanta on August 10, Attorney General Janet Reno reflected upon the string of events that led up to the establishment of that first drug court:

> In 1989 in Miami we were dealing with a system that rotated people through the system one after another and then back again. People charged with possession of a small amount of cocaine, first time offenders, were simply getting credit for time served. They were not getting treatment, they were not getting punished, and they were coming back in six weeks, or in a year. The Supreme Court and the chief judge of the circuit came together and authorized a judge to have a sabbatical for a year to set up the drug court. The ingredients of the drug court were a manageable caseload and resources that matched the caseload, and the court controlled it so that it was never spread too thin.

And further:

> There was authority in the judge. The judge knew the treatment resources, knew what to do with the treatment resources. The judge cared and had some expertise. The latest knowledge in terms of treatment was used. It was a tough road to get that drug court established, but about two months ago I appeared in Miami for the tenth anniversary of drug courts. There are now 359 drug courts across the country with some 200 on the drawing boards. Courts can solve problems if given the authority and the resources and the expertise, and there are evaluations now that indicate that the drug court in its various forms is working across the country. Let us use that example and show what can be done and let the courts lead the way. (Reno 1999:3)

It is clear from these comments that the Clinton administration was firmly behind the drug court and appeared convinced of the efficacy and utility of its operation. However, claims of the effectiveness of drug courts by members of the Clinton administration and others should be viewed skeptically. A website devoted to providing information about drug courts (www.drugcourt.org) reports that the American University Drug Court Clearinghouse published a report whose findings suggest that recidivism has been significantly reduced for drug court participants. Additionally, a National Institute of Justice study reported a 33 percent decrease in recidivism over an eighteen-month period among clients of the Miami drug court, while those diverted to the Oakland drug court experienced a 35 percent reduction in recidivism over a forty-eight-month period (General Accounting Office 1997; Goldkamp, White, and Robinson 2001). The important question, however, is compared to what or to whom?

First of all, it is important to note the sorts of defendants who are typically accepted for the drug treatment courts. Although these guidelines
vary somewhat by state and by particular drug courts, most drug courts
accept defendants with substance abuse problems who are currently charged
with drug possession and/or other nonviolent offenses such as property
crimes (Danziger and Kuhn 1999). Importantly, most drug courts do not
accept defendants currently charged with a violent offense. This is because
under the 1994 Crime Act, federal grants cannot be awarded to any drug
court that allows violent offenders to participate in its programs.[4] Also, as
Kassebaum and Okamoto (2001:95) have recently reported with regard to
screening procedures of the Hawaii Drug Court, persons who "repeatedly
had evaded programs and restraints on drug use" were likely to be rejected
as viable candidates for admittance to the drug court.

Because most evaluations of drug courts have fallen short of the classical experimental design in which a group of subjects are randomly assigned
to experimental and control groups, the design most frequently employed
is quasi-experimental (Hoffman 2000; Nolan 2001:131). Here, instead of random assignment of subjects to experimental and control groups, the experimental group—in this case, defendants diverted to the drug court—are
simply compared to a "comparison" group whose members are considered to have some of the same essential characteristics of the experimental
group. In most evaluations of the drug court, then, defendants who come
before the drug court are compared against substance abuse defendants
who come before traditional courts. In order to assess whether drug courts
"work," these evaluations tend to focus on rates of reoffending or of substance abuse, that is, rates of recidivism. Most of the claims of success with
regard to evaluations of the drug courts amount, then, to the rather modest claim that substance abuse defendants before the drug courts have
lower rates of recidivism in comparison to substance abuse defendants
who come before traditional courts (see, e.g., Peters and Murrin 2000).

The reason we must remain cautious about such claims of the effectiveness of the drug court goes beyond the limitations of the research design,
however. Even more importantly, it must be kept in mind that the drug
courts, by limiting the types of defendants that are eligible to be adjudi-
cated, have effectively self-selected defendants who are least likely to reoffend anyway, regardless of the intervention of the drug court. By
selecting only the least serious offenders, and especially by eliminating violent offenders, drug traffickers, and the like, the drug courts can make
startling, but in reality relatively empty, claims of the success of their drug
abuse interventions. It is likely that many defendants who come before the
drug court fall into the category of marginal or technical violators of existing drug or alcohol abuse regulations. These represent relatively minor violations that happen to involve drugs and/or alcohol, such as first-time

DUI offenders, technical violations of probation, or the discovery by law enforcement of small amounts of marijuana or drug paraphernalia used ostensibly for recreational purposes (Peyrot 1985). Because law has incorporated and thereby reified the "certainties" of the welfare, health, and behavioral sciences (White 1998), especially with regard to the prevailing assumption of the medical model of disease (Chriss 1999b), defendants with drug-related charges who come before the drug court, however minor or peripheral to the complex of factors that brought them to the attention of formal agents of social control in the first place, are assumed to be ill and in need of "treatment." However, as Maxwell (2000:554–55) has reported, defendants who are mandated into drug treatment for the sort of relatively minor offenses mentioned above are at a significantly higher risk of dropping out of treatment early than those referred into treatment after sentencing.

Another claim about the positive benefits of the drug court is the suggestion that they are cost-effective; that is, that it costs less per person to divert defendants into alcohol and other drug (AOD) treatment than to incarcerate them or place them under traditional forms of probation. In one article that cited a study of the drug courts conducted by the State of California (California Department of Drugs and Alcohol Programs 1994), the claim was made that "AOD treatment provides a $7 return for every $1 spent on treatment."[5] If this were true, it would mean that California's criminal justice system could net $6 billion by spending only $1 billion on treatment. But why stop there? After all, the more you spend, the more you save.

It is this sort of questionable logic that makes claims of the cost-effectiveness of the drug court suspect. It is strikingly similar to a claim made in 1994 by the chief economist of the Governor's Office of Planning and Research in California that each incarcerated offender saved the state about $200,000 annually (cited in Skolnick 1995). As Livingston (1996:543) notes, following this logic, if the state of California were to incarcerate an additional 4,500 prisoners in the next year it would save the state an additional billion dollars.

Even more astonishing is the way the drug court operationalizes "recovery" or "sobriety." Staying true to the assumptions of the medical model of disease and the tenets of therapeutic jurisprudence, Hora, Schma, and Rosenthal (1999:451) cite approvingly the American Society of Addiction Medicine (ASAM) definition of addiction as a "disease process characterized by the continued use of a specific psychoactive substance despite physical, psychological or social harm." However, defenders of the drug treatment court conveniently overlook how the treatment industry inflates its rate of treatment success. The trick is not to count *relapse*—the recurrence of psychoactive substance-dependence behavior in an individual who has previously achieved and maintained abstinence for a significant period of time (ibid.:454)—as program failure, but to incorporate it into the definition as an acceptable part of drug treatment. That is, from the therapeutic jurisprudence and drug court perspective, relapse must not be viewed as the *failure* of treatment but as an *inevitable stumbling block* on the road to abstinence (ibid.).

This definitional fiat has important implications for understanding the seeming "failure" of traditional probation and the criminal courts in dealing with substance-abusing defendants. As we have seen, proponents of the drug court are quick to point out the purported failure of traditional approaches in dealing with drug-related crime. One particular Office of Justice Programs (OJP) document explains how the drug court has improved upon the traditional adjudication process because of its greater capacity to deal promptly with relapse and its consequences. There it is stated:

> It is particularly common for defendants on probation for drug offenses to fail to comply with probation conditions entailing attendance at treatment programs or abstaining from drug use. Frequently, their failure to comply is evidenced by a new arrest for a drug or drug-related offense, generally becoming known to the justice system months after the defendant's drug use has resumed, if it ever ceased in the first place. This violation hearing, which generally results in imposition of the original sentence suspended when the defendant was placed on probation, and (2) conviction for the new offense, often resulting in an additional sentence of incarceration. It is common for this cycle to continue indefinitely once the defendant is released, with an enhanced incarceration sentence imposed each time to reflect the defendant's lengthening criminal history. At least 40% of offenders incarcerated in 1995 were imprisoned for drug related offenses and over 60% of the correctional population had substance abuse problems. ("Looking at a Decade of Drug Courts" 1998:5)

What we see, then, is simply a change in definition. Under the traditional adjudication system, an offender who fails to get or stay sober is a recidivist, while in the context of the drug court this same behavior is labeled merely a relapse and not a program failure. Indeed, it is clear to see that reductions of recidivism under the drug court system are assured because of the way the definition of sobriety (or recovery) is manipulated by the smuggling in of relapse.

THE IDEOLOGY AND RHETORIC OF THE DRUG COURT

The Gouldnerian program of critique guides us into investigating claims made by proponents of the efficacy, utility, morality, goodness, or cost-effectiveness of any policy, project, or theory. Even further, however, the program of critique asks the question, Whose interests are being served by current arrangements? Along with this, the social critic must be sensitive to the history of contentious policy issues so that contemporary lines of discussion or argument can be traced back to the same or similar lines of reasoning that have appeared in the past but, for whatever reasons, have been forgotten, neglected, or repackaged in an attempt to make them appear "new" (see Chriss 1999a:1–4; Gouldner 1965).

First, to the issue of whose interests are being served, certainly those who stand to benefit the most from the drug court or drug treatment court movement are practitioners associated with the various psychotherapeutic helping professions, including social work, occupational therapy, marriage and family therapy, school counseling, medicine and nursing, psychiatry, psychology, educational psychology, mental health counseling, Alcoholics Anonymous and other 12-step treatment programs, and correctional counseling (Chriss 1999b). The economic payoffs are staggering for those who are successful in diverting federal funds earmarked for the criminal justice system to drug court treatment personnel as well as to consultants who are hired to assist in the establishment or maintenance of these courts.

Close behind this group are judges who have become increasingly frustrated with the backlog of court cases resulting from the war on drugs and who are desperate to remedy what they perceive to be the failings of traditional probation in dealing with defendants with drug-related charges. As a result, many judges are now turning to treatment professionals of the helping and psychological sciences—collectively referred to as the "psy complex" (Ingleby 1985; White 1998)—who these judges believe hold the key to reducing recidivism rates among this group of offenders. But even further, drug court judges who buy into the vision and rhetoric of the psy complex tend to view themselves as trustees or good stewards of the psychotherapeutic ethos. This is especially reflected in the push to move the court into a nonadversarial direction where proper and fair treatment of "clients," including of course the goal of "curing" these persons of their "illness," rather than the adjudication and punishment of "criminals" if found guilty, becomes the order of the day.[6]

Though there is evidence that the legal field has largely incorporated (thereby reifying) the "certainties" of the welfare and psychological sciences (see Chriss 1999b:11; White 1998), it is within the drug court context that judges and other court personnel have become thoroughly imbued with the psychotherapeutic ethos (Nolan 1998, 1999). Take, for example, a recent news story on National Public Radio's (NPR) "Morning Edition." Reporter Wendy Kaufman is providing background on the King County Drug Court in Seattle, Washington, which includes several sound bites of actual courtroom proceedings. To one particular drug court participant standing before her, Judge Nicole McGuiness explains:

I'm a social worker here. I mean, I put people in jail, so I guess I'm a judge. But I'm really operating as a social worker. And I get to know these people. We get invested in people's success. We get upset with people's failures. And it's a very direct process that we have here.[7]

The remarkable thing about this passage is Judge McGuiness's difficulty in admitting that she is actually a judge. In earlier forms of rehabilitation, judges were firm in making clear distinctions between themselves and court personnel on the one hand, and treatment professionals who happened to be working for or in conjunction with the court on the other. Now, however, many drug court judges have acquiesced to—or perhaps better, "consented to" (see Nolan 1999)—the egalitarian notion of the therapeutic alliance where members of the treatment team comprise a "helping alliance" whose primary aim is to set the offender on the path of virtuousness and "clean living."

As we have seen, the drug court judge operates within a diversity of roles, including those of social worker, judicial officer, and psychologist. This attempt to maintain bonds of respect and caring between drug court personnel and their clients is close to Braithwaite's (1989) notion of "reintegrative shaming." In reintegrative shaming, although community members express disapproval toward offenders, they nevertheless allow reformed members back in to the community after they have served their time or completed treatment. This overcomes the problem of "stigmatizing shaming," which is simply the application of a deviant label on an offender (e.g., delinquent, ex-con, child molester, pusher or drug user). Offenders who have been shamed in this way find it difficult to reintegrate into conventional society after release because the deviant or criminal label sticks to them, thereby becoming a master status. According to Braithwaite, justice systems or approaches that practice or promote reintegrative shaming (such as the drug court) should have lower rates of crime and recidivism than standard justice approaches, which tend to follow the principle of stigmatizing shaming.

However, the rhetoric of the drug court may not comport well with how it actually operates. Among a random sample of AOD defendants taken from drug court and the general district courts of Las Vegas, Miethe, Lu, and Reese (2000) found that drug court participants had substantially *higher* recidivism risks than non–drug court participants. What might account for this unanticipated finding? The authors explain:

Contrary to this structural image of drug court as following the principles of reintegrative shaming, our field observations gave the clear impression that drug court was far more stigmatizing than reintegrative in its orientation toward offenders. This was indicated by a common hostile attitude toward some defendants who had failed to comply with court practices, a degradation of these offenders in a public arena, and only a rather token recognition of the defendants' efforts to successfully complete the program. (ibid.:536)

Miethe et al. (ibid.:537) observed that whereas the district courts of Las Vegas provided criminal defendants with an assembly-line type of treatment characterized as routinized, impersonal, and anonymous, it was also much less intrusive and paternalistic. The drug court judge, on the other hand, in taking a "personal," "hands-on" interest in his "clients" and their "well-being," felt emboldened to scold and berate them, much like a father to a child. In effect, the personal, intimate approach of the drug court may actually be exacerbating rather than reducing stigmatizing shaming, thereby unwittingly promoting secondary deviance among drug court defendants.

COMBINING COERCION AND COMPASSION

Presumably the drug court program works because it brings to bear the full weight of all interveners—judges, probation officers, correctional and law enforcement personnel, prosecutors, defense counsel, treatment specialists and other social service providers, and even family and friends—thereby forcing the offender to deal with his or her substance abuse problem or suffer consequences (Maxwell 2000). The problem with this position, however, is that coercion into therapy or treatment violates one of the sacred tenets of the therapeutic alliance, namely, that persons must enter into treatment voluntarily. Persons who acknowledge of their own free will that they have a "problem" with drugs or alcohol are the best candidates for this kind of treatment (Kress 1999:557; Maxwell 2000; Winick 1994). No matter how much proponents claim otherwise, however, the criminal justice system simply cannot combine coercion and compassion in this way in its dealings with reticent clients or defendants.

This is not to say, however, that attempts to combine coercion and compassion have never occurred. Nisbet notes that humanitarianism, which arose in the early nineteenth century, can be defined as the "gradual widening and institutionalization of compassion" (1966:8). Modern democratic constitutional states have concomitantly developed the notion of *parens patriae*, or the "state as parent" (Kittrie 1971). Initially, the humanitarian impulse of the constitutional state appeared in the form of caring for and tending to members of society who could not care for themselves, namely, prisoners and the mentally ill. Somewhat later, children were brought under the umbrella of the compassionate state as well, giving rise to the juvenile justice system. The problem with the drug courts' application of *parens patriae* is that, with the continuing expansion of categories of "mental illness" (see Chriss 1999b), more and more persons are being dealt with formally (coerced as they are into treatment under the threat of more severe sanctions), but without the constitutional protections afforded to defendants appearing before traditional criminal courts. This problem of "net widening" and the circumventing of due process for the defendant's "own good" are but two of the more serious problems associated with the drug courts' attempt to combine coercion and compassion.

Another problem with the drug court's acceptance of the medical model of disease is simply the fact that, as Erving Goffman (1959) has shown, persons are adept at self-presentation and impression management. This is especially the case under harsh conditions where a self is under siege and placed within the context of a total institution such as the drug court. Once admitted to the total institution, persons easily come to understand the prevailing protocols and definitions of "sickness" and "recovery" employed by members of the treatment team. Clients learn to fashion responses to inquiries from the treatment team that comport with their expectations of progress toward recovery. Contrary to popular belief, the clinical tools used by treatment professionals to ascertain whether a client has "recovered" and is ready to be released back to the community are simply not that reliable (see Breggin 2000; Stravynski and O'Connor 1995; Watters and Ofshe 1999). Rosenhan's (1973) famous study clearly illustrated that clinical staff cannot readily distinguish "sanity" from "insanity." As mentioned above, this is important insofar as a growing number of deviant, criminal, or simply "odd" behaviors are being redefined as DSM category mental illnesses, including of course drug and/or alcohol use or abuse.

There is also a need to examine more closely the history of policy discussion regarding the use of psychiatric (i.e., medical) or psychological expertise and personnel in the criminal court. The most important thing to note is that although the drug treatment court is a relatively recent innovation, talk of replacing judges with psychiatrists or the judicial system with "treatment tribunals" has been around since the establishment of psychiatry in the late 1800s. More than thirty years ago, for example, psychiatrist Karl Menninger published a book, *The Crime of Punishment,* in which he argued that in light of the "certainties" or "truths" that psychiatry has discovered about human behavior, there simply is no need to invest more time, effort, or resources in the current criminal justice system. The idea is to replace criminal justice, an antiquated and outdated system of social control, with the more "scientific" system of social control represented by psychiatry. Menninger (1968:139) cites approvingly a recommendation made by Sheldon Glueck, who suggested that criminal court procedure should be guided by a professional treatment tribunal composed, say, of a psychiatrist, a psychologist, a sociologist or cultural anthropologist, an educator, and a judge with long experience in criminal trials and with special interest in the protection of the rights of those charged with crime (1936).

Although Glueck includes members from other professions such as so-ciology, anthropology, education, and the judiciary in the proposed treat-ment team, it is clear that Glueck expects these other members to readily acquiesce or consent to the prevailing medically based expertise of psy-chiatrists. Ideas about normality, deviance, and its control deriving largely from Freudian psychoanalysis were prevalent among intellectuals from the 1920s and the rise of the "mental hygiene" movement through the 1950s in the United States (see Clausen 1966; McLaughlin 1998; Wrong 1994:110–15), so it is not surprising that Glueck, writing in the 1930s, would expect this. Menninger and other proponents of psychotherapeutic prac-tice and theory are implying that medically based knowledge is superior to, and has greater utility than, legal procedures as currently conceptual-ized and implemented for dealing with all kinds of defendants, especially those who can be shown to be suffering from some form of "mental illness" such as drug or alcohol addiction.

Jeffrie Murphy has provided an important critique of Menninger's po-sition, which deserves to be revisited anew, for although written more than twenty years ago, it is nevertheless directly relevant and applicable to the similar position being taken by proponents of the drug treatment court to-day. Like Gouldner's program of critique, Murphy set about to crack open the tacit or unstated assumptions underlying the policy recommendations of Menninger and others advocating the ascendancy of the vision of treat-ment professionals over that of judges and traditional criminal law. The main difficulty of the drug treatment court position is that its proponents are confusing two types of considerations relevant to moral evaluation that often come into conflict with one another: *utility* and *justice*.

In law and social policy, utilitarianism refers to programs, policies, or orientations that promote the greatest amount of happiness and well-being for the greatest number of people. Proponents of the drug court promote utilitarian values when they suggest that making people sober will in-crease the well-being of society (by reducing accidents, increasing pro-ductivity, decreasing depression, and other negative health consequences of drug use), or that drug treatment administered and overseen by health specialists produces better results (i.e., lower rates of recidivism) than do traditional forms of criminal sanction.[8] On the other hand, considerations of justice act to check social utility, because the unbridled promotion of happiness and well-being of all means that some will be treated unfairly or suffer as a result of others' pursuit of happiness. In order to ensure that persons are treated fairly, due process becomes one of the abiding value el-ements of justice.

The underlying assumption of the medical model of disease adhered to by members of the psy complex and the drug courts leads to an embrace of "public safety" as the predominant political value. Further, this utilitarian value of public safety (or health) actually overrides due process, which as we have seen is one of the mainstays of criminal justice. Menninger (1968:53) and others who champion psychotherapeutic intervention and the expertise of members of the psy complex over the legal expertise of judges, especially with regard to the latter's role in assuring that due process is extended to AOD-related defendants who come before the criminal court, believe that due process protection for such defendants actually interferes with the efficiency of securing public safety.

As Murphy (1979:151) explains, this tension between the justice value of due process, on the one hand, and the utilitarian value of public safety on the other, reflects a long-standing and persistent contradiction built into our criminal justice system. This is a contradiction between two models or perspectives of criminal justice, namely, the *crime control model* and the *due process model* (Packer 1968). The crime control model represents the standard view of the function of the criminal justice system, which is to do something about crime. Under the Constitution, states are empowered to designate agents (police, courts, and corrections) with powers of coercion for the ultimate purpose of enforcing criminal laws and punishing those who are found guilty of violating such laws. The due process model, however, reflects the constitutional decree that suspects arrested and being tried in the criminal court must be dealt with fairly. A range of guaranteed due process rights is afforded defendants through every stage of their processing through the criminal justice system.

The philosophy of the drug courts is the same philosophy underlying civil commitment and the notion of *parens patriae,* namely, that the state has the obligation to divert certain defendants who pose a threat to themselves or others into treatment, in the process circumventing due process. For example, defendants who come before the drug court may be "fast-tracked" into drug treatment rather than be allowed the usual range of presentence hearings routinely extended to criminal defendants.[9] Defendants are generally provided a choice, of course: they may choose to "voluntarily" waive their right to due process provisions and enter treatment on the fast-track "for their own good," or they may opt for the standard due process provisions and pay the consequences in the form of imprisonment or other appropriate criminal sanctions. Rather than being provided a real choice, however, drug defendants accepting the conditions of the drug court can best be described as victims of "coerced voluntarism" (Peyrot 1985) rather than as recipients of the good graces and compassion of the drug court.

Quinn (2000–01) has pointed out yet another problem with fast-tracking drug court defendants into treatment. Most often when a waiver of rights occurs in a criminal court—for example, in the plea-bargaining context (see Hora et al. 1999)—the defendant and his or her defense attorney are relatively certain of what they are getting in return for a guilty plea.

However, because the drug court experiment is still relatively new, and because of variations in procedures from drug court to drug court, defense attorneys in drug courts may not be able to supply their clients with the same definitive answers they would generally be able to supply to clients who are considering such offers of waiver in a traditional criminal court. Drug court judges and proponents of therapeutic jurisprudence expect defense attorneys to take on faith the notion that the waiver of defendants' rights for purposes of fast-tracking them into treatment is indeed for their clients' "own good." However, "without knowing with certainty all that a treatment modality and regime of sanctioning entails, the attorney may not be able to assist meaningfully a drug court client considering a guilty plea" (Quinn 2000–01:55).

Indeed, in an ironic twist, involuntarily committing or diverting into treatment defendants who come before drug courts does not reflect a new level of compassion whereby the scientific insights of the psy complex replace the archaic, crude, and inhumane methods of punishment of the criminal court. That is to say, by doing away with due process, or rather, by elevating the values of social utility over the values of justice, the drug courts are actually much closer in spirit to the crime control model of criminal justice than to the due process model.

The problem with this, of course, is that if the primary aim of a policy or intervention is crime control—which I have argued is the case in the drug court's tacit opting for the utilitarian value of public safety over the justice value of due process—then those who are best equipped to implement these policies and oversee the handling of cases before the court are criminal justice experts, that is, judges or other members of the judiciary. That is to say, the vision of treatment professionals and others whose purported altruistic aims are to help defendants who presumably cannot help themselves should not guide or inform the work of the judiciary. Members of the psy complex are concerned not with justice, but rather with assuring that the world is safe and that harm resulting from the actions of individuals who are deemed "sick" is reduced or eliminated. Justice professionals, however, must resist this purported moral and altruistic vision of the helping professions, for it is inimical to the business of assuring that criminal defendants are dealt with fairly, that is, that justice is served.

CONCLUSION

The program of critique aims not only to analyze the tacit assumptions underlying any theory or public project, but also to offer policy initiatives that are closer in spirit to the self-reflexive and liberative program of inquiry Gouldner (1970) envisioned for both sociology and society. Here, then, are several policy recommendations regarding the operation of the drug court specifically and the criminal justice system in general.

First, although proponents of the drug court acknowledge the deficiencies of current drug policy, they do not go far enough in their critique of the criminal justice system. This is understandable given that members of the judiciary, as agents of the criminal justice system, must seek to uphold the current laws and statutes of their jurisdictions. This points to the conservative nature of agents of the system (whether police, lawyers, judges, or corrections officials), because even while they may seek change in the system, their primary responsibility of course is to maintain and defend the status quo.

Judges who buy into the pronouncements of representatives of the psy complex on such issues as the purported large and growing numbers of defendants who are suffering mental illness or in need of AOD treatment are not seeing the whole picture, that is, they are not critically examining whose interests are being served. We must look at the situation in this way: President Reagan's "war on drugs" was a policy that of course ended up sending an unprecedented number of Americans to prison for AOD-related crimes. Eldredge reports (1998:112), for example, that today over half of all arrests are drug-related, and that "the number imprisoned for drug offenses is increasing thirteen times faster than adult drug arrests" (see also Cole et al. 1993; Schlosser 1997; Wells and Triplett 1992; Zawitz 1992). With the continuing expansion of influence of the medical discourse of disease in American culture and social institutions (see Chriss 1999b, 1999c), alcohol and drug use or abuse have now been incorporated into the vast pantheon of DSM mental illnesses, and as a consequence judges are feeling pressure on two fronts: to deal with the "criminal justice" problems of trying and sentencing defendants who come before their courts for violating stricter and stricter antidrug laws; and to placate medical and mental health experts who, in effect, want a piece of the windfall that has been produced as a result of these new tough antidrug laws.

I agree in spirit with critics of the war on drugs who argue that criminalization of drug use has not worked. But where the drug courts and drug treatment professionals seek to replace criminalization with medicalization of AOD defendants, I suggest that medicalization will not alleviate the problems associated with "illicit" drug use, and in fact, could even make the situation worse. In other words, it is not enough simply to critique the legacy of Reagan's war on drugs and replace "criminalization" with "medicalization" of drug users (because of all the problems of the latter approach discussed above).[10] Short of *decriminalizing* certain drugs (marijuana in particular), we must attempt, at the very least, to reinstate the lower enforcement levels and the less harsh sentences for drug use of the pre-Reagan era (see Berridge 1996).

Certainly there are illicit drugs that are truly addictive and that warrant medical intervention, such as detoxification to manage withdrawal or methadone treatment for heroine addiction (Anglin and Hser 1991). But in keeping with the medical model of disease, "addiction" has become a cottage industry and is being illegitimately applied to a growing list of drugs—both legal and illegal—as well as such social and recreational activities as gambling, love and friendship, eating, working, the internet, and sports to name a few (Peele 1995). The attempt to bring marijuana under the umbrella of addictive substances is dubious, however, as there is no clear evidence that marijuana acts as a "gateway" to the use of harder, more dangerous, and legitimately addictive drugs, nor that heavy users of marijuana who cease use at higher levels suffer from withdrawal, a classic symptom of addiction. This is important because when we speak of drug and drug-related arrests, the population with which we are dealing is overwhelmingly marijuana users. According to the U.S. Department of Health's 1996 report on household drug abuse, an estimated 12.8 million Americans were current illicit drug users and 77 percent of these (9.8 million) were marijuana users (Gray 2000:174 note 7, 235–36). This leaves only a relatively small percentage of Americans who are using or abusing powdered or crack cocaine, heroine, or other illicit narcotics, barbiturates, or hallucinogens.[11] It is this latter group of users over which proponents of criminalization or medicalization of drugs can perhaps legitimately fight. Regardless, decriminalization of marijuana, the linchpin of the war on drugs crusade, would make moot the issue of whether medicalization or criminalization of the drug is more appropriate. It would also make moot the need to create a bridge—the drug court—between criminal justice and mental health services (Wenzel, Longshore, Turner, and Ridgely 2001).

Second, along with repealing or restricting current marijuana laws, the whole concept of the drug court itself will need to be rethought. The most serious threat that the drug court, as currently conceived, poses to American society is its uncritical expansion and extension of the *parens patriae* doctrine to a growing number of American adults. If indeed therapeutic jurisprudence is the theory lying behind the practice and operation of the drug treatment court, as Hora et al. (1999) suggest, then it would be instructive to look at the implications of therapeutic jurisprudence for the *parens patriae* doctrine, and specifically, for the problem of paternalism.

Therapeutic jurisprudence (TJ) is a movement or perspective within law and legal studies that is concerned with using social science research to study the extent to which a legal rule or practice promotes the psychological or physical well-being of participants in the criminal justice system, whether as defendants, plaintiffs (in civil or tort litigation), attorneys, judges, jurors, witnesses, or even family and friends of participants (Slobogin 1996:767). In essence, the aim of therapeutic jurisprudence is to understand how law itself may act either therapeutically or antitherapeutically with respect to individuals, and attempt to maximize the psychological well-being of individuals impacted by the law.

Let us look at an example of therapeutic jurisprudence in action. Bruce Winick (1994), a prominent proponent of therapeutic jurisprudence, has argued that a mentally ill person's opting to refuse mental health treatment actually supports the therapeutic value of choice. That is, persons who have a say in their treatment options are more likely to accomplish treatment goals. From this perspective, laws that support mandatory commitment (civil or otherwise) of the mentally ill would be seen as antitherapeutic insofar as they "infantilize" the person and seem to deny the basic human need of self-determination (ibid.:108–9).

However, one must also consider the possibility that "option" itself is not necessarily an unmitigated psychological good, because empowering some defendants to make choices with regard to their hospitalization or treatment may cause anxiety and even be debilitating to them (Slobogin 1996:773). This then leads to the suggestion that a particular law could very well have therapeutic consequences for some persons and antitherapeutic consequences for others. What to do then?

Since therapeutic jurisprudence seeks to promote therapeutic and reduce antitherapeutic outcomes of law, the logical response to this dilemma is to attempt to individualize the law. As Slobogin explains, "More specific to an assessment of TJ, abandoning 'the rule of law' may well work to the ultimate detriment of those affected, because it places so much authority in the hands of practitioners" (ibid.:782). In other words, the therapeutic jurisprudence approach must reject the traditional rule of law, including such notions as the universality of law and "equal treatment under the law," and opt instead for an individualized treatment model where rules will be applied or waived depending on their predicted outcomes on defendants. This means handing over important decision-making powers to treatment tribunals that presumably possess the expertise to assess the likely impact of a law on a particular defendant so as to ensure or maximize therapeutic outcomes.

This returns us once again to the idea that psy complex practitioners should replace judges—or at the very least, that judges should be thoroughly imbued with the psychotherapeutic ethos—when it comes to dealing with AOD-related defendants. Although David Wexler states that "therapeutic jurisprudence in no way supports paternalism, coercion, or a therapeutic state" (Wexler 1996, cited in Slobogin 1996:784), the exact opposite is more likely to be the case. By suggesting that AOD-related defendants are "addicted" or suffer from the "mental illness" of drug use or abuse, therapeutic jurisprudence and the drug court attempt to make the case that a whole new group of citizens—most of whom are nonviolent marijuana or alcohol users—are "sick" or "ill" and cannot fend for themselves. Instead of applying the rule of law to these defendants, they must instead be "treated" by a team of treatment professionals that, through individualized assessment and diagnosis, attempts to achieve sobriety and instill prosocial adjustment in these individuals. This is, as I argued earlier, a powerful and far-reaching invocation of the doctrine of *parens patriae*, with all the paternalism that attends to it. As Slobogin (ibid.) states,

> The empiricism of TJ and its alluring call for therapeutic results may combine to create a tendency to support proposals that, although not necessarily "bad" in an ultimate sense, are thoroughly paternalistic.[12]

A third and final policy recommendation derives from the above discussion. We see clearly now, contrary to Wexler's pronouncement, that the therapeutic values of utility, public safety, and prosocial adjustment "trump" the justice value of due process, thereby undermining the aims and operation of the criminal justice system. To rectify this situation, judges should seek to limit the influence of psy complex practitioners in their courtrooms so that they may once again oversee the important work of assuring justice and due process for AOD-related defendants. This task would be made much easier, of course, if and when a reasonable set of drug enforcement laws is put into place.

NOTES

1. In Appendix C of the *National Drug Control Strategy* a list is provided of the public interest groups that were consulted or otherwise helped shape the language or ideas contained in the document (Office of National Drug Control Policy, p. 195). It is no surprise that a number of these are drug, alcohol treatment, or therapeutic organizations, and it is of course drug companies and drug treatment facilitators or agencies that stand to benefit most from the establishment and expansion of drug courts. Some of the groups listed are American Institute on Drug Prevention, Broward County Commission on Substance Abuse, California Association of Alcoholic Recovery Homes, Community Anti-Drug Coalitions of America (CADCA), D.A.R.E. America, Elks Drug Awareness Program, Family and Medical Counseling Services, Inc., National Asian Pacific American Families Against Substance Abuse, Inc., National Association of Alcoholism & Drug Abuse Counselors (NAADAC), National Association of State Alcohol and Drug Abuse Directors, Inc., National Council on Alcoholism & Drug Dependence, Inc. (NCAAD), Operation PAR, Inc., Prevention, Intervention & Treatment Coalition for Health (PITCH), UCLA Drug Abuse Research Center, and Wholistic Stress Control Institute.

2. The war on drugs has disproportionately affected black males. For example, 41.5 percent of all drug arrests involve African-Americans, which has contributed to an alarmingly high black incarceration rate (Eldredge 1998:124). In their study of the relationship between the criminal justice and mental health systems, Liska, Markowitz, Whaley, and Bellair (1999) found that as the percentage of blacks in a city/county increases, jail capacity in that population increases as well. Further, as jail capacity increases, admissions to public mental hospitals increase. Indeed, as Wagenaar (1989) has argued, urban mental hospitals are fast becoming jails for poor and minorities charged or convicted of drug and other nonserious offenses.

3. For a thorough summary of the rise and evolution of the contemporary American drug court, see Nolan (2001).

4. This information is contained in a briefing report to the Committee on the Judiciary, U.S. Senate, and the Committee on the Judiciary, House of Representatives, May 1995. The Senate committee was presided over by Orrin G. Hatch, Chairman, and Joseph R. Biden, Jr., Ranking Minority Member. The House Committee was presided over by Henry J. Hyde, Chairman, and John Conyers, Jr., Ranking Minority Member. This text was found in the Schaffer Library of Drug Policy, located at www.druglibrary.org/ schaffer/govpubs/gao/gao75.htm.

5. This passage was found in a publication entitled *Defining Drug Courts: The Key Components*, published January 1997 by the National Association of Drug Court Professionals and the Drug Court Standards Committee. (The document contains no page numbers.)

6. Here, the assumption is that certain criminal behaviors should be redefined as illnesses, and instead of these mentally impaired defendants having punishment meted out, they ought to receive treatment [see Hoffman (2000:1469–73) for a scathing critique of the disease model of addiction]. However, an even more radical perspective suggests that *all* forms of crime fall under the category of psychopathology insofar as crimes can be considered not "normal" whether in a statistical, moral, or legal sense. The psychopathology of crime perspective (see Raine 1993) would indeed require the most extreme form of *parens patriae,* where treatment tribunals would replace judges and criminal courts, much to the delight of advocates such as Karl Menninger, whose ideas we will consider shortly.

7. The transcript of this program was retrieved via a Lexis-Nexis keyword search of "drug courts." The program aired Friday morning, July 9, 1999, with the headline "King County Drug Court Program Working With Those Addicts Who Would Rather Have Treatment Than Serve Jail Time." The Lexis-Nexis Academic Universe website address is http://web.lexis-nexis.com/universe.

8. The drug treatment court can be placed within the broader "public health" approach or model for dealing with illicit drugs. As Weisheit and Klofas argue, in contrast to criminal justice, the public health approach "is far more utilitarian, relying more on empirical judgments about harm than on moral judgments about offensiveness" (1998:199). With its focus on harm, the public health approach emphasizes prevention, which assumes it pos-

sesses a proactive set of practices or knowledge base that presumably trumps the mere "reactive" mechanisms of traditional criminal justice. Indeed, *proactivity* stands as one of the most fundamental rhetorical ploys or features of public health theory, research, and policy, whether as applied to drugs, education, violence, or a host of other concerns.

9. As Hora et al. note, "In the preadjudication [drug treatment court] context, the court may direct that a defendant waive the right to a speedy trial, but only so the individual can participate in treatment" (1999:521).

10. Fishbein (1991) favors the medicalization of the drug war because of research she cites that indicates that certain psychological traits, specifically antisocial personality, psychopathy, impulsivity, and affective and conduct disorders are more prevalent among substance abusers than in non–drug abusing populations. Fishbein goes on to suggest that there is a "strong" likelihood that these traits may *antedate* drug use and place the individual at risk for later drug use (ibid.:329). With the "discovery" of such antecedent factors, public health proponents such as Fishbein proclaim that members of the psy complex are better prepared to deal with AOD defendants than are criminal justice system personnel. The only problem with Fishbein's argument is that it is merely wishful thinking: positing that certain factors "may" antedate drug use and abuse does not mean that they actually do; indeed, it is the drug use that may just as plausibly be producing the manifested psychological traits. The lesson to be learned here is: *correlation is not causation*.

11. Somewhat different data on the numbers and types of drug users have been reported. Vago (2000:232), for example, reports that there are an estimated 20 million Americans who are regular users of marijuana, 5 to 10 million cocaine abusers, and an estimated 200,000 to 900,000 heroin addicts (see also Abadinsky 1997; Goode 1998; Walker 1993). Using the median figures of 7.5 million for cocaine users and 550,000 for heroine addicts, this suggests that 71.3 percent of Americans using or abusing drugs are marijuana users, reasonably close to the 77 percent figure cited above.

12. Obviously I have found Christopher Slobogin's discussion of the "dilemmas" of therapeutic jurisprudence helpful in informing my own views on the drug court and therapeutic jurisprudence. Slobogin, although critical of certain aspects of therapeutic jurisprudence, is actually sympathetic in spirit to its aims. Interestingly, however, Slobogin makes the following assessment of therapeutic jurisprudence near the paper's end: "These suggestions, or others like them, are needed to goad therapeutic jurisprudence into a critical self-consciousness" (1996:792). Here Slobogin's position dovetails sharply with Gouldner's program of critique and self-reflexivity, a program that I of course have attempted to follow throughout this chapter.

REFERENCES

Abadinsky, Howard. 1997. *Drug Abuse: An Introduction*, 3rd ed. Chicago: Nelson-Hall.

Alexander, Jeffrey C. 1982. Theoretical Logic in Sociology. Volume 1, Positivism, Presuppositions, and Current Controversies. Berkeley: University of California Press.

Anglin, M. Douglas and Yih-Ing Hser. 1991. "Criminal Justice and the Drug-Abusing Offender: Policy Issues of Coerced Treatment." *Behavioral Sciences and the Law* 9:243–67.

Berridge, Virginia. 1996. "Drug Policy: Should the Law Take a Back Seat?" *Lancet* (Feb. 3):301–5.

Braithwaite, John. 1989. *Crime, Shame and Reintegration.* Cambridge: Cambridge University Press.

Breggin, Peter R. 2000. Reclaiming Our Children: A Healing Plan for a Nation in Crisis. Cambridge, MA: Perseus.

California Department of Alcohol and Drug Programs. 1994. Evaluating Recovery Services: The California Drug and Alcohol Treatment Assessment (CALDATA) General Report. Sacramento, CA: Author.

Chriss, James J. 1999a. Alvin W. Gouldner: Sociologist and Outlaw Marxist. London: Ashgate.

Chriss, James J. 1999b. "Introduction." Pp. 1–29 in *Counseling and the Therapeutic State*, edited by J. J. Chriss. Hawthorne, NY: Aldine de Gruyter.

Chriss, James J. "The Family under Siege." Pp. 187–98 in *Counseling and the Therapeutic State*, edited by J. J. Chriss. Hawthorne, NY: Aldine de Gruyter.

Clausen, John A. 1966. "Mental Disorders." Pp. 26–83 in *Contemporary Social Problems*, 2nd ed., edited by R. K. Merton and R. A. Nisbet. New York: Harcourt, Brace & World.

Cohen, Eric. 1999. "The Drug Court Revolution." *Weekly Standard,* 27 December, p. 20.

Cole, Charles G., et al. 1993. *The State of Criminal Justice.* Washington, DC: American Bar Association.

Danziger, Gloria and Jeffrey A. Kuhn. 1999. "Drug Treatment Courts: Evolution, Evaluation, and Future Directions." *Journal of Health Care Law and Policy* 3(1): 166–90.

Eldredge, Dirk Chase. 1998. *Ending the War on Drugs: A Solution for America.* Bridgehampton, NY: Bridge Works.

Fishbein, Diana H. 1991. "Medicalizing the Drug War." *Behavioral Sciences and the Law* 9:323–44.

General Accounting Office. 1997. *Drug Courts: An Overview of Growth, Characteristics, and Results.* Washington, DC: Office of Justice Programs, U.S. Department of Justice.

Glueck, Sheldon. 1936. *Crime and Justice.* Boston: Little, Brown.

Goffman, Erving. 1959. *The Presentation of Self in Everyday Life.* Garden City, NY: Doubleday/Anchor.

Goldkamp, John S., Michael D. White, and Jennifer B. Robinson. 2001. "Do Drug Courts Work? Getting Inside the Drug Court Black Box." *Journal of Drug Issues* 31(1):27–72.

Goode, Erich. 1998. *Drugs in American Society,* 5th ed. Boston: McGraw-Hill College.

Gouldner, Alvin W. 1965. Enter Plato: Classical Greece and the Origins of Social Theory. New York: Basic Books.

Gouldner, Alvin W. 1970. *The Coming Crisis of Western Sociology.* New York: Avon.
Gouldner, Alvin W. 1974. "Marxism and Social Theory." *Theory and Society* 1(1):17–35.
Gouldner, Alvin W. "The Dark Side of the Dialectic: Toward a New Objectivity." *Sociological Inquiry* 46(1):3–15.
Gouldner, Alvin W. *The Two Marxisms.* New York: Oxford University Press.
Gray, Mike. 2000. *Drug Crazy.* New York: Routledge.
Hoffman, Morris B. 2000. "The Drug Court Scandal." *North Carolina Law Review* 78:1437–1534.
Hora, Peggy F., William G. Schma, and John T. A. Rosenthal. 1999. "Therapeutic Jurisprudence and the Drug Treatment Court Movement: Revolutionizing the Criminal Justice System's Response to Drug Abuse and Crime in America." *Notre Dame Law Review* 74(2):439–537.
Ingleby, D. 1985. "Professionals as Socializers: 'The Psy Complex.'" In *Research in Law, Deviance and Social Control,* edited by A. Scull and S. Spritzer. Greenwich, CT: JAI.
Kassebaum, Gene and Duane K. Okamoto. 2001. "The Drug Court as a Sentencing Model." *Journal of Contemporary Criminal Justice* 17(2):89–104.
Kittrie, Nicholas N. 1971. The Right to Be Different: Deviance and Enforced Therapy. Baltimore: Penguin.
Kress, Ken. 1999. "Therapeutic Jurisprudence and the Resolution of Value Conflicts: What We Can Realistically Expect, in Practice, from Theory." *Behavioral Sciences and the Law* 17:555–88.
Liska, Allen E., Fred E. Markowitz, Rachel Bridges Whaley, and Paul Bellair. 1999. "Modeling the Relationship between the Criminal Justice and Mental Health Systems." *American Journal of Sociology* 104(6):1744–75.
Livingston, Jay. 1996. *Crime and Criminology,* 2nd ed. Upper Saddle River, NJ: Prentice Hall.
"Looking at a Decade of Drug Courts." 1998. Prepared by the Drug Court Clearinghouse and Technical Assistance Project. A Program of the Drug Courts Program Office, Office of Justice Programs, U.S. Department of Justice. Website address: www.ojp.usdoj.gov/dcpo/decade98.htm.
Maxwell, Sheila Royo. 2000. "Sanction Threats in Court-Ordered Programs: Examining Their Effects on Offenders Mandated Into Drug Treatment." *Crime and Delinquency* 46(4):542–63.
McLaughlin, Neil G. 1998. "Why Do Schools of Thought Fail? Neo-Freudianism as a Case Study in the Sociology of Knowledge." *Journal of the History of the Behavioral Sciences* 34(2):113–34.
Menninger, Karl. 1968. *The Crime of Punishment.* New York: Viking.
Miethe, Terance D., Hong Lu, and Erin Reese. 2000. "Reintegrative Shaming and Recidivism Risks in Drug Court: Explanations for Some Unexpected Findings." *Crime and Delinquency* 46(4):522–41.
Murphy, Jeffrie G. 1979. *Retribution, Justice, and Therapy.* Dordrecht: Reidel.
National Drug Control Strategy: Strengthening Communities' Response to Drugs and Crime. Office of National Drug Control Policy, Washington, D.C. 1995.
Nisbet, Robert A. 1966. "Introduction: The Study of Social Problems." Pp. 1–24 in

Contemporary Social Problems, 2nd ed., edited by R. K. Merton and R. A. Nisbet. New York: Harcourt, Brace & World.

Nolan, James L., Jr. 1998. *The Therapeutic State: Justifying Government at Century's End*. New York: New York University Press.

Nolan, James L., Jr. 1999. "Acquiescence or Consensus?: Consenting to Therapeutic Pedagogy." Pp. 107–29 in *Counseling and the Therapeutic State*, edited by J. J. Chriss. Hawthorne, NY: Aldine de Gruyter.

Nolan, James L., Jr. 2001. *Reinventing Justice: The American Drug Court Movement*. Princeton, NJ: Princeton University Press.

Packer, Herbert. 1968. *The Limits of the Criminal Sanction*. Stanford, CA: Stanford University Press.

Peele, Stanton. 1995. Diseasing of America: How We Allowed Recovery Zealots and the Treatment Industry to Convince Us We Are Out of Control. New York: Lexington.

Peters, Roger H. and Mary R. Murrin. 2000. "Effectiveness of Treatment-Based Drug Courts in Reducing Criminal Recidivism." *Criminal Justice and Behavior* 27(1):72–96.

Peyrot, Mark. 1985. "Coerced Voluntarism: The Micropolitics of Drug Treatment." *Urban Life* 13(4):343–65.

Quinn, Mae C. 2000–01. "Whose Team Am I on Anyway? Musings of a Public Defender About Drug Treatment Court Practice." *New York University Review of Law and Social Change* 26(1–2):37–75.

Raine, Adrian. 1993. The Psychopathology of Crime: Criminal Behavior as a Clinical Disorder. San Diego, CT: Academic Press.

Reno, Janet. 1999. "Comments before the Convention of the ABA, Atlanta, Georgia, August 10." Reported by Lori T. Donovan, Certified Court Reporter and Notary Public. American Bar Association.

Rosenhan, D. L. 1973. "On Being Sane In Insane Places." *Science* 179:250–57.

Schlosser, Eric. 1997. "More Reefer Madness." *Atlantic Monthly* (April):90–102.

Skolnick, Jerome H. 1995. "1994 Presidential Address: What Not to Do About Crime." *Criminology* 33 (1):1–15.

Slobogin, Christopher. 1996. "Therapeutic Jurisprudence: Five Dilemmas to Ponder." Pp. 763–93 in *Law in a Therapeutic Key*, edited by D. B. Wexler and B. J. Winick. Durham, NC: Carolina Academic Press.

Stravynski, Ariel and Kieron O'Connor. 1995. "Understanding and Managing Abnormal Behavior: The Need for a New Clinical Science." *Journal of Psychology* 129(6):605–20.

Wagenaar, Hendrik. 1989. "Ironies of Inclusion: Social Class and Deinstitutionalization." *Journal of Health Politics, Policy and Law* 14:503–22.

Walker, Samuel. 1993. "Reform the Law: Decriminalization." Pp. 569–79 in *Deviant Behavior: A Text Reader in the Sociology of Deviance*, edited by D. H. Kelly. New York: St. Martin's.

Watters, Ethan and Richard Ofshe. 1999. Therapy's Delusion: The Myth of the Unconscious and the Exploitation of Today's Walking Worried. New York: Scribner.

Weisheit, Ralph A. and John M. Klofas. 1998. "The Public Health Approach to Illicit Drugs." *Criminal Justice Review* 23(2):197–207.

Wells, Tim and William Triplett. 1992. *Drug Wars: An Oral History from the Trenches.* New York: Morrow.

Wenzel, Suzanne L., Douglas Longshore, Susan Turner, and M. Susan Ridgely. 2001. "Drug Courts: A Bridge between Criminal Justice and Health Services." *Journal of Criminal Justice* 29:241–53.

Wexler, David B. 1996. "Applying the Law Therapeutically." Pp. 831–42 in *Law in a Therapeutic Key,* edited by D. B. Wexler and B. J. Winick. Durham, NC: Carolina Academic Press.

White, Susan. 1998. "Interdiscursivity and Child Welfare: The Ascent and Durability of Psycho-legalism." *Sociological Review* 46(2):264–92.

Winick, Bruce J. 1994. "The Right to Refuse Medical Treatment: A Therapeutic Jurisprudence Analysis." *International Journal of Law and Psychiatry* 17:99–117.

Wrong, Dennis H. 1994. The Problem of Order: What Unites and Divides Society. New York: Free Press.

Zawitz, Marianne W. (ed.). 1992. *Drugs, Crime, and the Justice System.* Washington, DC: U.S. Department of Justice.

10

Drug Control and the Ascendancy of Britain's Therapeutic Culture

Frank Furedi

Since 1998, support for drug courts and related programs has steadily grown in Britain. Leading figures involved in devising antidrugs policies appear to have become converted to the idea that special courts oriented toward treating offenders is an effective alternative to existing methods of law enforcement. Keith Hellawell, the Government's antidrugs coordinator has been an enthusiastic advocate of drug courts. He believes that it is "excellent that magistrates are getting together to discuss the important issue of how to deal with drug offenders and look for solutions to help break the cycle of drugs and crime." Jack Straw, the former secretary of state responsible for law enforcement, was also impressed by drug courts and predicted in September 1999 that the Home Office was likely to extend the pilot schemes established a year previously in the two West Yorkshire towns of Pontefract and Wakefield (Syal and Bamber 1999).

Participants at a "drug summit" held at Downing Street in February 2000, were enthusiastic about the drug court experiment. Prime Minister Tony Blair reportedly expressed considerable interest in the pilot schemes established in West Yorkshire (Hibbs 2000). This discussion was motivated by the belief that fresh ideas are needed to tackle Britain's formidable drug problem. It was argued that drug courts, often presented as an American success story, were one possible answer to this search for ideas. Supporters of the drug court movement received a further boost to their cause when Tony Blair indicated in March 2001 that he wanted to introduce a network of drug courts throughout England and Wales. After this announcement it was widely expected that the Home Office would actively promote the establishment of new drug courts (Mitchell 2001).

From the outset, Home Office officials appeared to believe that drug courts would prove to be an effective alternative to more traditional methods of handling drug offenders. This experiment has been strongly endorsed by the recently devolved government in Scotland. After a U.S. fact-finding mission in April 2000, Deputy Justice Minister Angus MacKay stated that U.S.-type drug courts could be introduced into Scotland. A United Nations report promoting this initiative was discussed and debated at a conference on drugs courts at a Scottish police forces' college in Tulliallan, Fife. "Drug courts are an excellent example of best practice that does work," argued Andrew Wells, a senior adviser to the United Nations group that produced the report. Ten months later, McKay's successor, Iain Gray, announced that Glasgow would be the location for Scotland's first drug court (BBC 2001).

Increased interest in the American experience with drug courts by the British law enforcement community is in part a response to the widely held perception that the methods available for dealing with the drug problem are less than effective. The Home Office takes the view that traditional forms of punishment have failed and is therefore looking for a new approach. The consensus around traditional punishment has broken down. Lack of certainty about how to tackle the drug problem is most clearly exposed in the erosion of a consensus about how drug offenders ought to be viewed and treated. In the past, Conservative party politicians often called for tougher sentencing and decried attempts to wean offenders off drugs through treatment. Today, the Conservative party is divided on the issue and some of its prominent figures have even called for the decriminalization of cannabis. It has been suggested that the approach of American drug courts is strongly compatible with the "classic Blairite balancing of opportunities and responsibilities" and explains the appeal of this approach to New Labour (Wintour 2001).

In addition to the two West Yorkshire drug courts, the British government also announced in December 1997 that it would spend one million pounds on a pilot program, called Drug Treatment and Testing Orders (DTTOs). Much like the British drug courts, DTTOs offer convicted drug offenders the alternative of court-monitored treatment. In September 2000, the then home office minister Paul Boateng indicated that courts all over England and Wales would be allowed to compel offenders to undergo treatment for their drug problems (Davies 2001). DTTOs, which were also directly inspired by the American drug court experience, have been widely endorsed by individuals involved with drugs policy. In a DTTO program, offenders who refuse to comply with these court orders, risk returning to the court to face a tougher sentence. The Government's ten-year program designed to fight drug abuse is committed to extending DTTOs and has committed forty million pounds to implement drug treatment and testing. The Howard League for Penal Reform argues that DTTOs should be used more widely, as an alternative to jailing many women offenders. The League's director, Frances Crook, has called on government to expand the use of DTTOs nationally (BBC 2000).

The swift embrace of drug courts and DTTOs by the British law enforcement community is only in part an outcome of the belief that the existing system for dealing with offenders is ineffective. The shift toward treatment is integral to a clearly discernible trend within the legal system as a whole. In a wide variety of circumstances, members of the judiciary have begun to advocate therapeutic intervention and its integration into the system of justice and law enforcement. Lord Chief Justice Lord Bingham, for example, has called for the introduction of behavior therapy in jail to treat violent offenders. Lord Justice Thorpe has also advocated resolving disputes between parents over custody through investing in therapeutic services (Dyer 2000; Taylor 2000).

That drug courts and DTTOs are perceived to be so uniquely effective must in part be influenced by cultural sensibilities that hold therapy in high regard. Such sensibilities predispose advocates of therapeutic intervention to evaluate these schemes in a one-sidedly positive light. One study commissioned by the Home Office, *Doing Justice to Treatment*, argues that well-organized schemes offering treatment to offenders are effective in reducing drug abuse and crime. However, a close inspection of the methodology used by this study indicates that the majority of responses came from clients who were easy to contact and thus more likely to provide positive stories about their experience (Edmunds, Hough, Turnbull, and May 1999).[1] Recent reports calling into question the effectiveness of DTTOs have not dampened the enthusiasm of its supporters. It was reported in December 1999 that in the three pilot programs, two-thirds of the treatment orders imposed by the courts had been breached and one-third had been revoked. The response of the cabinet office that coordinates the government's antidrugs program was to concede that these figures were puzzling, but for a pilot scheme not disappointing (Wintour 1999).

Campaigning journalist Nick Davies has questioned claims regarding the efficacy of DTTOs. In September 2000, Home Office Minister Paul Boateng justified the expansion of DTTOs on the grounds that among those taking part in the pilots, there has been a "dramatic" fall in the number of offenses committed. Davies has shown that this claim was based on ignoring inconvenient evidence and on the untested claims of offenders who knew that if they were caught taking drugs they would be sent back to jail (Davies 2001). This willingness to give DTTOs the benefit of a doubt is underpinned by a deeply held conviction in the validity of therapeutic treatment.

THE CULTURAL CONTEXT

That is, the public embrace of programs like drug courts and DTTOs cannot be understood simply on the grounds of their purported efficacy, which, as noted above, has been called into question. Rather, the essentially therapeutic orientation of DTTOs and drug courts is consistent with broader changes afoot in British political and legal culture. This chapter highlights various developments in the United Kingdom to illustrate the extent to which drug courts and DTTOs are in keeping with the changing currents of contemporary British culture. That is, the evident shift from "punishment" to "treatment" is driven by widespread cultural and legal change oriented toward the institutionalization of the therapeutic ethos. This legal innovation, like other areas of law, is embedded in contemporary cultural sensibilities (Friedman 1989) Consistent with developing cultural currents, new ideas about personal responsibility have become assimilated into law. The feminist legal scholar Helen Reece, for example, argues that the Family Law Act 1996 expresses a radically new conception of responsibility, which she characterizes as that of "post-liberal" responsibility. She believes that whereas responsibility formerly was measured by our level of self-control, it is now assessed by our level of self-awareness. Reece notes that this focus on self-awareness encourages a view that part of the task of the legal system is to help people reflect on their responsibility. She cites Lord Mackay's proclamation that people "may need help with reflection" as an illustration of the therapeutic turn in British legal culture (see Reece 2000:84–85).

Reece's discussion of the shifting definition of personal responsibility is particularly relevant for grasping contemporary conceptions of crime and criminality. Criminality is systematically interpreted through a medical discourse and antisocial behavior is often presented as an outcome of a psychological disorder. Lord Justice Thorpe has argued that custody battles are "often driven by personality disorders" and that they ought to be "treated therapeutically, where at least there would be some prospect of beneficial change" (Dyer 2000). Helping people to reflect on their responsibility is viewed as essential for tackling antisocial behavior. More broadly, the therapeutic turn in Britain has stimulated the reinterpretation of crime as the violation of victims by people who have lost control over their emotions. In Britain, recently constructed high profile crimes—stalking, hate crimes, road rage, bullying, date rape—are associated with acts perpetrated by psychologically destructive individuals who lack self-awareness and who are not quite in control of their emotions (Best and Furedi 2001). This problem of rage is built upon a cultural foundation that regards social problems as rooted in psychologically destructive behavior.

Antisocial behavior is increasingly interpreted as the outcome of emotional dysfunction that can be put right through therapeutic intervention. The New Labour government's consultation document *Supporting Families* claims that criminal behavior can be substantially reduced through an ambitious program of therapeutic intervention in the lives of families (HMSO 1998). Therapeutic intervention is often presented as a solution to the problem of law and order. Offenders who are fined or sentenced to community service can now be ordered to attend a rehabilitation program. It seems that "rehabilitation" is now associated with various forms of counseling and therapy. Failed parents are the targets of "parenting orders," a new scheme enacted by the Blair government to deal with fathers and mothers whose children fail to turn up in school. The core requirement of a parenting order is that "the parent attends counseling or guidance sessions" as specified by the courts (Home Office 2000). This approach has been anticipated by numerous local pilot projects that have experimented with the treatment model for dealing with antisocial families. For example the Dundee Family Project, launched in 1996, has sought to handle antisocial tenants on local authority housing estates through the provision of family therapy. In order to avoid permanent eviction, problem families are sent to a residential unit, where they live for an average of nine months. These families have to agree to a "personally challenging supervisory regime," including three visits per day. During the course of their residence, the families are offered modules on domestic and anger management, addiction counseling, and parent/child therapy (McKay 1999).

THE THERAPEUTIC TURN

Again, the development of programs such as these must be understood in the context of wider cultural processes. One of the most important cultural expressions of the shift toward the therapeutic is the radical redefinition of the human condition as that of vulnerability (Furedi 1998). In recent years, many experiences, previously regarded as normal parts of one's life have been redefined as harmful and traumatic. Adults and particularly children are said to be prone to a bewildering variety of injuries, abuses, and illnesses. Stress has become a common term to describe the state of people in virtually every conceivable setting. Students facing exams are said to face exam panic attacks. Delegates at the 1999 conference of the British Professional Association of Teachers denounced the examination system for the "sadistic" pressure it placed on children to perform well and called for its abolition on the grounds that it was little more than child abuse (Henderson 1999). The discovery that the age-old system of school examination is actually dangerous to children's well-being reflects the tendency to reinterpret difficult or challenging encounters as potentially damaging to the people concerned. It is not merely exams that have been given a health warning. Competition—particularly competitive sports—has been attacked because it is said to strike a blow at children's self-esteem. Pushy parents have been labeled as emotional abusers because they place "unacceptable" pressure on their children. In March 1998, a World in Action documentary about the Royal Ballet School alleged that this institution's regime caused widespread anorexia, bulimia, and bullying among the young students. It claimed that the dream of becoming a ballerina "has turned into a nightmare" for many children who go to the school.

Contemporary perceptions of vulnerability stand in sharp contrast to the way people viewed their engagement with adversity not so long ago. It is easy to forget that the systematic application of the therapeutic to make sense of how people handle misfortune is a relatively recent development. Today, minor tragedies have become the sites for the intervention of trauma counselors and therapeutic professionals. Counseling the bereaved, their relatives, and their friends has become almost mandatory. Commentators continually allude to hidden psychological damage that is likely to incapacitate people for considerable time, if not forever. But not so long ago, people who went through harrowing events were simply the recipients of sympathy and solidarity and not of therapy. Take the case of one of the most devastating industrial tragedies in postwar Britain: the Aberfan disaster of 1966. Despite the horror of a village school engulfed by a coal-tip slide, nobody demanded compensation for their trauma or their psychological distress. The relatives of the 116 children and 28 adults who died during this tragedy took the view that they did not want to pursue prosecution because that would be to "bow to vengeance." The surviving children resumed their education a fortnight after the tragedy "so that their minds may be taken off the disaster." A year after this disaster, Mary Essex, a family and child psychologist from the University of Wales, noted that the surviving children seemed normal and adjusted. The *Times* observed that "the villagers had done admirably in rehabilitating themselves with very little help" ("Coping Well" 1966). Today, such a response to a major disaster would be unthinkable. There would be an automatic assumption that every survivor in the area was deeply traumatized and inevitably scarred for life. Sending young pupils back to school so soon after a tragedy would be scorned as bad practice. The very attempt by the community to cope through self-help would be denounced as misguided since such victims could not be expected to deal with such problems on their own.

Since the 1990s the history of Aberfan is being rewritten in line with today's therapeutic ethos. Researchers are busy helping survivors to reinterpret their experiences through the language of trauma. A collection of recently conducted interviews of Aberfan survivors suggests that retrospectively people have discovered past traumas. A survivor who has authored a recollection of this disaster echoed this sentiment, when she remarked that "one crucial area where I feel we were badly let down in Aberfan was in the lack of proper counseling" (Madgwick 1999). Such is the power of present-day sensitivity to emotional injury that past events can only make sense through the language of trauma. Instead of exploring the resilience of this Welsh mining community, commentators are far more likely to treat the survivors as hidden victims whose emotional needs were ignored by a callous officialdom.

THE CULTURE OF EMOTIONALISM

As we enter the new millennium, British society appears drawn toward a conception of human behavior that is radically different from what it possessed at the beginning of the twentieth century. Important cultural and intellectual influences suggest that the model of individual autonomy is seriously flawed and that people are not nearly as self-sufficient, resilient, and capable of making responsible decisions as was once believed. Helen Reece has noted that the new version of responsibility posits the proposition that individual autonomy is illusory (Reece 2000:84). The condition of vulnerability is now seen not as a dimension of the human condition but as its defining feature. This state of vulnerability has acquired formidable social prestige. The victim is no longer simply someone to be pitied—it is a status to which many aspire. As an object of cultural empathy, the victim serves as an affirmation of the belief that human existence represents a state of vulnerability to forces beyond individual control. As an object of veneration, the privileged status of the victim testifies to a moral shift of emphasis from being judged on one's achievements to being defined by what one has suffered.

In intellectual terms, the ascendancy of the cult of vulnerability is reflected in the way that moral and social problems tend to be interpreted through a therapeutic paradigm. Consequently, the model of the individual as a rational calculating actor is gradually being displaced by a cultural framework that insists that human experience is best understood through the prism of emotion. The therapeutic imperative continues to alter the language of our times. Terms like stress, self-esteem, and emotional literacy have acquired everyday usage and continually highlight the trauma of simply coping with everyday life. Explanations oriented toward the emotions are now used to make sense of problems that in the past were illuminated through socioeconomic or philosophical analysis. Academics applying for financial support of their research are far more likely to gain funding for a project on "unemployment and mental health" than for a proposal to study "structural unemployment." When the *Guardian* published a major report on the crisis in Britain's education system, its emphasis was on the emotional damage suffered by poor children, rather than on their social conditions or the failure of the system of education: "Poverty does its worst damage with the emotions of those who live with it" (Davies 1999). It seems that society is far more comfortable in dealing with poverty as a mental health problem than as a social issue. This approach is driven by a widely held premise that adverse circumstances, even relatively banal ones, are stress inducing and cause trauma and various forms of mental illness.

The influence of the therapeutic worldview is particularly striking in deliberations around old social problems such as racism. Whereas in the past critics of racism emphasized the salience of economic inequality, discrimination, and violence, today there is a tendency to adopt the therapeutic language of victimization. A recent study conducted by the Joseph Rowntree Foundation focused on the "devastating stress" suffered by victims of racial harassment. The report self-consciously sought to win public sympathy for victims of racism by playing the therapeutic card. Its focus was on the "anger, stress, depression, sleepless nights" of the respondents to the survey (Joseph Rowntree Foundation 1999). In this instance, the therapeutic idiom provided a new vocabulary to express an old problem. In other cases, the emotionalist perspective has the unfortunate consequence of actually distorting the issues at stake.

The adaptation of the discourse of emotionalism in relation to wars and international conflict has been criticized for distorting the situation people face in very difficult circumstances. The application of the trauma perspective to international conflict has inspired the exportation of psychotrauma programs costing millions of pounds to places like Rwanda and the Balkans. According to Derek Summerfield of the Medical Foundation for the Care of Victims of Torture, this discovery of trauma as a humanitarian issue in wars "owes much to the medicalization of distress within western cultures and to the rise of 'talk therapies'" (Summerfield 1998:1581). Claims that 1.4 million people were traumatized in Bosnia and Croatia have been questioned by Summerfield, who is concerned about the trend to transform a brutal war into a psychological issue. He points out that these programs are driven by the therapeutic assumptions of Western professionals. He writes:

> The assertion that PTSD is universally valid will come as news to Rwandans, whose language does not even contain words comparable to "stress" and

"trauma." In Cambodia, it is expatriate workers who believe that the trauma of the Pol Pot years has not been processed, and talk about a "culture of silence" which blocks what they see as a necessary expression of painful feelings about memories. Cambodians do not share these ideas about themselves and point instead to their socio-economic problems.(ibid.)

The globalization of the therapeutic worldview to war torn regions of the world is driven by a cultural impulse that imagines that damage to the emotion constitutes the fundamental problem of humanity.

So what drives the culture of emotionalism and the consciousness of vulnerability? It appears that at a time of social fluidity and moral uncertainty, the question of belonging is posed in a particularly acute form. Important questions are continually posed about what it means to be British. National identities throughout the Western world have become problematic. The rise of regional and ethnic movements suggests that the capacity of traditional national identity to inspire people has diminished. These developments have been reinforced by an unprecedented dynamic toward individuation, which forces more and more people to ask the question, Where do I belong? Such questions do not refer merely to the phenomenon of the diminishing influence of historic national identities. The forces of global economic change and of geographical mobility encourage the fragmentation of communities. Coincidentally, the family form and gender relations have become subject to a relentless process of transformation. The individual's place in the world has become characteristically uncertain. What defines the contemporary question, Where do I belong? is that there are no obvious answers at either the collective or individual level.

In an era of unprecedented individuation, the outlook of emotionalism allows people to make sense of their lives and to continually reinterpret their biographies. The very act of universalizing the condition of vulnerability helps provide a focus for shared experience. That is why community established through suffering provides the foundation for those unique instances of collective solidarity that make an impact on people's lives. Mourning for individual victims such as Princess Diana or for those who lost their lives in tragedies, such as the fourteen children who were killed in their school by a crazed gunman in Dunblane in 1996, provide for exceptional occasions of collective solidarity. The community of feeling, where people can share in each other's pain appears to provide a provisional solution to the question of belonging. The very normalcy of suffering allows everyone to share in either their own or other people's pain. That is why victim television and confessional writing have become so pervasive in popular culture. Emotionalism not only allows for collective sharing, it also endows those who have suffered with moral status and a sense of identity. It is a form of identity that appears to suit the individuated temper of our times.

THERAPEUTIC POLITICS

The ascendancy of the culture of emotionalism is one of the most remarkable developments in Anglo-American societies during the past decade. Society's celebration of the victim, preoccupation with suffering, and the public display of emotion has been widely commented upon (Furedi 1997; Mestrovic 1997; Nolan 1998). There is a growing tendency for public figures to adopt an emoting style. They demonstrate their humanity by revealing to the world details of their broken families, alcoholic mothers, abusive fathers, or the tragic afflictions of their children. Revelations of private hurt and suffering are likely to receive the full approval of the media. This sympathetic response is in striking contrast to how society views individuals who refuse to display their emotions in public. "Cold," "aloof," and "inhuman" are likely epithets used to describe the self-contained individual who insists on keeping private emotions and life just that—private. During the recent negotiations around the peace process in Northern Ireland, one of the main criticisms directed at the Unionist political leaders was that they refused to adopt an emotional style and were therefore not worthy of trust.

The culture of emotionalism is strongly associated with a therapeutic ethos and a focus on the self. It seems that with the self as the dominant point of reference, conventional politics is experienced as an alien irrelevant phenomenon. The politics of emotion directly competes with politics driven by ideologies, philosophical principles, or social causes. Professional politicians have been quick to adapt to the politics of emotion. Politicians have come to recognize that their political, ideological, and moral links with the electorate are characteristically fragile. Traditional forms of party politics, political values, and identities have little purchase on an evidently disenchanted public. Popular mistrust of authority is confirmed by the growing alienation of people from the system of elections. American-style voting apathy has become a fact of life in the New Europe, where a significant proportion of the electorate believes that voting is a waste of time (Dogan 1998). The turnout at the British general election in June 2001 was the lowest since universal suffrage was introduced in 1918. And Blair received the lowest share of the eligible electorate of any prime minister for more than a century (Johnston 2001).

Politicians throughout the Western world have begun to look for new forms of legitimization. Such a search needs to engage with a highly individuated electorate that has distanced itself from traditional values and indeed from any commonly held beliefs and ideologies. An ethos, with its emphasis on the self-referential individual and on the domain of emotion has provided an obvious focus for the energies of the political classes. In an important study of this process, the American sociologist James Nolan has argued that the strength of therapeutic consciousness has been clearly recognized by U.S. politicians concerned with mobilizing popular support. It is the combination of the manifest decline of so-called traditional moral and social norms and the emergence of a highly individuated and self-referential consciousness that provides the point of departure for therapeutic politics. "Because of the devaluation of former cultural codes of moral understanding and the rise of the therapeutic cultural system, the conditions are ripe for the infusion of the latter into the various programs and policies of the American state," writes Nolan (1998:45).

Politicians have sought to adapt to this therapeutic culture in order to connect with the mood of the times. This political style was perfected by the Clinton administration, and successfully copied by New Labour. Blair's New Labour has drawn heavily on the Clinton experience. The 1996 Labour party convention demonstrated that the therapeutic worldview had become thoroughly assimilated into British political life. The high point of this conference was the speech made by Ann Pearston, the main public figure of the Dunblane-based Snowdrop campaign against gun ownership. Evoking memories about the Dunblane school tragedy, Pearston succeeded in stunning the conference into silence. Delegates wept openly as Pearston recounted the details of the tragedy. Her speech was followed by an enthusiastic standing ovation. And Tony Blair led the conference in a minute's silence to mourn the Dunblane victims. This was political theater at its best. Carefully orchestrated, Pearston's speech was patiently rehearsed by New Labour spin-doctors. It demonstrated the power of political emotionalism. Indeed, it was the only memorable moment of the conference. It is worth recalling that the Tories had declined to accept Pearston's offer to address their conference. Their ineptitude in engaging with the politics of emotion may in part explain their subsequent defeat at the polls and their current exile in the political wilderness.

Tony Blair has perfected the art of emotional politics. His speeches are littered with the language of therapy, emphasizing how much he "feels" and "cares" and promising to "share" and "reach out" to the people. A misty eye is now a highly prized political asset. Blair's political style continually exploits an opportunity for establishing a point of contact with public emotion. His response to the Omagh bomb tragedy in Northern Ireland, in August 1998, was to tell the public about the depth of his feeling. With a pained expression, he furrowed his brow and stammered, "I am very full of emotion, I just kept thinking last night of those poor murdered people." Only a few maverick journalists picked up on this exploitative theatrical performance. "To draw attention to one's own feelings publicly, while others lie murdered or are dying or are suffering, is grotesque self-indulgence," wrote Paul Goodman of the *Daily Telegraph*. He added that Blair was "focusing attention not on them, but on him, him, him" (Good-man 1998). And yet it is precisely the act of drawing attention to oneself that finds such a strong resonance with today's cultural elite. Such displays merit praise while those who refuse to disclose their feelings are treated with fierce suspicion.

The significance attached to public emotionalism was vividly confirmed during the events surrounding Princess Diana's funeral. The promoters of the politics of emotionalism were particularly vitriolic against members of the royal family who did not wish to share their inner pain. Sections of the media took it upon themselves to instruct Queen Elizabeth and Prince Charles on the form of grieving the public expected from them. One did not have to be particularly sympathetic to the royal family to be struck by the way in which these commentators assumed they possessed the moral authority to intrude into the private lives of the royal family. The desire to mourn in private and in accordance with one's individual feeling was pathologized and denounced as cold and inhuman. In particular, Prince Charles, was hysterically lectured for not putting his arm around his boys in public.

The propagation of emotionalism is public life is vigorously pursued by its supporters. The 1997 Labour party conference saw the launch of a new campaign by Antidote, set up by "psychotherapists and other members of the caring professions" to promote the cause of emotional literacy among British politicians. Antidote aims to encourage public figures to become more "comfortable" with their emotions. This project of colonizing the public space with psychopolitics has been widely endorsed by New Labour politicians.

During the year leading up to New Labour's 1997 election victory, there were clear signs that the party had opted for the politics of emotionalism. Joy Johnson, one of Labour's leading spin doctors resigned from her post in 1996, on the ground that she did not want a job that was primarily about "selecting 'real people' with emotional stories to tell" (Thynne 1996).

Consider, for example, Tony Blair's emotional "off-the-cuff" tribute to his seventy-three-year-old father Leo at the October 1996 party conference. Blair also recalled the funeral of a leading union leader, Sam McCluskie. He remarked that a family member gave him a strip of red ribbon belonging to McCluskie, a keepsake that the Labour leader still treasured. Such tearful demonstrations of emotion are emblematic of the new style of therapeutic politics. "This isn't a time for sound bites," Blair remarked just before the signing of the Northern Ireland Agreement, before adding "but you know, I feel that the hand of history is really on our shoulder, I really do."

Northern Ireland is an important testing ground for the institutionalization of therapeutic politics. Throughout the peace process, the British government has sought to endow its initiatives with legitimacy through establishing a point of contact with the victims of the Irish war. In November 1997, the government established a Victims Commission, which published its report shortly after the signing of the Good Friday Agreement, in April 1998. The report, titled "We Will Remember Them," written by Sir Kenneth Bloomfield, Northern Ireland Victims Commissioner, is inspired by the therapeutic ethos. The report proposed establishing a "champion" post for victims and their support groups, greater advice and counseling, and high priority for the treatment of pain and trauma. The secretary of state for Northern Ireland quickly announced that the government would appoint a "minister for victims," who will be there "to understand and listen." One of the first initiatives to be announced by Adam Ingram, the newly appointed "minister for victims," was the allocation of seven hundred thousand pounds to establish a trauma unit in Belfast for young people and families affected by the Troubles (Breen 1998). In turn, Tony Blair announced a grant of several million pounds to underwrite "comprehensive and effective counseling initiatives." The therapeutic ethos now dominates the Northern Irish political landscape. Sinn Fein leader Gerry Adams has repeatedly apologized for the pain and hurt caused by the Republican movement, while constantly reminding others that the nationalist community has suffered too. Adams even borrowed Bill Clinton's election slogan, "I feel your pain." Unionist politicians have also jumped on the bandwagon. Banners claiming that the Protestant community was the real victim of the troubles were prominent in Unionist protests organized throughout 1999.

While the institutionalization of therapeutic policymaking received a major boost in the eighties under the conservative Thatcher and Major regimes, it was under the Blair government that the therapeutic idiom came to exercise an important influence on the presentation of public policy. One of the principal underlying assumptions that informs New Labour policymaking is the importance of connecting with people's emotional needs and offering measures that can boost the electorate's self-esteem. New Labour rhetoric is deeply embedded within the therapeutic idiom. Concepts like the Third Way, social inclusion, and exclusion are directly wedded to the objective of offering public recognition to the emotional needs of the British public. For example, according to Prime Minister Blair, the problem of social exclusion is not so much about material poverty as about destructive influences that are "damaging to self esteem" (Blair 1997). Not surprisingly, almost every initiative promoted by the Blair government's Social Exclusion Unit is designed to raise people's self esteem.[2]

The language of therapy permeates the British government's domestic policy initiatives. Officials and politicians regularly use expressions like "raising self-esteem" and promoting "emotional literacy." So a government initiative designed to tackle underachievement by girls promised to "boost girls' self-esteem" (BBC Online 1998). Getting people to feel good about themselves influences government policy in education and health. Margaret Hodge, former undersecretary for education and employment, remarked that "developing self confidence, self esteem and social skills is as vital as learning to hold a pencil and count to ten," when the government announced its plan to spend eight billion pounds on an integrated early-years and childcare strategy (Hodge 1999). An integrated health care initiative launched in February 1999 was promoted on the grounds that the real health problem in many communities was "lack of self esteem."

Some of New Labour's most highly publicized initiatives—teenage pregnancy, employment schemes, parenting initiatives—prescribe the raising of self-esteem as its main objective. The June 2000 government-sponsored "Body Image Summit" is paradigmatic in this respect. During the months preceding this event government ministers spoke out on the alleged danger that the pressure to be thin posed for young women's self-esteem. According to Tessa Jowell, then minister for women, young women are "being held back from fulfilling their aspirations and reaching their potential because they lack confidence and self-esteem" (Cabinet Office 2000). According to recent government statements, low self-esteem is a common factor associated with child prostitution, homelessness, teenage pregnancy, drug abuse and a variety of antisocial and destructive behaviors. Consequently social problems are increasingly presented as rooted in psychological pathologies that require therapeutic treatment. Even the hard-nosed Treasury has adopted this approach. One of its consultation documents, *Enterprise and Social Exclusion,* argues that local development policies will be marginal unless they help foster "people's skills and self-esteem." Other consultation papers argue that people can be "removed from economic deprivation" through "raising poor self-esteem" (H. M. Treasury 2000).

The role of therapy has acquired an important dimension in New Labour's social policy toward the unemployed. The practice of counseling the unemployed was adopted during the Thatcher era, albeit in a hesitant and unsystematic manner. Since the election of the Blair government in 1997, this approach has become a key component of welfare policy. The Gateway program, which is designed to assist the government's project of modernizing the welfare state, offers guidance and counseling. In September 1998, it was reported that officials of the Department of Social Security were expected to switch their role from that of officers to that of counselors. "The ability of civil servants to switch from paper-bound administrators to flesh-and blood counselors is one of the New Deal's most crucial aspects," argued one analysis of this development (MacErlean 1998).

The term *self-esteem* lacks any scientific precision, and it is far from clear how it can be raised (Hewitt 1998). Supporters of the politics of raising self-esteem claim that they are not so much interested in hard facts as in following their intuition. Their reaction is not surprising since proponents of the self-esteem ideology believe that adopting an emotional political style toward the goal of making people feel good is valuable in and of itself. And although their various initiatives are unlikely to have any significant practical consequences, they contribute toward a political climate that privileges emotionalism. Consequently, there is now a tendency for political socialization to take the form of emotional training. It is worth noting that a British Government Advisory Group on Education for Citizenship and the Teaching of Democracy in Schools considers self-esteem as an important core skill (Smithers 1998). And the therapeutic style of governance is continually animated by the vision of healing people and society.

The importance that the political class attaches to self-esteem represents a major reorientation in the activities of the state. The incorporation of the policy of raising self-esteem into the business of the state shifts governmental focus from the public to the private sphere. The conviction that how people feel about themselves is the business of government indicates that therapeutic politics is gaining an important institutional dimension. It is the search for legitimization that has stimulated the absorption of a therapeutic imperative by the state. Through a complex process of accommodation and borrowing, politicians and policymakers alike have come under the influence of therapeutic political culture. In some cases individuals have adopted the rhetoric of healing, while the state sometimes presents itself as a collective healer.

MORAL POLICING

The institutionalization of the therapeutic ethos can also be interpreted as the constitution of a regime of social control. Those who run afoul of the norms of the therapeutic ethos often discover that they are not just offered but are coerced into receiving "help." This authoritarian impulse in public policy is clearly focused on a small group of "irresponsible parents." Between September and December 1999, 122 parenting orders were imposed by the courts. These orders require the parents of convicted children to discipline them and to attend courses on parenting. These courses "help" parents to come to terms with their emotions, whether they like it or not.

The "whether you like it or not" approach also informs Britain's antidrug strategy. Steven Todd, the operational director of Addaction, a charity running a treatment program in Derby, argues that research shows that "even forcing people to take treatment worked" (BBC News Online 1999). Forcing people into therapy indicates that emotionalism can be an intensely coercive cultural phenomenon.

In Britain, corporate counseling has become a powerful instrument for maintaining managerial control. In some cases, managers have called in employees to an interview at which they were given the sack, asked to leave the premises immediately—and offered counseling (Charlton 1999:15). PPP Healthcare employee assistance programs offer a compulsory option for employers who want to force their employees to receive counseling. If employees refuse to participate in this program, they can face disciplinary sanctions including the sack (1999). The gradual expansion of mandatory counseling—"We'll help you whether you like it or not"—indicates that the line between therapeutic intervention and policing has become blurred.

The phenomenon of mandatory counseling illustrates how the domain of feeling and emotion has been invaded by the therapeutic ethos. The very idea that how people feel about themselves and others is the business of government has helped to politicize the sphere of the emotion. Measures are enacted to help the emotionally illiterate and to train those who deviate from the new therapeutic consensus to adopt an acceptable, emotionally correct form of behavior. New so-called hate crimes are oriented toward policing unacceptable forms of individual thought on the grounds of protecting the emotionally vulnerable target groups from prejudice. Such laws have little practical purpose since there are already plenty of legal means for prosecuting different forms of violence and incitement to violence. Nevertheless, they serve an important symbolic role of indicating which forms of thoughts and emotions are acceptable and which are beyond the pale.

The politics of emotion is by definition arbitrary in its public impact. It is extremely difficult to objectively grasp concepts like intention, hate, emotional damage, trauma, or an act of abuse. The elevation of feeling means that the subjective offense a victim claims to have suffered need have little to do with the objective actions of the offender. If you feel that someone's words or behavior are offensive, that is enough to end the discussion, regardless of what was intended. After all, nobody can reasonably argue that you are not really offended, just as nobody can get inside your heart and check if you are pretending to be upset. The very act of disagreeing with a victim can bring a charge of secondary victimization. The politics of emotion contains a disturbing authoritarian potential for encroaching upon people's lives. The claim of victim expertise is not open to contestation. To challenge such claims is to insult or offend the victim. "I'm the expert. I know," was how one secondary victim of homicide asserted the right to moral authority on a British television chat show (Rock 1998:193).

Supporters of the therapeutic turn of the state welcome this orientation as a reflection of society's greater awareness of hitherto unrecognized problems. The institutionalization of emotionalism is often interpreted as representing a greater sensitivity to people's feelings. Officials and professionals committed to this outlook take the view that far more can be done to extend the therapeutic ethos into the institutions of public life. "We feel that it is important that the law should be able to develop incrementally as relevant experts learn more about psychiatric illness and society further recognizes its debilitating consequences," states a report published by the British Law Commission (Law Commission 1998:3). The authors of this report clearly anticipate a future where even greater recognition will be accorded to problems of the emotion.

In light of these cultural, political, and legal developments, the emergence and expansion of British drug court and DTTO programs should be no surprise. Like other government programs, these new approaches to handling drug offenders are fully commensurate with increasingly pervasive therapeutic sensibilities and practices in British culture more broadly. Moreover, in keeping with the rationales offered for the various government schemes reviewed above, British drug courts and DTTOs are likely to experience little resistance in their essential advancement of "coerced treatment." Even if the drug court movement in the United States did not exist, British criminal justice would have discovered a therapeutic approach for dealing with the problem. Cultural sensibilities dictate and justify an approach that stresses the importance of treating the emotional illness of the drug offender. When all social problems are liable to be reinterpreted from a therapeutic perspective, why should crime be exempt? A system of justice inspired by the therapeutic ethos is likely to be with us for some time to come.

NOTES

1. One would have expected that a significant reduction in drug use and criminal activity would have been reflected in some tangible change in the respondents' lifestyle. However, the authors of this study noted that the people surveyed did not experience any significant change in their employment status, accommodation, or personal relationship (see ibid.:2).
2. It is worth noting that a recently published government-commissioned report acknowledges that there is no agreed definition of the term self-esteem nor is there any British research that can be used to justify self-esteem-raising policies. See Dennison and Coleman (2000).

REFERENCES

BBC News Online. 1998. "Government to Boost Girls' Self-Esteem." 9 November.

BBC News Online. 1999. "Drug Treatment Orders Offer Alternatives to Prison." 25 May.

BBC News Online. 2000. "Call to Scrap New Women's Jails." 5 April.

BBC News Online. 2001. "Glasgow to Trial Drugs Court." 21 February.

Best, J. and Furedi, F. 2001. "The Evolution of Road Rage in Britain and the United States." In *The International Diffusion of Social Problems*, edited by J. Best. Hawthorne, NY: Aldine de Gruyter.

Blair, T. 1997. Speech at Stockwell Park School, Lambeth, December.

Breen, Suzanne. 1998. "Trauma Unit to be Set Up for the Victims of Violence." *Irish Times* 1 July.

Cabinet Office. 2000. "Pressure To Be Thin Affecting Young Women's Self-Esteem: Body Image Summit." Press Release 20.

Charlton, B. 1999. "Corporate Counselling." *LM* 18(March).

"Coping Well." 1966. *Times* 15 November.

Davies, N. 1999. "Crisis, Crisis, Crisis: The State of Our Schools." *Guardian* 14 September.

Davies, N. 2001. "Demonising Druggies Wins Votes. That's All That Counts." *Guardian* 15 June.

Dennison, C. and Coleman, J. 2000. *Young People and Gender: A Review of Research. A Report Submitted to the Women's Unit, Cabinet Office and the Family Policy Unit, Home Office.* London: Women's Unit.

Dogan, M. 1998. "The Decline of Traditional Values in Western Europe; Religion, Nationalism, Authority." *International Journal of Contemporary Sociology* 39(1).

Dyer, C. 2000. "Judge Attacks Waste in Custody Battles." *Guardian* 20 June.

Edmunds, M., Hough, M., Turnbull, P, and May, T. 1999. *Doing Justice to Treatment: Referring Offenders to Drug Services.* London: Drug Prevention Advisory Service.

Friedman, L. A. 1989. *The Republic of Choice: Law, Authority, Culture,* Cambridge, MA: Harvard University Press.

Furedi, F. 1997. *The Culture of Fear: Risk Taking and The Morality of Low Expectations.* London: Cassell.

Furedi, F. 1998. "New Britain—A Nation of Victims." *Society* 35(3).

Goodman, Paul. 1998. "Omagh and Him, Him, Him." *Daily Telegraph* 19 August.

H.M. Treasury. 2000. *Enterprise and Social Exclusion.* London: Author.

Henderson, Mark. 1999. "Exams Criticized as 'Child Abuse.'" *The Times* 28 July.

Hewitt, J. P. 1998. *The Myth of Self Esteem: Finding Happiness and Solving Problems.* New York: St Martin's.

Hibbs, J. 2000. "Downing Street Hosts Drugs Summit as Crime Figures Soar" *Daily Telegraph,* 17 February.

HMSO. 1998. *Supporting Families: A Consultation Document,* London: The Stationery Office.

Hodge, Margaret. 1999. "Time for a Fresh Game Plan." *Guardian* 16 March.

Home Office. 2000. "The Crime and Disorder Act. Guidance Document: Parenting Order." 2 June.

Johnston, P. 2001. "Low Poll Takes Shine Off Win." *Daily Telegraph,* 9 June.

Joseph Rowntree Foundation. 1999. "The Experience of Racists Victimization." *Press Release,* 21 June.

Law Commission. 1998. *Liability For Psychiatric Illness.* London: The Stationery Office.

MacErlean, N. 1998. "New Deal—So Play Your Right Hand." *Observer* 13 September.

Madgwick, Gaynor. 1999. "A Plea to the People of Dunblane from a Survivor of the Aberfam Disaster." *Daily Mail* 19 March.

McKay, Reg. 1999. "Keeping the Doors Open." 21 July.

Mestrovic, S. J. 1997. *Postemotional Society.* London: Routledge.

Miller, G. and Holstein, J. A. (eds.). 1993. *Constructionist Controversies: Issues in Social Problems Theory.* Hawthorne, NY: Aldine de Gruyter.

Mitchell, D. 2001. "Idea for U.S.—Style Drug Courts Gains Momentum." *Guardian,* 13 March.

Nolan, J. L. 1998. *The Therapeutic State: Justifying Government at Century's End.* New York: New York University Press.

Reece, H. 2000. "Divorcing Responsibly." *Feminist Legal Studies* 8.

Rock, P. 1998. "Murderers, Victims and 'Survivors': The Social Construction of Deviance." *British Journal of Criminology* 38(2).

Smithers, Rebecca. 1998. "Citizenship Lessons Urged for Pupils." *Guardian* 23 September.

Summerfield, D. 1998. "'Trauma' and the Experience of War: A Reply." *Lancet* 23 May.

Syal, R. and Bamber, D. 1999. "'Soft Option' Drugs Court to Be Extended." *Daily Telegraph,* 19 September.

Taylor, D. 2000. "Judge Targets Sick Crimes." *Express,* 24 January.

Thynee, Jane. 1999. "Spin Doctors Polish the Party Image as Election Looms. *Daily Telegraph* 25 October.

Wintour, P. 1999. "Crackdown on Drug Crime Fails." *Observer,* 5 December.

Wintour, P. 2001. "Big Shake-Up Aims to Break Cycle of Crime." *Guardian,* 23 February.

11

Drug Courts, the Judge, and the Rehabilitative Ideal

Philip Bean

INTRODUCTION

Drug courts continue to enjoy a burgeoning growth and with every prospect this will continue, along with the same high level of public and political support they have enjoyed from their inception in 1989. So great has been the scope and influence of drug courts we can reasonably talk of a drug court movement. Drug courts can be defined as a slow-track, court-based treatment program (Bean 1996), where the key features are dedicated courtrooms that provide judicially monitored treatment, drug testing, and other services to drug-involved offenders (Belenko 1998).[1] Drug court is predicated on the assertion that crime and all other manifestations of unacceptable behavior come from the offender's addiction. Accordingly, drug court theory does not consider the nonaddicted offender, the addict who is not an offender (although the illegal use of drugs may classify him as an offender), or the once-addicted offender who after successful treatment continues to commit offenses.

The U.S. Department of Health and Human Services says that "judges play a crucial role in planning and operating the treatment based drug court program" (1997:13). They do so in a number of ways, although here I want only to concentrate on the judge's powers and the manner in which judges deal with offenders, linking these to traditional notions of justice, and to the courtroom team. I want to consider these in terms of links with rehabilitation, that is, to ask to what extent drug courts mark a return to the rehabilitative ideal of a generation ago, and if so, to examine some of the consequent implications.

DRUG COURT AND TRADITIONAL NOTIONS OF JUSTICE

The drug courts claim to be reinventing justice is manifested inter alia in the fundamental transformation of courtroom procedures. Anyone new to drug court would be astonished by its informality, where the center stage is fully accorded to the judge. This contrasts with the traditional approach where the judge takes a more neutral position, is a detached figure protecting the dignity of the office, and is nonpartisan in the resolution of conflict, although he or she may be more partisan at the sentencing stage.

Drug court offers a different approach, with the judge becoming more than a stylistic figure. He or she will frequently engage in a dialogue with the offender, and may stand in the body of the court, where—if progress is good—he or she will as likely as not lead the courtroom in a round of applause, perhaps even embracing the offender. Also, he or she may conduct the dialogue in language more familiar to those of the streets than the courtroom, using more informal terminology than is usually expected from a member of the judiciary. These inclusive personal contacts can produce affection and loyalty from some offenders; they will often say, with admiration, that no other judge has ever bothered to discuss with them the details of their personal lives. Responses from two surveys of four hundred drug court participants in the final phase of their program confirm this. Results show that close supervision and encouragement provided by the drug court judge, coupled with intensive treatment, rehabilitation, and ongoing monitoring within the program, were critical in promoting their success (U.S. Department of Justice 1999:7).

Canvassing the opinions of offenders on the merits and worth of judges is unusual, yet such is the intimacy of drug court and the interaction between judge and offender that those familiar with drug court do not see it as unusual or strange. In drug court, the judge is recognized by his or her decisions and personality; the cult of personality has from inception been close to the drug court culture. In drug court the tone, the reputation, and style of the program are determined by the judge; it is his or her court and is known to be such. The idiosyncrasies of individual judges are famed, and where stories are told about this or that drug court they invariably center on the judge's personality. Supervision becomes a highly personalized affair, given over to the preferences, likes, and dislikes of the particular judge.

In drug court the judges place themselves on the offender's side, or rather this is how they may appear to the offender. In practice things are more complex, as drug court also presents itself as being concerned primarily with community safety. Drug court judges offer control mixed with sympathy, acting as a paternal or maternal figure, and able to show that their punishment (medicine) is always for the offender's own good. As an exercise in social control it is masterly; rarely has a social control system been better packaged, or presented in such an effective and sophisticated way.

In drug court the judge directly controls the offender, which may involve coercing him or her into treatment, praising and rewarding when treatment succeeds, but sanctioning when treatment fails. In drug court the judge does not hand over the supervision and control to criminal justice agencies such as the probation service, for a central tenet of the drug court philosophy is that the traditional adversarial system has been tried and has failed. The addicted offender was seen to have manipulated the system, to have avoided sanctions and not to have come to terms with his or her offending behavior. Moreover, agencies such as the probation service were thought to lack the status of the court, have fewer powers, lack the prestige of the judge, and not act decisively when things went wrong.[2] Illustrating this basic sentiment, one drug court judge said, "There is nothing the probation service can do that I cannot, and I can do a lot more than the probation service can do" (Bean 1996).

In drug court the rules of evidence are largely suspended, along with other procedural rules. The judge may cite the results of the latest drug test, showing he or she is pleased or disappointed about the offender's progress, but there is no attempt to determine the validity of the tests, or allow defense lawyers to put any plea of mitigation. The offender's family may corroborate or discount the offender's story, again with little or no apparent concern for evidential or procedural rules. In some courts the offender's "significant other," usually a close partner, may participate in the program, again with no apparent regard for the rules of evidence or other procedural matters, including matters of jurisdiction where "significant others" become subject to the same sanctions as the offenders.

Understandably, drug court has not always been viewed sympathetically by those holding a more traditional jurisprudential view. Cooper and Trotter, not always the harshest critics of drug court say:

> Essentially these drug courts are not courts at all, but diversion-to-treatment programs which are supervised through regular (usually monthly) quasi-judicial status hearings at which the drug court judge enters into a dialogue with each defendant about his or her progress in the treatment/rehabilitation program. (Cooper and Trotter, quoted in Boldt 1998:1252)

Other critics might go further and say that drug court cheapens the judicial office, placing the judge at the level of a ringmaster in a judicial circus. Drug court invariably meets these criticisms with a pragmatic response; it claims that drug court works, it produces clean addicts, and its results compare favorably with other systems notorious for their failure to deal with addicted offenders. That of course raises the obvious question: Is a pragmatic response sufficient to answer a question that is central to the philosophical basis of the judicial system? The answer is clearly no. The debate is not about the effectiveness of a system; were that to be so ends would always be more important than the means. The debate is about those means, which for these purposes involve the role of the judge and the direction of the legal system.

Criticisms of drug court, based as they are on drug court's apparent disregard for justice, are likely to be of little consequence, for the stated aim of the court practitioners is not to realize justice but to solve problems, this in spite of some claims about "reinventing justice." Justice in Aristotelian terms is about treating equals equally and unequals unequally. Justice requires that all differences must be disregarded except those that accord to the relevant criteria in each field (Benn and Peters 1975:173). In Aristotelian terms the relevant criterion is the offense, so that the judge must establish the link between an act or omission, the crime, and the punishment. This is not the major concern of drug court. Nor are precedents or comparisons with earlier omissions of interest. Equality before medicine is not the same as equality before the law. Every sick person is different, so that precedents and comparisons are out of place in their way. The judge in drug court is concerned to remove addiction, and he or she makes choices about different treatment options. He or she is not wanting to treat equals equally and unequals unequally, but to provide opportunities and facilities to deal with each offender (patient) according to his or her treatment needs. This places judges in an unusual position, for they hold judicial office, and preside over a court, yet do not appear to be administering justice.

JUDICIAL MEASURES OF CONTROL

Drug courts require the judge to make and enforce decisions where the ostensible aim is not to punish but to reinforce positive client behavior (Belenko 1998:7). Or as Deborah Chase and Peggy Hora say, "Sanctions for program failures are not primarily for punishment; rather sanctions are tools for program compliance to enhance treatment and recovery" (Chase and Hora 2000:12). The judge draws less on his or her legal training than on his or her knowledge of the natural history of the problem, in this case substance abuse. The central question the drug court judge must address is how to remove or reduce the offender's dependency on drugs. In this respect there is little legal theory on which to draw, or assistance from an adversarial process that presents stark but apparently certain alternatives, nor is there a sound jurisprudential base from which to seek ethical guidance on questions about treatment. The judge will, however, have considerable knowledge about substance abuse as most judges are experts in this, especially in the disease model of addiction, and he or she may have sought training in drug addiction treatment. Advice is also available from other court officials including those responsible for treatment, which taken together will, it is hoped, produce the required outcome. On that basis the judge will make a decision, but always seeking a solution to the offender's drug problem, without concern for matters that affect traditional legal concerns, such as fairness or comparability with the decisions made on other offenders similarly placed.

Measures of informality ought not to disguise the serious intent or the powers used by the drug court judges. Informality does not equate with leniency. The judge may congratulate, but will also condemn, and condemnation can and often does lead to regular periods in jail. The drug court program is not a soft option; it can last up to two years, during which time the offender must report regularly to court, and failure to do so can invoke a range of sanctions including imprisonment. The offender must also receive treatment, where again failure to respond positively may lead to the same sanctions. The drug court method involves persistent surveillance by the court, supported by frequent monitoring through drug testing, and active participation in a treatment program. The offender may be drug tested three or four times per week, depending on progress and length of time in the program. These therapeutic interventions are critical: "In effect drug treatment courts invoke the moral authority of the judicial office to show defendants the seriousness with which their behavior is being taken" (Boldt 1998:1262).

There is little data on the extent of sanctions used; Steven Belenko in his review of drug court evaluations reports that only three studies have examined the way judges use sanctions (Belenko 1999:21). In one study in Cumberland, Maine, researchers observed courtroom hearings for a twenty-five-week period and found that a total of eighty-two sanctions and thirty-seven incentives were used. (Belenko gives no data on the numbers of offenders in the study.) Of the sanctions, 44 percent involved spending time in the dock, 31 percent had to spend some time in jail, and 7 percent were required to increase the number of attendances at AA/NA meetings. Among the incentives, 38 percent involved being advanced to the next treatment phase, 30 percent were given other rewards such as gift certificates, and 16 percent had a reduction in the frequency of court status hearings. In another study in Washington, D.C., of those receiving sanctions nearly 75 percent had to spend three days in the jury box, 50 percent spent three days in jail, 34 percent were sent to a detoxification program, and 22 percent were ordered to spend at least one week in jail. The third study compared the sanctions of graduates and nongraduates and need not concern us here.[3]

Offenders may be subject to multiple sanctions, i.e., receive more than one sanction while on the same program—Belenko gives no data on their use in the three courts he examined. Sanctions can be imposed for a number of failings, among them testing positive for substance abuse (which in some courts includes alcohol) or when the offender is adjudged to be at risk, e.g., when the offender is found to be associating with other drug users.

Whatever the reason, the use of multiple sanctions illustrates one of the major differences between drug court and traditional systems. Allowing a judge to sentence an offender for a second or third time while under the same court order is almost unheard of in common law jurisdictions. In Britain, for example, the courts have no powers to impose multiple sanctions, and for the court to be granted those powers new legislation would be required. Interestingly enough, the nearest the British system gets to multiple sanctions occurs with violations (or breach) of probation or parole, i.e., within a rehabilitative sentence, but even here the offender could receive only a small financial penalty if the order were to continue. There would not be a sentence of imprisonment, however short, nor would a violation be considered for a second time without the order being revoked. Notwithstanding the suitability of continuing with a probation or parole order if the offender repeatedly broke the conditions, it would be regarded in Britain as unjust to punish repeatedly an offender in that way. Better therefore to deal again with the original offense for which the offender was placed on probation, or revoke parole altogether. The difference, of course, is that nowhere in Britain is there a rehabilitative program of the type and duration as in drug court, although once drug courts (which more closely approximate the American model) are introduced, as they recently have been in Glasgow, multiple sanctions can be expected to follow.

The length of time spent in prison, whether on a multiple sanction or not, will be comparatively short in drug court, although the aggregate time over a two-year period might be extensive. It will almost certainly be less than had the sentence been from a court operating with a three-strikes policy, yet it will often be longer and more frequent for the first-time offender convicted of possession of a small amount of drugs for personal use. In that sense, drug court is a net-widening court. The most extreme sanction I have seen in drug court was three months in prison for an offender who tested positive for a number of drugs, and who in the judge's view was making no progress on the program. However, the critical issue here is the power of the drug court judge to impose multiple sanctions, not the length of the sentence per se. It is surprising that there have been no formal legal appeals to a state or to the U.S. Supreme Court, where a writ of habeas corpus would surely be upheld had the offender been repeatedly imprisoned.

Yet drug courts have always presented themselves as successful innovators able to benefit all and sundry, including the offender by reducing his or her level of addiction, and aiding the community by reducing the number of predatory criminals. It becomes difficult therefore to criticize, legally or otherwise, a system that is so obviously beneficial. Drug court uses a coherent therapeutic paradigm predominantly based on the "thank you theory" of psychiatry, where the patient (the offender) will eventually appreciate the help and care offered. The patient may find the current situation unpalatable, but like everyone else knows that what is being done is for his or her own good. And of course that is what invariably happens, as any graduation ceremony in drug court will testify. Offenders *are* grateful, and invariably thank the judge and everyone else for the help given. For most offenders the "thank you theory" of psychiatry is entirely acceptable. Opponents may see it as patronizing, demeaning, and protecting the powers of the state, but not everyone shares this view. Many accept Plato's view that the medicine is "unpalatable but wholesome" (quoted in Bean 1980a:54). Most long-term addicts know that giving up their habit is difficult, and find themselves wanting contradictory things. They want to give up drugs but do not want to be coerced into doing so. Yet they recognize that they will not give up drugs without some form of coercion, which they will neither like nor accept. Drug court deals with this: it sees offenders when they at their most vulnerable, and convinces them that this is the only way forward.

There is no available data showing the comparable effectiveness of drug court judges. It is not known, for example, whether the actions of one judge produce a more favorable outcome than another. Evaluations, where they exist, have been more concerned with the impact of sentencing on post-program outcomes than on the relative success rates of individual judges. Nor have there been many attempts to examine the variations and likely disparities in sentencing, where, say, one judge might prefer one type of sanction for noncompliance, prison perhaps, while another might prefer a different one, say a detoxification center. However, one such study conducted in Denver found interesting results. It seems that over the course of a year one drug court judge gave 66 percent of the participants "good and passable" reviews, but sent 14 percent to jail. Under his successor only 40 percent received "good and passable" reviews and 40 percent were sent to jail. It was reported that the drug court program was stable over the years examined save for the switching of judges (quoted in Boldt 1998: 1260). Such disparities, will of course, do little to enhance the reputation of drug court because they reveal the precarious and fickle nature of the courtroom practices. Such disparities may stem from the predilections of the drug court judge, or from the unique constitution of the drug court team, which will be examined below.

THE DRUG COURT TEAM

Adversarial judicial systems are not suited to drug court, as players in the adversarial system have their own specializations and functions, which do not encourage cooperation and a team approach. In drug court the adversarial system is replaced by the team, directed by the judge, where the professionals agree on outcomes that may involve actions that coerce, encourage, or bully the offender to complete the program. This team approach encourages and forces the offender to accept the expectations placed on him or her to make the necessary changes to his or her behavior and lifestyle (U.S. Department of Health and Human Services 1997:13). The judge, however, remains the public face of the court, and as team leader receives whatever acclaim or opprobrium is granted.

A great deal has been made of the team approach, where prosecutor, defense lawyer, probation officer and other court staff work together under the judge as team leader. Richard Boldt describes it thus:

> Almost without exception these courts seek to accomplish these goals by muting the traditional adversarial positions of prosecutor and defendant, and by making the process judge driven rather than lawyer driven. (Boldt 1998:1252)

The required changes to the role and status of the defense lawyer, prosecutor, probation officer, and the newly acquired status of the treatment provider have been well-documented (see Boldt 1998; Hora 1999; Nolan 2001:61–89). Briefly, the prosecutor finds him- or herself wearing the new mantle of therapeutic team member, where the "public safety and punishment orientated goals of the prosecution are not naturally compatible with drug treatment perspectives" (Goldkamp quoted in Hora 1999:477). The defense lawyer faces a similar dilemma for he or she "must put aside the adversarial mindset and engage in the collaborative efforts of the treatment team" (ibid.:479). Treatment providers find themselves in the unusual position of acting as employees of the court, which in effect means undertaking and completing treatment as directed by the judge, yet also offering expertise and advice. This also represents a radical departure from the traditional court system where only officers of the court have a right to a formal input into the adjudication process (ibid.:480).

Drug court supporters laud the team approach, where defenders, prosecutors, and others work together for the betterment of the offender. Others have responded with alarm. Critics fear that the offender's rights are disregarded in the enthusiasm of the court to provide treatment, for the state always has a tendency to overreach itself and provide ever greater levels of control. To redress that balance, or rather to prevent the state from operating excessively, a vigorous and formal set of procedures is required to buttress the offender from state control (Boldt 1998:1216). Drug courts lack this, leaving them open to the obvious criticism that the offender remains unprotected. Procedural rules are seen as a drawback in drug court for they promote and maintain social distance, isolate the parties, and limit their social interactions. They also inhibit treatment and hold back the offender, limiting participation in the program.

The team approach can extend beyond the court to include social services staff, health providers, job training representatives, and even the local educational establishments (Weitzman undated). "Establishing an open flow of communication between members of the drug court *team* will strengthen the partnership and help it flourish" (ibid.:6, emphasis in original). Problems of confidentiality appear to be unrecognized here, where intimate details of the offender could be handed to all team members who have a stake in his or her recovery. The problem is similar to that of probation reports in Britain, which are handed round to all and sundry, to prison officers, medical officers, etc. However, information is given to the probation officer in the British context on the basis that it relates only to the current offense, and it is restricted to the court. In drug court, all team members say they have an equal right to the data because all have a stake in the offender's recovery, and on that basis all have a legitimate claim. The effect, of course, is that the offender's personal details are widely known to those who would not otherwise have this level of access.

Another result of the team approach is to merge legal and sociomedical models so that the actions of the court are changed in a way that hides their meaning. This is a common feature of systems where individuals, who would otherwise represent different viewpoints, are merged into a partnership. The effect, as seen by Richard Boldt, is that the drug court team "undermines the institutional mechanisms ordinarily used to maintain societal blaming practices" (Boldt 1998:1241), and it is no longer clear which organization should accept the blame for the offender's failure. Teams cannot easily accept blame; they prefer to see any failure as the fault of the offender. Defense counsel, traditionally the voice of the offender, is similarly muted, for as an active team member the defense counsel must take the same institutional position as other team members. The team approach may have the advantage of pooling resources, but has the disadvantage of sometimes producing a paternalistic approach, with decisions made in the offender's "best interests." The language of the team can readily replace the language of the judge so that sanctions are no longer punishments, but adjustments that the court uses to teach addicts responsibility for their actions (quoted in ibid.:1249).

As team leader, the judge receives support from the team, to the apparent benefit of his or her health and disposition. Considerable attention has been given to this matter, especially by supporters of therapeutic jurisprudence, who point to a reduction in job stress among drug court judges, many of whom express pride in a job well done and claim to have a brighter outlook since taking the drug court assignment. These benefits also extend to other team members producing "increased job satisfaction and possibly overall mental health" (Chase and Hora 2000:13). Improvements of this order are always to be welcomed, but is this what we should be concentrating on? Does it really matter whether judges have greater job satisfaction? (And incidentally one of the fundamental weaknesses of therapeutic jurisprudence is that it *does* concentrate on these matters rather than on the rights of those who are disadvantaged.) Ought we to be thinking more about the impact of the team approach on notions of justice, rather than concern ourselves with the well-being of judges, an occupational group quite capable of protecting its own interests? Certainly a careful examination of the role of judge as team leader is overdue; for example, we need to know whether the team controls the judge or the judge controls the team. These, however, are the types of questions we should be asking rather than about the welfare of the judge or the job satisfaction of the team members.

THE DRUG COURT JUDGE AND REHABILITATION

There are many good reasons to suspect that drug court has returned to the rehabilitative ideal of the earlier part of the twentieth century. Its aims and objectives support this, as noted by the former president of the National Association of Drug Court Professionals (NADCP), Judge Jeffrey S. Tauber: When asked if drug courts were leading a broader movement away from purely punitive incarcerative approaches back to rehabilitation, he replied that drug courts were in the initial wave of a movement that addresses rehabilitation issues. He added that the drug court model has been duplicated in domestic violence courts, juvenile courts, and other courts using comprehensive treatment, supervision, and judicial monitoring (quoted in Boldt 1998:1213). Other senior figures in the drug court movement make the same point: drug court and rehabilitation are inextricably bound together. "Treatment based drug courts present an alternative to the traditional method of handling cases by providing eligible defendants with treatment and other social services under close judicial scrutiny" (Weitzman, undated:6). Treatment within a court setting becomes the sine qua non of rehabilitation whether in its earlier forms or in its current manifestation.

Briefly, rehabilitation is a theory of crime control that was dominant up to the late 1970s (Bean 1976). The central proposition is that the causes of crime can be found in the personal and social defects of the offenders. The offense, in this case addiction, becomes the justification for intervention, but the offense is merely a symptom of an underlying disease condition found in the offender's individual psyche or social background. It is the disease rather than the symptoms that need treatment, which in this case is not the addiction, but the social and behavioral problems that caused the addiction.

Rehabilitation has remained embedded within the medical model as illustrated in the language used and the terminology it embraces. If the cure requires treatment in the form of an infliction of pain (punishment) then so be it, for in Plato's terms wickedness is a disease, ultimately fatal unless cured. Punishment may be unpalatable, but is nevertheless wholesome[4] where retribution and deterrence proceed directly from the crime to the punishment, rehabilitation takes a more circuitous route, taking account of the offender's circumstances, and his or her social world. Rehabilitation was always more than a theory of disease, it was a moral theory of crime control, applied whenever someone was failing to achieve acceptable moral standards, whether socially, personally, financially, or professionally.[5]

Many accounts have been given about the development of drug court and its links with rehabilitation. Richard Gebelein, a drug court judge in Delaware argues that rehabilitation, which was all but abandoned as a sentencing goal in the 1970s, was revived for drug-involved offenders through the institution of drug courts. He suggests that drug courts were created initially to relieve court dockets burdened by the rising number of drug cases in the late 1980s and to relieve prison overcrowding. He adds, "Most notably they offered a treatment based alternative that also mandated judicially involved sanctions. For drug involved offenders drug courts replaced what was lost when indeterminate sentencing was eclipsed as a means of rehabilitation" (Gebelein 2000).

Paradoxically, research results in the 1970s, which failed to show that rehabilitation was effective in reducing crime, aided the growth of rehabilitation in drug courts some two decades later. Numerous research studies began to show close links between drug taking and crime, and others showed that treatment, whether coerced or voluntary, works. Moreover, research results showed that the longer the patient remained in treatment the greater the chance of success (Gebelein 2000; Bean 2001; Anglin 1988). If treatment reduced addiction, so then it would reduce crime; the link provided one of the many justifications for drug court.

As a consequence, a central tenet of the drug court philosophy is that addiction is a disease, with all the attendant medical inferences. In keeping with this defining perspective, the drug court judge is put in a position akin to that of a therapist. The structure of drug court supports this; it has become a problem-solving court, it involves a measured shift in the adjudication process toward outcomes rather than inputs, with considerable flexibility in its decision-making. It also takes a recognizable interest in the concerns of the offender and victim, and considers what is best for the community (Rotman 2000).

Steven Belenko describes drug court as "using the various components of the criminal justice and substance abuse treatment system to work together to try and use the coercive power of the court to promote abstinence and prosocial behavior" (Belenko 1998:6). If this is so, and this seems to be confirmed by others (Chase and Hora 2000), we should recognize that drug court closely resembles the rehabilitative ideal of an earlier period. Accordingly, we should be cautious that drug court violates some basic canons of justice by extending the scope of law beyond that which can be reasonably expected. Liberal theorists have always wanted to prevent law from intruding into those areas of personal space in which they believe it has no business, and the conception of drug court should raise those fears.

Promoting abstinence and pro-social behavior, as Belenko puts it, is language that distorts the fundamental distinction between punishment and welfare. With this line blurred, coercion is readily used to justify "doing good to the offender," i.e., promoting abstinence. Again, drug court becomes closely aligned with an earlier form of rehabilitation in which sanctions were no longer punishments, but a therapeutic reply to the personal and social problems of the offender, who had been transformed from someone who made rational decisions to an irrational or diseased patient.

The structure of drug court makes the judge the main point of contact. His or her task, like that of all therapists, is to interpret the world, and provide the means and route by which treatment is secured. The judge decides the appropriate way forward, determining when treatment is complete—and that can only occur when the judge (therapist) and offender (patient) agree about the patient's condition. The judge as therapist is recognized by supporters and critics alike, who variously applaud or accuse (depending on their point of view) the drug court judge as being a "judicial social worker." The aim, direction, and method are therapeutic in intention, where some form of therapeutic relationship develops between offender and drug court judge, however weak that might be.

A key feature of all therapies is the claim that decisions are made according to the pace set by the patient. Drug court follows this therapeutic practice by allowing for flexibility in its decision-making processes. The judge who is released from traditional role expectations supposedly operates at a pace set by the offender/patient, but in practice that pace is largely determined by the judge. Structurally, the drug court gives the judge powers to retain "leverage over the offenders as they navigate between relapse and recovery" (Boldt 1998:1209), which he or she maintains through frequent contacts. Outwardly, drug court, like other rehabilitative regimes, requires flexibility in sentencing, for rehabilitation cannot operate where sentencing guidelines are strict. Accordingly, it is best served where the model is a determinate or semi-indeterminate sentencing structure, and where outcomes are decided on the basis of soft criteria such as "the offender's needs," which in this case means reducing a dependency on drugs. Offenders who progress will be rewarded, perhaps by a shorter sentence, those who are recalcitrant will pay with a longer sentence, or may be removed from the program. Flexibility becomes a necessary tool for those using a disease model, for as with all diseases, individual treatment must proceed at the pace at which treatment can be successful.

However, drug court like other rehabilitative regimes also has within it a rigid orthodoxy where the judge controls events and the offender (patient) follows. The judge lays down the terms, decides when they are violated, and determines the nature of the sanctions. The therapeutic approach in drug court presents the offender with a monolithic structured ideology with little room for disagreement. The paradox contained in all rehabilitative practices is evident in drug court; on the one hand it eschews rigidity and welcomes flexibility, but on the other it operates according to a deep authoritarian structure, which brooks no disagreement. It allows only the therapist to make the decisions, in this case the judge, albeit often in collaboration with the drug court team.

While there are clear parallels with drug court and the rehabilitative ideal, there are differences. The judge can never be a therapist in the full sense of that term; he or she has limited social and personal contacts with the offender, which are brief and infrequent compared with most therapeutic relationships. Most judges would claim to have little more than a quasi-therapeutic relationship with the offenders. A few may still see themselves as judges first and social workers/therapists second. Most if not all seem happy to retain the title and status accorded to them as judges, and, I would suspect, remain more comfortable with their judicial colleagues than with professional therapists. Most return to standard judicial practice after a spell in drug court, and presumably return to earlier ways. Richard Gebelein argues that

> the advantage drug court has over "plain old" rehabilitation is the focus on one problem (addiction) that is causally related to crime committed by one group of offenders (addicts) Treatment is reinforced with a healthy dose of specific deterrence as a motivation to achieve a specific result—abstinence. (Gebelein 2000)

That may be only partly true. "Plain old" rehabilitation focused on one problem, crime, but such is its nature that it can be extended to include everything in the offender's (patient's) lifestyle. So too with drug court. Abstinence might be the aim, but that also includes being crime free, which means the offender must acquire prosocial attitudes, including being a productive member of society, i.e., being in full employment, having the appropriate friends, adopting acceptable attitudes toward others, and leading a good and useful life. The apparent reach of drug court may be restricted to curing addiction but in practice it is all embracing, as were other rehabilitative programs.

The system clearly relies on the ability, integrity, and goodwill of the drug court judge. Drug courts have been designed for judges with high levels of imagination, insight, and moral integrity; there are few controls and few formal constraints. Drug court has not seen fit to impose many restrictions on the judges. What then of an overly enthusiastic judge, a sadistic judge, or an incompetent judge? They seem not to exist, or rather they have not been officially recognized in drug court. For example, at a seminar in 1998 with a number of drug court judges the question was asked about the existence of procedures to deal with an unsatisfactory judge. The answer offered by one drug court judge was interesting: the matter had not been considered. Unsatisfactory judges, it was said, would not want to sit in drug court, for drug court attracts only those of goodwill, with the energy to solve the offender's problems. Yet it is difficult to see why such optimism exists, for one would have thought all judicial procedures should provide safeguards against the simpler forms of corruption and the subtler forms of administrative vices (Benn and Peters 1975:131). The nearest we get to any suspicion about the quality of drug court judges is from Richard Gebelein, who notes that "when a drug court judge steps down it is not always possible to find a sufficiently motivated replacement. Without a highly motivated judge the drug court approach simply does not work well" (Gebelein 2000). However, he says nothing about how best to screen out those who are not highly motivated or about what to do with those whose motivation while in office has diminshed.

SOME CONCLUDING COMMENTS

The links with drug court and the rehabilitative ideal are clear. As a problem-solving court, drug court emphasizes dispositional events; this in contrast to the more traditional courts, which emphasize the case rather than the person. The great strength of drug court is that it points to the importance of producing treatment within a framework that also provides close supervision, seen as necessary when dealing with addicted offenders. Drug court broke the mold, and came to terms with a group of offenders who were persistent criminals, making a heavy drain on the criminal justice system. The solution was to provide a measure of treatment with an equal measure of close supervision that required sanctions if progress was not maintained. It has led to a treatment program supported by judicial sanctions, or what Richard Boldt calls "the blending of punitive and therapeutic functions in drug courts" (1998:1266). Whether that approach needs to be refined is a question underlying the main thrust of this chapter.

There is little doubt that drug court has provided the most important idea in criminal justice for a decade. It is, however, in serious danger of reproducing many of the earlier rehabilitative practices that had previously been so roundly criticized. If it is to survive, it must avoid falling into those traps, some of which are powerful and well baited. It will need to learn from that earlier experience. There will always be a place for rehabilitation in the criminal justice system, but unbridled rehabilitation will never be accepted. Rehabilitation has its place but not a prominent one; drug court should accept this, and tailor its coat to that type of cloth.

Claims to be "reinventing justice" are hyperbolic and do drug court little good. They create the impression that earlier forms of justice have not worked, or at worst are illegitimate and should be abandoned, giving way to this new and untried form. This will lose drug court valuable support. In light of what has been said above, it has certainly broken the mold, but it is not clear if this is a reinvention of an earlier outmoded form. It could as easily be seen as taking a step back to an earlier age when judges assumed greater prominence. The system was discarded, in part, because the judges assumed roles that were too partisan. In this sense drug court marks a return to a pre-Benthamite era of discretionary justice where the judge assumed a more central and powerful position, what Bentham referred to somewhat disdainfully as "judge & Co" (see Bean 1980a). Modern neo-classical jurisprudence following Bentham has insisted that judicial decision-making follows the Aristotelian dictum of "passionless reason." That is, the judges are not partisan, and do not decide cases in the light of personal considerations, where decisions are not made by the unfettered discretion of judges acting as arbitrators producing discretionary justice. For to do so is to turn the exercise into a matter of prejudice, promoted by selfish interests, irrelevant preferences, or administrative self-assertion. Critics of drug court see it as moving in that direction, sometimes getting dangerously close to a system that offers scope for accusations of bias and favoritism.

One of the earlier criticisms of rehabilitation was that it debased the language; "punishment" was not punishment but a form of "therapy" unpalatable but wholesome (Cohen 1985). That debasement has continued; the judge does not "punish" but "provides the external structure needed until participants can develop their own internal structure to be able to maintain sobriety" (Chase and Hora 2000:12). Sending a convicted offender to prison for whatever reason, and in this case because he or she has violated a court code is punishment in any term. Prisons are prisons; incarceration is incarceration. Prisons are not therapeutic institutions concerned to address therapeutic difficulties, though they may do this while they are punishing the offender by detaining him or her there. The offender sent to prison for three days, three weeks, or three months is being punished, and a clear recognition needs to be made of that.

Another pertinent criticism of rehabilitation was that it gave therapeutic groups and individual therapists undue measures of power justified on the grounds that they were doing the offender good. Critics pointed to the obvious dangers, one of which was the possibility that some therapists might abuse those powers. Those of us who fear that corruption is endemic to all systems, especially where claims are made that those wielding power are acting in others' best interests, insist that checks and balances be built into every system, with additional vigilance required when those in power have as much power as do drug court judges. It may well be true that drug court judges are currently beyond reproach, but that does not mean they always will be. Drug court should attend to this matter by adding more controls over judges, even allowing procedural rules to inhibit the judiciary, i.e., allowing a lawyer to represent the offender, or allowing a right of appeal against an order. When claims are made that the adversarial system is entirely out of place then the matter has become serious. The adversarial system may act as an impediment to those who want to dispense with a system they see as ineffective, but it was developed and sustained because it inter alia protects offender's rights. It also avoids casting offenders as amoral, for amoral offenders tend to end up being ignored, or worse, being punished excessively and with fewer rights. It is those rights that need protecting.

There are other problems. In the 1970s rehabilitation was heavily criticized, especially by the American Friends Service Committee (1971) because offenders could and often did finish up serving longer sentences than they would have otherwise. Again, drug court can easily fall into that trap. Appearing before it are many first-time offenders who would not have received prison sentences under the traditional system. For these offenders, spells in prison, however short, are commonplace, and are often justified by the judge on the grounds that these offenders would otherwise become persistent recidivists. "Nipping the problem in the bud" is what drug courts say they are doing. However commendable this might be (and Francis Allen warned against the way rehabilitation used arguments about saving taxpayers money when the moral justifications were weak), we do not put people in prison for what they might become but for what they have done.

This determination to promote welfare (for which read "free from addiction") rather than justice leads drug court into additional problem areas. It appears sometimes to ignore existing legal regulations. For example, the prerelease program for prisoners who enter drug court prior to parole (i.e., so-called re-entry courts) is justified on the basis that parole and other forms of statutory release are rarely available, and those that are appear to have little impact on the exprisoner, who on discharge invariably returns to drugs. Drug courts offer an entirely worthwhile approach, by providing control and sanctions linked to therapy prior to the offender being offered parole. The difficulty is that in doing so they come up against another set of questions about the nature of jurisdiction. That is, the offender in custody is outside the jurisdiction of drug court, or any court for that matter. Some drug courts, as in Nevada, solve the problem by requiring the offender to agree to transfer jurisdiction back to the court while in prison and before being granted parole, i.e., while remaining a prisoner. Jurisdiction, however, cannot be transferred by agreement, it can only be transferred by legislation and that has not been forthcoming. In the same way that psychiatrists and social workers in Britain were severely criticized for ignoring the legislative framework in the way they detained patients under the former Mental Health Act (Bean 1980b) so drug court is likely to invite the same condemnation. Bentham argued that we must distinguish between "is" and "ought," that is, we must operate according to what the law is, not what we may think it ought to be. The eagerness to do good often leads to a failure to appreciate that Benthamite prescription.

Add to this the other matters noted above, such as failing to protect confidentiality, and comparisons with the rehabilitation of earlier years are evident. That should also sound a warning: the rehabilitative ideal of earlier times was jettisoned because it failed to meet required standards of justice. One hopes drug court does not meet a similar fate.

It is not the aim here to produce a catalog of failings: quite the reverse, for drug court has achieved too much for it to be reduced in that way. Rather, the intention is to seek modifications, which in effect means amending some of the ideological positions from which drug court operates. It is to bring it back to being a court, and the judge back to being a judge, and not someone involved in a therapeutic endeavor that controls people for their own good. If that means a reduction in the level of certainty then so be it. Certainty has always been a dangerous commodity in those determined to help others.

NOTES

1. In December 1999 the Office of Drug Control Policy for the United Nations convened an Expert Working Group whose primary goal was to develop

key principles for drug courts in member nations. The twelve-key principles provide the most succinct account of the aims and methods of drug
court:

(1) The programs integrate substance dependency treatment and rehabilitation services with justice case processing.

(2) Using a nonadversarial approach, prosecution and defense counsel
promote public safety while protecting offenders' due process rights.

(3) Eligible offenders are identified early and promptly integrated into the
program.

(4) The program ensures access to a continuum of substance dependency
treatment and other rehabilitation services.

(5) Frequent substance abuse testing objectively monitors compliance.

(6) A coordinated strategy governs responses of the court to program noncompliance (and compliance) by offenders.

(7) Ongoing judicial interaction with each offender in the program is
essential.

(8) Monitoring and evaluation measures the achievements of program
goals and gauges effectiveness.

(9) Continuing interdisciplinary education promotes effective planning
implementation and operations of these court-directed programs.

(10) Forging partnerships between courts directing treatment and rehabilitation programs, public agencies, and community-based organizations generates local support and enhances program effectiveness.

(11) Ongoing case management includes the social support necessary to
achieve social reintegration, if necessary including the family of the offender or those who have close relationships with the offender.

(12) There is appropriate flexibility in adjusting program content including incentives and sanctions, to better achieve program results with
particular groups, such as women, indigenous people, and minority
ethnic groups.

2. In this respect it is interesting that in Britain legislation has used many of
the features of drug court in its Drug Treatment and Testing Order, but the
court, operating from a more traditional stance, hands the supervision over
to the probation service. Critics say this will not work; the probation service
has neither the status, influence, power, nor ability to respond rapidly or to
have any impact on treatment outcomes. These critics are correct in my
view; the Drug Treatment and Testing Order will not work, at least in the
way that drug court has succeeded, but that should not be a justification for
introducing drug courts in Britain or elsewhere in the form in which they
exist in the United States.

3. A jail sanction was imposed for 46 percent of graduates and 77 percent of
nongraduates in a Florida-based drug court program(Belenko 1998:22).

4. Francis Allen, one of the most ardent critics of the rehabiliative ideal, sees it
as a complex theory that almost defies definition (Allen 1964). There are, he
says, numerous subdivisions of rehabilitation, some of which are antitheti-
cal to each other, whether in doctrine or method, and others are extensions
or variations on a central proposition. Rehabilitation has a long distin-

guished history going back at least to Plato, who saw wickedness as a disease, ultimately fatal, but that required the medicine of punishment if it was
to be cured (see Bean 1980a). We find strains of the same argument in St.
Thomas Aquinas, who spoke of *poena medicinalis*, "We can also look at punishment as medicinal and then not simply as a cure for past sins but as a pre-
ventative of future sins or even as an inducement to some good" (ibid.:54).
Rehabilitation was subject to intense criticism from the mid-1960s onward
(Allen 1964; American Friends Service Committee 1971; Bean 1976). The
medical model in which it resided was seen as inappropriate for understanding offending behavior, failing to encapsulate the essential nature of
crime. The humanitarian guise it fostered was also found wanting; some
saw it as hypocritical when offenders served longer sentences under a rehabilitative regime than they would have otherwise. In addition, a lack of
procedural rules posed threats to civil liberty. Moreover, the research evidence was poor; rehabilitation was found to be largely ineffective in reducing crime. Under such a sustained attack it was not surprising that it
surrendered its earlier preeminence, finally giving way to a theory of 'just
deserts,' which made fewer claims to solve the problems to which flesh is
heir, yet appeared more honest and in keeping with the spirit of the times
(von Hirsch 1976).

5. In Samuel Butler's *Erewhon,* surely the most complete parody on rehabilita-
    tion, there were those trained in soulcraft, the "straighteners," literally
    translated as "one who bends back the crooked." Their task was to cure all
    forms of mental indisposition. It was hardly necessary, said Butler, to say
    that the office of straightener required long and special training, for it stood
    to reason that those who would cure mental ailments must be practically ac-
    quainted with all its bearings. Their familiarity with long names gave as-
    surance they understood the case (Butler 1960:87).

REFERENCES

Allen, F. A. 1964. *The Borderland of Criminal Justice.* University of Chicago Press.
American Friends Service Committee. 1971. *Struggle for Justice.* Hill and Wang.
Anglin, M. D. 1988. "The Efficacy of Civil Commitment in Treating Narcotic Ad-
    diction." In Leukefeld, C. G. and Tims, F. M. *Compulsory Treatment of Drug
    Abuse; Research and Clinical Practice.* National Institute on Drug Abuse. Re-
    search Monograph Series 86, pp. 8–34.
Belenko, S. 1998. "Research on Drug Courts: A Critical Review." *National Drug
    Court Institute Review.* Vol. 1 Issue 1 (Summer).
Bean, P. T. 1976. *Rehabilitation and Deviance.* London: Routledge and Kegan Paul.
Bean, P. T. 1980. *Punishment: a Philosophical and Criminological Inquiry.* Oxford: Mar-
    tin Robertson.
Bean, P. T. 1980b. *Compulsory Admissions to Mental Hospitals.* Chichester: John Wi-
    ley and Sons.
Bean, P. T. 1996. "America's Drug Courts: A New Development in Criminal Jus-
    tice." *Criminal Law Review.* pp. 718–719.

Bean, P. T. 2001. *Drugs and Crime.* Devon: Willan Publishing.

Benn, S. I. and Peters, R. S. 1975. *Social Principles and the Democratic State.* London: George Allen and Unwin.

Boldt, R. C. 1998. "Rehabilitative Justice and the Drug Court Movement." *Washington University Law Quarterly,* vol. 76, pp. 1205–1306.

Butler, S. 1960. *Erewhon.* London: Jonathon Cape.

Chase, D. J. and Hora, P. 2000. "The Implications of Therapeutic Jurisprudence for Judicial Satisfaction." *Court Review.* (Spring), pp. 12–20.

Cohen, S. 1985. *Visions of Social Control.* London: Polity Press.

Gebelein, R. S. 2000. "The Rebirth of Rehabilitation; Problems and perils of Drug Courts." *National Institute of Justice* (May).

IADCP News. 2000. *UNDCP Designs Drug Court Standards,* vol. 11, issue 1, pp. 1 and 4.

Nolan, J. 1998. *The Therapeutic State: Justifying Government at Century's End.* New York: New York University Press.

Nolan, J. 2001. *Reinventing Justice: The American Drug Court Movement.* Princeton: Princeton Unversity Press.

Rotman, D. 2000. "Does Therapeutic Jurisprudence Require Specialised Courts (and Do Specialised Courts Imply Specialist Judges)?" *Court Review* (Spring), pp. 22–27.

U.S. Department of Justice. 1999. "Looking at a Decade of Drug Courts." Washington, DC: Drug Courts Program Office.

U.S. Department of Health and Human Services. 1997. "Substance Abuse Treatment Planning: Guide and Checklist for Treatment Based Drug Courts." Washington, DC: U.S. Dept of Health and Human Services.

Von Hirsch, A. 1976. *Doing Justice.* New York: Hill and Wang.

Weitzman, J. (undated). Drug Courts: A Manual for Planning and Implementation. American Bar Association.

Index